VETERINARY

Related titles:

John Butler: *The Ethics of Health Care Rationing*

Anthony Dyson: *The Ethics of IVF*

Bernard Hoose (ed.): *Christian Ethics: An Introduction*

Andrew Linzey and Dan Cohn-Sherbok: *After Noah: Animals and the Liberation of Theology*

Stephen Wilmott: *The Ethics of Community Care*

VETERINARY ETHICS
An Introduction

Edited by Giles Legood

CONTINUUM

London and New York

Continuum
Wellington House
125 Strand
London WC2R 0BB

370 Lexington Avenue
New York
NY 10017 – 6503

First published 2000

British Library Cataloguing-in-Publication Data
A catalogue record for this book is available from the British Library.

ISBN 0 8264 4784 8

Typeset by York House Typographic Ltd
Printed and bound in Great Britain by Creative Print and Design Wales, Ebbw Vale

Contents

Contributors

Michael C. Appleby is Senior Lecturer in Farm Animal Behaviour and Welfare at the Institute of Ecology and Resource Management, University of Edinburgh. He is co-editor of *Animal Welfare* and author of *What Should We Do About Animal Welfare?*

John Bower is a Senior Partner in the Veterinary Hospital Group small animal practice in Plymouth. A former President of both the British Veterinary Association and the British Small Animal Veterinary Association, he is co-author of *Veterinary Practice Management.*

Stephen R.L. Clark is Professor of Philosophy at the University of Liverpool and sometime Fellow of All Souls. He is a member of the Farm Animal Welfare Council and has written extensively on animals: his books include *The Moral Status of Animals, The Nature of the Beast* and *Animals and their Moral Standing.*

Jane C. Hern qualified as a solicitor and is Secretary and Registrar of the Royal College of Veterinary Surgeons.

Mac Johnston is Professor of Veterinary Public Health and Head of the Animal and Public Health Division at the Royal Veterinary College, University of London. He has been a member of a number of advisory committees in the UK and elsewhere in the European Union, and Veterinary Advisor to the Humane Slaughter Association. He is an Honorary Fellow of the Royal College of Veterinary Surgeons and an RCVS Specialist in Veterinary Public Health.

James K. Kirkwood is Scientific Director of the Universities' Federation for Animal Welfare, Honorary Director of the Humane Slaughter Association, Visiting Professor at the Royal Veterinary College, University of London and was formerly Head of the Veterinary Science Group at the Zoological Society, London. He has published widely on wild animal welfare, medicine and conservation.

Martin P.C. Lawton is senior partner of an exotic animal and ophthalmic referral centre and is a Fellow of the Royal College of Veterinary Surgeons. He is an RCVS Recognised Specialist in Exotic Animal Medicine and a holder of its Diploma in Zoological Medicine (Reptilian).

Giles Legood is Chaplain and Honorary Lecturer in Veterinary Ethics at the Royal Veterinary College, University of London. He is editor of *Chaplaincy: The Church's Sector Ministries* and co-author of *The Godparents' Handbook*.

Anna Meredith is Head of Exotic Animal Services and is the Named Veterinary Surgeon at the Royal (Dick) School of Veterinary Studies, University of Edinburgh, Veterinary Surgeon for Edinburgh Zoo, an Inspector under the Zoo Licensing Act and a holder of the RCVS Certificates in Zoological Medicine and Laboratory Animal Science.

Bob Moore is a graduate of the Royal (Dick) School of Veterinary Studies, University of Edinburgh and has worked in agricultural practice since graduating in 1967. He is a past President of the British Cattle Veterinary Association and has served on British Veterinary Association committees. In 1999 he was elected to the council of the Royal College of Veterinary Surgeons.

Mike Radford is a Lecturer in Law at the University of East Anglia, where he teaches a course on animal welfare law. He is a Council Member of the Universities' Federation for Animal Welfare (UFAW), an academic adviser to the Royal College of Veterinary Surgeons and a founder member of both the Animal Welfare Science, Ethics and Law Veterinary Association (AWSELVA) and Lawyers for Animal Welfare (LAW).

Kate Rawles was formerly Lecturer in Philosophy at the University of Lancaster and now works freelance, specializing in environmental and animal welfare ethics. She is particularly interested in working with professionals in other fields, especially conservation and veterinary medicine, and in combining environmental ethics with outdoor pursuits.

Diane Sinclair was formerly Assistant Registrar and Head of Professional Conduct of the Royal College of Veterinary Surgeons. She is now a consultant and an Honorary Associate of the RCVS.

Paul Townsend is Head of the Animal Services Unit at the Veterinary Laboratories Agency, Weybridge and a holder of the RCVS Diploma in Laboratory Animal Science.

John Webster is Professor of Animal Husbandry, and formerly Head of the School of Veterinary Science at the University of Bristol. He was a founder member of the Farm Animal Welfare Council and is currently Chair of the independent Food Ethics Council. He is the author of *Animal Welfare: A Cool Eye Towards Eden.*

For Victoria with love

Introduction

Giles Legood

Why veterinary ethics?

For many years in Britain there has been widespread and deep interest in issues of animal welfare. This has been especially true in the period since the Second World War, when books and films such as *Ring of Bright Water* and *Born Free* have both stimulated and given expression to this interest. In 1976 the cause of animal welfare and its calls for better treatment of animals was given impetus with the publication of Peter Singer's *Animal Liberation*. Since then, whilst many supporters of better animal welfare have devoted their time to campaigning, either through law reform, by bringing economic pressures to bear on those who abuse animals or through direct action, philosophers have increasingly turned their attention to considering the moral status of animals.[1] As a consequence, questions such as whether we can speak of animal 'rights' or what, if anything, are the duties of humans towards animals have become issues thought of and discussed by a large proportion of the general population. The effects of such stimulation are seen in the changing patterns of diet (especially the number of people following a vegetarian diet), attitudes towards animals being used for recreation, clothing or cosmetic purposes and, not insignificantly, through the increasing preponderance of television producers to make programmes about animals and the veterinary profession. Historically the United Kingdom has been at the forefront of the deliberation and action concerning the protection of animals (traditionally we have been seen to be a nation of 'animal lovers') and this is reflected in the fact that there are today literally hundreds of UK charities dedicated to animal welfare.

Over the same period of this recent interest in animal issues, there has been an equally dramatic new interest in professional ethics. A generation ago the now well-established discipline of medical ethics virtually consisted of two rules: don't advertise and don't sleep with your patients. Today, metres of shelving in bookshops are dedicated to medical ethics and all the newly devised medical curricula in medical schools must now include formal and assessed ethical components. Other professional groups too have looked towards issues of what it is to be a profession and what standards are required. Nurses, lawyers, journalists and others in the media, as well as social workers, those in advertising and PR, amongst others, now address ethical and professional issues in formal, structured ways. There has however, thus far, been little or no public debate over veterinary ethics. In a world of self-regulation and the increasing need for transparency of this regulation, the time for the professional and ethical issues of the veterinary surgeon is upon us. Cynics might say that professions only become interested in ethics, transparency of regulation and other professional issues as society becomes more litigious. Whether this is true or not, increasing debate over such matters will, nevertheless, improve not only animal welfare but will also improve the way in which animal owners and those who have anything to do with animals, even as consumers, are treated. Several recent crises, such as fears over the BSE outbreak and over genetic engineering, bear witness to this.

The importance of veterinary ethics

In order to practise as a veterinary surgeon in this country membership of the Royal College of Veterinary Surgeons is required. On admission to membership of the RCVS every veterinarian must make the following declaration: 'Inasmuch as the privilege of the Royal College is about to be conferred upon me, I PROMISE AND SOLEMNLY DECLARE that I will abide in all due loyalty to the Royal College of Veterinary Surgeons and will do all in my power to maintain and promote its interests. I PROMISE ABOVE ALL that I will pursue the work of my profession with uprightness of conduct and that my constant endeavour will be to ensure the welfare of animals committed to my care.'

This declaration is contained in the RCVS's *Guide to Professional Conduct* which is issued to all veterinary surgeons.[2] For veterinarians it has a similar value and status as the Hippocratic Oath did for many centuries for physicians. The Hippocratic Oath has been revised by successive generations and today is represented in the World Medical Association's *Declaration of Geneva* (original version 1948, current version

1983). Similarly the RCVS declaration is formally revised and re-issued every three years to all veterinary surgeons registered and working in veterinary activity in the UK. The *Guide to Professional Conduct*, of which the declaration is part, sets out the obligations required of veterinarians arising from: the treatment of animals; the use of veterinary medicinal products; the veterinarian-client relationship; the veterinary practice; relationships between veterinarians; post-graduation responsibilities and continuing professional development. The *Guide* shows, both implicitly and explicitly, that the highest ethical obligations are laid upon all those working as veterinary surgeons in the UK.

It is not intended that this book be considered by these veterinarians apart from the *Guide*, but alongside it. Neither, too, is this book intended to supply answers to the multitude of ethical dilemmas faced by veterinarians. The book does, of course, contain thoughts and stances of its individual contributors, but they should been seen as tools to enable veterinarians to address their various situations, rather than weapons with which to defeat them. The chapters are written to inform and stimulate reflection, not to be the final word on their individual topics. Although individual veterinarians, and the profession as a whole, will have to draw lines in prescribing what is and is not permissible, because ethics are culture bound (or at least appear to be), these lines will have to be drawn in pencil. This in no way, however, removes from any of us, whether veterinarian or not, the requirement to think seriously about the issues, nor does it allow us to delude ourselves into thinking that since things may be different in the future we may do as we please today.

Interest in this book

According to the RCVS statistics for 1999 there are over 18,000 veterinary surgeons registered in the UK. Only 2,000 of these are retired. There is, it has been acknowledged for some time, a shortage of veterinary surgeons working in the UK. Whilst the six UK veterinary schools are producing an additional 450 new graduates each year, a further 450 are recruited annually from the EU and other countries to work in the UK. There is certainly no shortage of well-qualified and experienced applicants to the veterinary schools and the schools them-selves would very much like to be able to offer places to more candidates. All six have argued to successive governments that they should be funded to educate and train more people for the veterinary profession. Members of the profession not only contribute to society through their work in general practice but also in a variety of other spheres. Whilst half work in full-time general practice in the UK, many others work in universities, government service, research institutes, for commercial organizations or for charities. There is then this large group of people, who are influential in a number of areas, of whom society asks a huge amount. In the culture described above, one of increasing public awareness of animal issues, veterinarians, like members of any profession, will need to think deeply about the specific role of their profession and what is required of it. In this task they will need not only to consult amongst themselves but be aware of what others are expecting of them and what others are thinking.

It is hoped that for the first time in the UK this book will be able to offer to veterinarians some introductory text to assist them in their thinking. Whilst there has been a growing number of books written on the moral status of animals, and issues of animal welfare and the law, there has not thus far been a book dedicated exclusively to veterinary ethics.[3] As well as this corpus of literature, in 1997 the Animal Welfare Science, Ethics and Law Veterinary Association (AWSELVA) was formed. Its aim is 'to establish a forum through which veterinarians and non-veterinarians can develop informed views on issues relating to animal welfare science, ethics and law, through a multi-disciplinary approach'.[4] Through an annual general meeting, regional and special interest groups and through a twice-yearly newsletter AWSELVA has already made a significant contribution to the studies of veterinary ethics. Indeed, two of the contributions to this book were given in an amended form to an AWSELVA ethics symposium held at the annual Congress of the British Veterinary Association. It is hoped that it is not only veterinary surgeons who will have an interest in the contents of this book but also philosophers, ethicists, theologians, lawyers and those involved in food production, as well as it being of relevance to those involved in animal welfare work and campaigning.

Contents of this book

As befits this multi-disciplinary approach, the contributors of this book come from a wide range of backgrounds and expertise. Over half of the authors are veterinary surgeons. These veterinarians work in general practice, in universities as teachers and researchers, as Named Veterinary Surgeons with statutory responsibilities, for the Ministry of Agriculture, Food and Fisheries or for charitable organizations. They have, too, a wealth of other experience gained from previous posts. Other chapters in the book are written by philosophers, theologians, lawyers, research scientists or administrators responsible for regulating the veterinary profession. While the authors do not wish to claim to be giving definitive texts it is their hope that their contributions will stand as introductions to the individual subjects and that, as a whole, the book will fulfil its purpose as an introduction to the various areas encompassed by the term 'veterinary ethics.' There is undoubtedly much to be thought about and written in this area, both as situations and science change and as the debates are further engaged with by others.

Part One of the book sets the scene for much of the thought and experience related in Part Two. It addresses fundamental questions as to why and how veterinarians specifically, and humankind generally, have treated and ought to treat animals. Philosophical and historical issues are related and tackled, as are the legal matters of animal protection legislation and the administration of justice. Also included, vitally, are the practicalities of the administration of the veterinary profession, including its self-regulation and examples of the ethical problems and dilemmas upon which the RCVS is called to adjudicate. Part Two is concerned with examining some of the specific, individual areas in which ethical issues arise. Matters that are faced by veterinarians on a weekly, even daily, basis in general practice are considered, as are ethical concerns which veterinarians face on a less regular basis. Here the topics of wild animal health, zoos and exotic animals are looked at. Part Two also includes deliberation on the issues which often catch the wider public imagination: animals used in sport, genetic engineering and animal experimentation. The list of topics considered makes no claim to be exhaustive (space prevents that this be so), but is offered as 'bread and butter' issues which are most often faced by veterinarians and issues upon which the public expect veterinarians to have an informed and coherent opinion.

Finally, I should like to thank a number of people who have assisted me in various ways in seeing that this book has been published. Joe Brownlie, Mark Fox, Douglas Stewart, John Taylor, and Paul Watson have been both friendly colleagues and offered useful ideas on the form and content of the book. Alex Hunte provided invaluable help when either my computer or my technical competence let me down. I have been very fortunate to have such a supportive and enthusiastic editor at Continuum in this and in a previous project – Ruth McCurry. Melanie Phillips has given great encouragement to the whole project and kindly spent time looking at my own contributions to the text. My greatest thanks, however, are due to the students of the Royal Veterinary College, University of London. Both in formal, timetabled teaching and in informal discussions (often taking place over the pool table – as befits a 'man of the cloth') they have influenced my thoughts on ethics and my understanding of the complexity of veterinary study and practice.

Notes

1. Examples of this genre include: Mary Midgley, *Animals and Why They Matter*, Athens: University of Georgia Press, 1983; Tom Regan, *The Case for Animal Rights*, London: Routledge, 1988; Bernard Rollin, *The Unheeded Cry: Animal Consciousness, Animal Pain, and Science*, Ames: Iowa State University Press, 1989; Michael Leahy, *Against Liberation: Putting Animals in Perspective*, London: Routledge, 1991.
2. Further discussion in Chapter 6.
3. A similar book to the current volume has been available in the American context for some years. Its usage is limited somewhat in the UK however, because of the market for which it was written. Its price and size also may not make it attractive to many veterinarians working in the UK. See, Jerrold Tannenbaum, *Veterinary Ethics: Animal Welfare, Client Relations, Competition and Collegiality*, St. Louis: Mosby, 2nd edn, 1995.
4. Further details of AWSELVA, including membership application forms, can obtained from:
    Department of Biomedical Science and Ethics
    Medical School
    University of Birmingham
    Edgbaston B15 2TT.

PART ONE

1

Why do vets need to know about ethics?

Kate Rawles

Some years ago, when I was still in Scotland, my colleague David became really quite ill, due largely to stress. However, after a break of only a few days he returned to work and carried on as before, apparently more or less recovered. One day I ran into his wife, Yvette. Yvette told me that David was more stressed than he seemed, that if anything this was getting worse, not better, and did I think there was any way his teaching load might be reduced.

Shortly after this conversation I encountered our head of department, Charles. I decided to seize the moment. 'Charles,' I said, 'I've been talking with Yvette, who says that David is still very stressed. Is there any scope for rearranging the timetable in order to reduce his load?' Charles looked, well, surprised. I assumed this was because of the unheard-of challenge to the stiff upper lip regime of the time. Nevertheless, he agreed to see what he could do. David's teaching load was duly reduced, and in time he recovered fully.

Several years later, Charles came up to me at a departmental dinner. 'Do you remember that discussion we had about David?' he asked. 'Well, for years I thought you'd said you'd been talking to a *vet* about David's health . . . .'

Vets as authorities

What continues to strike me about this incident, is that the head of a university department acted on advice about a colleague's health, and a suggestion for reduced workload, that he believed to have come from a vet. This introduces my first point, which is that vets have authority. Vets, and vets' opinions, are treated with respect across a wide range of issues. If I had said, 'I've been talking with a builder who thinks David needs to work fewer hours,' I would surely have received a different response.

More usually, of course, vets are taken to be authorities on matters concerning non-human animals rather than academics. For instance, vets may be appealed to as expert witnesses in alleged cruelty cases, such as the recent prosecution of Mary Chipperfield, the circus owner and animal trainer, or the less recent attempt to prosecute nuns for cruelty with regard to their intensively housed veal calves. Alternatively, the mere presence of vets, for example, at slaughterhouses or in the context of transporting livestock, may be taken by the public as reassurance that the system is all right. In both kinds of case, vets are credited with an authority that animal rights activists, for example, do not have: vets are respected figures within 'the establishment,' and are assumed to have knowledge and experience of animals. Moreover, while vets may work for industry, if push comes to shove, they are widely thought to be on the animals' side – though in a rational and informed way, rather than a sentimental or purely emotional one.[1]

Mink liberation: an issue with many ethical dimensions

What I want to argue is that the kinds of cases where vets might be consulted will typically have ethical dimensions. Hence the vet's authority is taken to include matters of ethics as well as those we might, very loosely, refer to as matters of 'fact'. There are currently a number of high profile, 'media-fied' issues which could be used to illustrate this. I will begin with one example: the liberation of mink from farm cages.

Debates about the release of mink inevitably raise a number of questions, many of which seem, quite straightforwardly, to be about matters of fact. Examples include the following: What is likely to happen to the mink after their abrupt change of scenery? What will be the impact of the mink on local ecosystems? How will they affect indigenous species? These are all, broadly, factual or empirical questions, questions about what is, was or will be the case. Inevitably, however, the liberation of mink raises ethical questions too. These, broadly, are questions about what should be the case or about what ought to be done. They are questions about the rights and wrongs of the matter. Examples include questions about whether the activists were wrong to let the mink out, and if so, why.

If vets are called to comment on the release of mink, it is unlikely that their questioners will neatly separate the two kinds of questions and ask for comment only on the empirical ones. The questions are more likely to combine both ethical and empirical aspects. Moreover, in many cases, the empirical and the ethical are in any case very hard to separate. For example, suppose that the vet is asked whether the release of mink should be condemned, because of the adverse impact mink may have on other species. This question clearly contains an ethical question within it – the query about whether or not the release *should be condemned*. But now suppose that the question is limited to the (apparently) empirical bit. The vet is asked what impact the mink *will have* on the surrounding ecology. The reply: the mink will probably have a devastating effect on local bird populations, particularly ground-nesting species, and that they will threaten otter populations with extinction. This is a judgement about what will be the case, not about what should or should not be. Yet, given the context in which it is asked, the vet is effectively contributing to the 'should not' point of view. The answer contributes to the condemnation of the activists who let the mink out. Thus, apparently factual information is used to make an ethical point.

In short, when vets or the veterinary profession are consulted about an issue like the release of farmed mink, it is unlikely that they will be asked to confine themselves to factual or empirical issues and keep clear of ethics – or even that such a thing would always be possible. Exactly the same point can be made about other cases, such as the export of live animals and the genetic modification of animals. In commenting on such issues, vets are, therefore, likely to have to make judgements about ethics as well as about 'facts'. Thus, one reason why vets need to know about ethics is that they may be asked to comment on various issues which clearly have ethical dimensions. (In this context, it is also worth noting the questions that were *not* asked by the media about the mink case, for example, about the conditions under which the mink were being kept, and the legitimacy of farming animals for fur.)

The way some questions are emphasized and others omitted can help to create and sustain an ethical point of view: in this case, that the behaviour of the activists was clearly unacceptable, while the practice of mink farming was exempt from discussion. A similar point can be made about what information is given and what withheld. In the example above the vet's answer about the otters contributes to the view that those releasing the mink were irresponsible and even cruel. But suppose we now add the information that otters are only threatened by mink if their populations are already precariously low, and that they are in this situation largely because of river pollution deriving from intensive agriculture. It then becomes much less clear that responsibility for the otters' predicament lies solely with those who let the mink out. It also opens up the possibility that a range of previously neglected questions, for example, about the costs and benefits of particular agricultural practices, might now be asked.

What are ethics?

What are ethics? I have already contrasted them with matters of fact. Matters of fact concern what is the case: ethics concern what ought to be done, what the rights and wrongs of the situation are.

This distinction between factual and empirical matters on the one hand and ethical matters on the other is very rough and ready, and it needs to be treated with some caution. Many people express reservations about it.[2] Nevertheless, I think it is useful to draw the distinction here. To use a general example, questions about what the welfare of an animal *is*, are empirical; questions about what the welfare of an animal *ought to be*, are ethical. The important point in this context is that answering the first kind of question, no matter how thoroughly, does not amount to answering the second kind. No amount of animal welfare science will yield answers to questions about what level of welfare is acceptable.

That, then, is a rough and ready contrast between facts and ethics. Here is a rough and ready definition of ethics, ethical principles, ethical issues and ethical dilemmas:

Ethics: a shorthand for 'ethical principles'.

Ethical principles: principles, or codes of conduct, which specify what counts as acceptable and unacceptable treatment of others (and oneself).

Ethical issues: issues around what constitutes acceptable and unacceptable treatment of others in particular contexts, and (crucially), issues around how we weigh up and balance the different values, principles and commitments involved.

Is it acceptable to keep mink in such a way that they cannot perform much of the behaviour in their natural repertoire? How does this, and the concern for animal welfare generally, weigh against the value we place on economic profit and on consumer freedom (including the freedom to buy fur coats)? These would all be examples of ethical issues. (NB: to say that something is an ethical issue is not to say that it is ethical in the everyday sense, i.e., that it is the right thing to do).

Ethical dilemmas: the particular kind of ethical issue which arises when values, principles and commitments conflict, or seem incompatible, or incommensurable.

The classic kind of ethical dilemma arises when someone is faced with a 'choice between two bads'; whatever they do will have an undesirable outcome. In the events narrated in *Touching the Void*, Joe Simpson's climbing partner, while climbing with Simpson in the Peruvian Andes, was abruptly forced to choose between cutting the rope that held them together and letting Simpson fall down a crevasse of unknown depth, or being pulled off the snow face and down the crevasse himself.[3] He thus faced a particularly acute dilemma, in virtue of the obvious conflict between his desire to stay alive and his commitment to his partner. Less immediate dilemmas often arise in the context of environmental issues. For example, a commitment to reduce pollution may be incompatible with a commitment to increase industrial production. The value of roads on the one hand and particular habitats on the other may be thought to be incommensurable, because there is no common scale on which to weigh the benefits of each ('like trying to compare decibels with kilometres', as someone once put it).

Ethics in everyday situations

Mink liberation, then, is a high-profile case with a clear ethical dimension, and one that vets or the veterinary profession might well be expected to have an authoritative opinion about. I have mentioned the export of live animals and the genetic modification of animals as other examples. The ethical issues embedded in cases like these certainly arise, but not on a daily basis. But ethical issues are not confined to the high-profile cases. Nor are they confined to vets. They pervade everyone's ordinary, everyday lives in all sorts of banal ways.

People in general

Consider, for example, decisions about what to eat, which we make, say, three times a day. Everyone who ever reads this chapter will have some conception of things they consider it ethically unacceptable, or wrong, to eat. Disagreement between us would not be about whether there are things it is unacceptable to eat but what those things are.

There is a wide range of ways of drawing the line between the ethically edible and the ethically out of bounds. Vegetarianism is the obvious example. There can be various reasons for becoming vegetarian. Ethical ones include the belief that it is wrong to collude in practices that cause animal suffering, especially when alternative sources of food are available and/or the belief that it is wrong to kill animals, especially conscious, sentient ones – which would include most if not all of the animals we commonly eat.

A common variant on vegetarianism is to avoid meat but eat fish. (I have always thought this a peculiar position until a student explained to me that 'fish are just silver vegetables'). Vegans avoid eating animal produce, as well as animals, including dairy produce, and sometimes honey. Fruit and nut-arians only eat things one might reasonably consider to be offering themselves up for consumption – such as fruits and nuts. At the other end of the spectrum, I have a friend who considers himself to have strong moral principles in this area on the grounds that he only eats *pâté de foie gras* if given to him as a Christmas present.

The point is that daily decisions about what to eat raise ethical issues. If you have not aligned yourself with any of the above ways of delineating ethically unacceptable food sources consider whether you think it right to eat white veal, frogs' legs, larks' tongues, poodles or people, or food produced under an apartheid system, or grown using slave labour, or flown from the other side of the world, with heavy use of fossil fuels. If the answer to any of these is, 'No', ask 'Why not?', and you will uncover ethical principles, or at least their prototypes.

Everyday life is riddled with ethical issues, even if they are not normally recognized as such. Other examples might include where we choose to put savings, and how we balance concern that our investments are not supporting, say, the production of landmines, with concern that they rise in value, or the issue of whether or not to tell the truth in a particular context, and how truth weighs against other things we value, such as not hurting someone's feelings. In sum, decisions about how we choose to live involve constant choices which often have an ethical dimension – the decision goes beyond self-interest and involves a concern for others and how our actions affect them.

Vets *in particular*

Ethics, then, pervade everyone's everyday life. In addition, vets are working in what you might call an ethically dense profession (double meaning not intended!): the nature of their work ensures that they face a constant stream of ethical issues. Again, some of these will be relatively high-profile cases, involving an ethical dilemma. A trusty example: do you agree to dock a dog's tail, even though you believe the surgery to be unnecessary and unethical, or do you refuse, while being pretty sure that the owner will simply go somewhere less scrupulous? There are no doubt hundreds of ethical dilemmas that vets may encounter, though not necessarily on a daily basis. But vets do not meet ethical issues only in the form of occasional dilemmas. Ethical issues constantly arise in routine veterinary work, because vets are constantly dealing with animal suffering and death. Both forms of ethical issue occur.

Questions about what counts as acceptable treatment in particular cases are extremely common. Is this level of post-operational suffering acceptable, or should more analgesic be given? Should this old, but much loved dog be subjected to a further operation or would the most humane treatment be to destroy him? Is a given kind of husbandry, involving a certain degree of suffering, acceptable or not? and so on. Neither is there any shortage of questions about how to balance the different values, commitments and interests involved in particular cases. How does reducing pain weigh against economic cost? How does the value of a dog's life weigh against the costs of surgery, the risks of surgery, and the feelings of the owners? How does farm animal welfare weigh against profit margins and employment? And so on.

A second reason why vets need to know about ethics is because they are constantly being asked to make judgements and decisions about ethical issues in their everyday working lives. These judgements are unavoidable, regardless of whether or not they are consciously made.

Why think critically about ethics?

In arguing that vets need to know about ethics, I am not arguing that they need to know about the philosophical discipline that Plato started. Instead, I am arguing that they need ways of thinking, explicitly and critically, about the ethical decision-making that we are all already doing. By 'critically' I mean, not 'criticizing', but considering the strengths and weaknesses of different points of view, re-evaluating one's own point of view, uncovering hidden assumptions, and so on. So, why do vets need to think critically and explicitly about ethics and ethical decision-making?

Ethical issues and decisions are often hidden

As I have implied, we do not necessarily think of ourselves as making ethical decisions every time we sit down to lunch, or every time we decide whether or not to use more analgesic. This does not mean that ethical decisions are not being made – just that they are not being consciously made. This may be because they are hidden.

Ethical decisions can be hidden because they are part of a routine, such as eating, that we no longer question, or perhaps never have. They may also not be thought of as ethical decisions because they are made within the context of guidelines – professional guidelines, for example – that we normally just accept. They are ethical decisions nonetheless. Clearly, they will not be removed just because they have not been noticed. Nor are they removed by the existence of guidelines that somebody else has provided. Guidelines typically fall short of giving absolutely clear answers in each and every case, and judgements still need to be made. Is this a case of acceptable suffering or not? Moreover, the guidelines themselves need to be open to constant review. Guidelines on racism within institutions might be an obvious example here.

Ethical issues are often hidden in a number of more general, social or cultural ways. For example, they may be hidden by particular practices or by the way institutions are organized or in language. Consider, again, the animals we eat. A cartoon shows a farmer leaning on a gate, next to a sign which says, 'Pick your own strawberries' and then, 'Strangle your own turkeys'. The cartoon works because of course we do not, as a rule, strangle our own turkeys and, if we did, we would be unlikely to do it for fun on a Sunday afternoon. Most of us let others kill our food for us. Of course, this has a lot to do with convenience, and with a division of labour not unique to this issue. But it also, presumably, has at least a little to do with various kinds of reservations and concerns that we have about killing. Our system of food production allows us not to face these, or have to think them through.

This kind of evasion continues in language. We often do not acknowledge the existence of killing in the way that we talk about it, and we certainly do not talk about it in a manner that suggests pain or fear. Pets are 'put to sleep'. We send chickens to the packing station. We talk about 'harvesting salmon'. We buy salmon, chicken and turkey in the supermarket neatly packaged in a style not exactly chosen to remind the consumer that the meal within was recently alive and swimming/ strutting. So the killing is neatly removed, and hence the ethical issues associated with killing, and/or with causing pain and fear, are glossed over and ignored.

Sometimes the presence of ethical issues is flatly denied. For example, it may be insisted that the debate about genetically modified organisms is a scientific one: it is about what will or will not happen when such organisms are released. This is indeed an empirical, scientific question.

But the debate also raises crucial ethical questions. What level of risk to human health, and to the wider environment, is acceptable? How do these risks weigh against economic gain? Who should be making these decisions? Whose interests does biotechnology really serve?

Alternatively, we may be told that something is inevitable, so that protesting or trying to change it is pointless. Reference to the inevitability of market forces, for example, can be used to deny the existence of – and therefore evade being called to answer – ethical questions about the pursuit of profit at the expense of human safety or animal well-being. Alleged inevitability is not infrequently a cover-up for a human institution that could be changed, but that some sectors of society have a vested interest in not changing.

The ethical issues embedded in a particular case may, then, be hidden in a variety of ways. Decisions may thus be made without anyone noticing that they are dealing with ethics. This will not, of course, make the ethics go away. It will simply mean that the ethical dimensions of the decision are made without much, if any, thought. The first thing that critical thinking about ethics can usefully achieve is thus to highlight the presence of ethical issues and, especially where they are hidden, bring them out into the light. It is then possible to take a hard look at them, and to open them out for discussion and debate. This, in turn, is important for two main reasons: ethical decisions are difficult and ethical principles can (and should) change.

Ethical decisions are typically hard to make. They are often complex, and there may be few clear guidelines. Thinking about them might result in making them better. Not thinking about ethical issues, or failing even to notice their presence, is unlikely to lead to doing them well. It simply means that our ethics are a hotchpotch of different beliefs and principles, often inconsistent, taken on board from a range of sources in our social background and upbringing.

Thinking about the ethics we subscribe to, and why we do so, makes them our own, in a way that acquiring them by osmosis does not. Moreover, it puts us in a better position to defend and explain the ethical decisions we make, and the ethical principles and values we try to uphold. This is important in many contexts, but may be particularly so in the case of vets or others positioned as advocates for improved animal welfare. Robust and well-thought-out arguments will often prove necessary if those who consider animal welfare to be a marginal issue are to be persuaded otherwise.

Ethics that are hidden and hence not open to debate are not likely to change. A second reason for bringing ethics out into the open and subjecting them to critical scrutiny is so that this might lead to their revision and, hopefully, improvement.

This is important in all contexts, not just animal ones. It is a commonplace observation that Victorian values and principles – let alone those of, say, the ancient Greeks – are not always appropriate now, and may need re-thinking. Where such re-thinking has already taken place, we are inclined to believe that progress has occurred. We may think this, for example, with regard to our ethical views about the keeping of slaves, (not banned in British colonies until 1833) or the treatment of women who, in Britain, received equivalent voting rights with men only in 1928.

At the same time, we may think that more such progress is required. We may think, for example, that consumerist and economic values are too often given priority over the interests of animals, the environment and certain groups of people: in short that the ethics and values of modern, industrialized cultures still stand in great need of improvement.

Critical thinking about ethics, as a prerequisite to bringing about change is, then, important in many cases. But it may be especially so with regard to animals.

Animals are a special case

Subjecting our ethics to critical scrutiny is particularly necessary in the context of our attitudes towards, and treatment of, non-human animals. A first point is that we are dealing with creatures who cannot voice their own ideas about how they should be treated. A second point concerns the difficulty caused by our own vested interests and human-centred approach.

Anthropocentrism

Peter Singer once wrote that, for many urban Westerners, the most common encounter they have with other animals is on their dinner plates.[4] Most of us routinely benefit from the use of animals for food, research, education and entertainment. Our vested interests in using animals, and our ideas about our own relative importance, make it hard to think about what we owe animals, ethically. Constant checking is necessary to ensure that we are not simply rationalizing in our own favour.

Take the set of beliefs known as anthropocentrism, or human-centredness. It is easy to see, and to be critical of the more extreme forms of this, as found in the past. Keith Thomas, in *Man and the Natural*

World, refers to Henry More's claim (made in 1653) that the only reason sheep are alive is to keep their meat fresh until we want to eat them.[5] Thomas goes on to detail the stunningly anthropocentric attitudes of the seventeenth century, including the widespread belief that all features of the non-human world were there for human advantage. Explaining the nature of this advantage was clearly more taxing in some cases than others. Horseflies, for example, were said to have been created to develop human ingenuity, while lobsters were carefully designed to provide, not just food but also, in the difficult process of cracking open their legs, exercise. Big fierce animals exist, it is true, but they only come out at night, when humans are safely in bed.[6]

Anthropocentrism is linked to ethics, because if you think that the whole world was created for your benefit then you are liable to think that you are entitled to treat it pretty much as you please. No doubt things have changed since the walking-fridge view of sheep, but perhaps not all that much. Anthropocentrism is still a pervasive attitude. We see it, for example, in the vastly different principles governing research on people and on other animals. We see it in the way we routinely use animals for our own economic and other purposes and in the way we inflict substantial suffering on animals to achieve our own ends – even when, in cases such as testing cosmetics or the production of a particular kind of pâté, those ends are trivial.

Anthropocentrism is still with us. The point here is not to debate its validity. Rather, it is to suggest that it is a phenomenon we must both acknowledge and keep an eye on, if we are to ensure that the way we think about animals, and what counts as decent treatment of them, is not overly biased in our own favour. Animals are a special case, because human-centredness and our own vested interests makes it hard to think fairly about how we should treat them.

Existing animal ethics are inadequate and inconsistent

This difficulty is compounded by the fact that the ethical principles about animals currently endorsed by society are profoundly inadequate and profoundly inconsistent.

Take inadequacy first. For most of the history of Western thought about ethics it has been assumed that we have ethical obligations only to other people. This is true from Aristotle onwards, with few exceptions. The idea that there might be ethical limits to what counts as acceptable treatment of non-humans is thus a very recent one. Within philosophical literature it has come to the fore only in the last two or three decades. Hence our thinking about what exactly we owe animals, which animals, why, and how this should be put into practice, is relatively undeveloped.

This may be one reason why the ethical principles we do have concerning animals are riddled with inconsistencies. We think it obvious that it is acceptable to eat pigs but not poodles. (But why is this so? Pigs are at least as sentient and as intelligent as poodles.) We give pets names, treat them as individuals and spend incredible amounts of money on their food and health – and we do not eat them. Farm animals, on the other hand, are increasingly given numbers, and treated as economic units rather than as family members.

Consider the mink case again. Some striking inconsistencies and hypocrisies emerged in the way this issue was discussed. For example, animal rights activists were criticized for not really caring about animals, because the released mink threatened the lives of nearby pheasants. But the pheasants, of course, were being reared to be shot! Similarly, the activists were held to have been cruel to the mink themselves whose intensive upbringing had not necessarily best equipped them for life in the wild. Farmers and others were then described as 'rescuing' the mink from their risky encounter with the big wide world – in order to put them back in their extremely small cages, thereafter to be killed for their fur.

Vets often have unique opportunities to witness such inconsistencies. I have a friend who works as a vet in a small animal practice in the morning and in a slaughterhouse in the afternoon. She once told me about a day in which she spent the morning setting a complex fracture in a dog's leg, which cost her client several hundred pounds, while in the afternoon she witnessed turkeys arriving for slaughter with legs broken in transit. These fractures were simply ignored.[7]

Why do we treat pigs and poodles, turkeys and dogs so differently? Part of the reason must be that the value we give them derives from their relationship with us. Pets are family, whereas our relationship with farm animals is economic. To an extent this differential valuing may be quite reasonable. But as the *only* factor determining the way we treat animals it is, in my view, inadequate. We need, and still lack, a counter to it in the form of consistent, coherent ethical principles, asserting that animals merit respect and decent treatment, independently of their usefulness to us. These assertions need defending, and I do not have space to do this properly here. My argument would be, however, that our treatment of animals should be grounded in, not (or not just) their relationship to us, but in whether and to what extent they are capable of experiencing pain – whether they are sentient. To put it another way, we need an approach which is based on recognition of features of the animals themselves –

such as their sentience – rather than on our needs for them: an animal-centric, rather than anthropocentric, ethic.

Such principles and ethics have been articulated, in different ways, by philosophers such as Mary Midgley, Bernard Rollin, Peter Singer and Stephen Clarke, and also by a wide range of people campaigning for improvements in animal welfare.[8] They can even be seen to be gaining some ground in society at large, for example in the phasing out of cosmetics testing. But they are by no means embedded in all the institutions and practices that use animals. The view that sentient animals have value in their own right, and that our treatment of them should respect this, is not yet widely accepted in theory and nor is it consistently manifested in practice.

A second set of reasons why critical thinking about ethics is important, is that critical thinking acts as an antidote to simply absorbing ethical principles which are inadequate. This may lead to improvements in ethics, particularly with regard to animals.

Vets are a special case

The fact that, as a society, we lack coherent ethical principles about other animals will affect anyone who has dealings with animals. Vets may find themselves placed in a particularly uncomfortable position here, through no fault of their own.

I have argued that vets are considered to be authorities, including on ethical matters. This is so even though the study of ethics is only slowly being introduced to vet schools, so that vets may have had no special training in ethics; and we are, as a culture, still at the early stages of thinking through and developing animal ethics. In other words, vets may be expected to have expertise in areas that they cannot possibly have – first because no one fully has it, and second because the existing expertise is not being offered, or at least, not routinely.

This observation does nothing to alter the fact that vets are often on the ethical front line. I have already suggested that presence of vets at slaughterhouses, or in the context of transporting livestock, may be taken by the public as reassurance that the system is acceptable. The vets, however, may feel themselves to be co-opted into institutions they have considerable reservations about: that are, for economic or other reasons, not in fact acceptable from an animal welfare perspective.

And of course, vets themselves have to earn a living. In short, vets are not just at the front line, they are also on an ethical high-wire, constantly balancing their concern with animal welfare against the demands of the industries, clients and practices they work for, without necessarily having been given any training in how to do this. All this is set in the context of a society that has inconsistent and self-serving views about what we owe animals ethically, and why.

The study of ethics is, of course, gaining ground in veterinary schools. This has to be a good thing. Ethics should be taught with due recognition of the limitations of our thinking when it comes to applying ethics to animals – perhaps partly in the spirit of research and development, rather than the simple handing down of received wisdom. There is some such wisdom, but it is in short supply. It would be in the interests of vets, as well as other animals, if they were to take an active part in increasing it, and in improving the standard of ethical debate about animals in society at large.[9]

Notes

1. In fact I disagree with the view that the presence of emotion automatically renders a person's argument or point of view invalid. In some cases it is appropriate, and even rational, to be emotional – feeling anger in the face of cruelty or exploitation would be an example. The debate about the role of emotion in ethics is not really the issue here, however. Here the point is that in many contexts a rational approach is assumed to be superior to an emotional one – and vets are often assumed to be rational.
2. For example, many postmodern writers, amongst others, claim that there are no value-free facts. Similarly many sociologists of science claim that 'facts' are always socially constructed.
3. Joe Simpson, *Touching the Void*. London: Jonathan Cape, 1998.
4. Peter Singer, *Animal Liberation*, New York: Avon Books, 2nd edition, 1990, chapter 3.
5. Keith Thomas, *Man and the Natural World*, Harmondsworth: Penguin, 1983, p. 20.
6. *Ibid.*, chapter 1.
7. Many thanks to Sue Haslam for this.
8. See, for example: Mary Midgley, *Animals and Why They Matter*, Ames: University of Georgia Press, 1983; Bernard Rollin, *Animals' Rights and Human Morality*, Buffalo, Prometheus, revised edition, 1992; Peter Singer *Animal Liberation*, New York, Avon Books, 2nd edn, 1990; Stephen Clarke, *Animals and Their Moral Standing*, London, Routledge, 1997.
9. This chapter is based on a paper given to a satellite meeting of the British Veterinary Association Congress in Nottingham in September 1998. Many thanks go to the Animal Welfare, Science, Ethics and Law Veterinary Association (AWSELVA) for arranging this event, and to those who were there for a great discussion and many helpful comments.

2

Ethics and the history of animal welfare

Giles Legood

Anyone who regularly reads the newspapers, listens to the radio or watches the television news will not have failed to notice that the reporting and discussion of human treatment of animals is both news-worthy and of great current interest. We may confidently say that every day there is in the media an item involving ethical or welfare issues surrounding animals. Such issues typically include hunting, genetic engineering, laboratory animals, veal crates, whaling, wearing of fur, dog fighting, puppy farms, badger baiting, stray dogs, fishing, intensive poultry farming, transportation, exotic pets, zoos and circuses. This interest is no new phenomenon, there is an extremely long history of debate and disagreement among humans as to what we may legitimately do to non-human animals and what are our duties and responsibilities towards them.

Ancient views of animals

For centuries philosophy did not defend very seriously the moral status of animals. The philosopher Pythagoras (born *c.* 570 BC) and his followers did show some care for animals but only on the basis that when eating some cooked pork one might inadvertently also be eating the implanted soul of an ancestor. This was their belief in the doctrine of metempsychosis, where the souls of the dead may enter not only bodies of humans but also those of animals and beans. Pythagoras is reported to have tried to prevent someone from whipping a puppy because when he heard it bark he recognized the voice of a dear, departed friend.

Many see Aristotle (384–322 AD) as being responsible for the superior attitude adopted by many in the West towards animals. Aristotle held that only those who were rational, i.e. had the power of reason, were entitled to special moral status. Animals, he believed, were without reason and therefore humankind had no responsibilities or duties towards them. In *Politics* he writes 'Since nature makes nothing without some end in view, nothing to no purpose, it must be that nature has made animals and plants for the sake of humans.' This view endured for centuries and indeed is still held by many today. Two thousand years after Aristotle wrote those words, Nicholas Fontaine in 1738 observed a practical working-out of such a view: 'They administered beatings to dogs with perfect indifference and made fun of those who pitied the creatures as if they felt pain . . . They nailed poor animals up on boards by their paws to vivisect them and see the circulation of the blood, which was a great subject of conversation.'[1]

Religious attitudes towards animals

Archaeological work has shown that Neanderthal humans living 150,000 years ago were intensely religious in their outlook[2]. Despite the claims of secularism religion has been, and for the majority of the world's population still is, a major force in human life. In discussing both the ethics and the history of animal welfare the influence of religion cannot be ignored, for it has motivated many of those working in the field of animal welfare and thus underlies and informs many of the theories and discussions around the issues of the human use of animals. Religious beliefs may raise questions about how agreement can be reached in disagreements as to how animals should be treated. Whilst what we might call 'humane' treatment of animals may well be motivated by religious belief, equally 'inhumane' treatment might also arise from religious conviction. Where human uses and abuses of animals take place from religious conviction, it is likely that discussion as to why an action has been taken might not go beyond, 'Because God/scripture says it is so.' In the world of veterinary science, where scientific enquiry is the usual discourse, such metaphysical claims (that is, claims which cannot be tested by experience or observation) may not sit easily with many. Nevertheless, to understand something of the motivations and beliefs of others is important, both in recognition that we are all different and to engender greater empathy amongst us all. Better understanding of clients and their animals makes for better veterinary surgeons. The following is a brief introduction to the main beliefs of the world's five major religions and their attitudes towards animals.

Judaism

Although there are only 17 million Jews in the world, adherents of this religion have had an enormous influence on world history. Not only has Judaism provided some of the world's greatest thinkers – Moses, Jesus, Freud, Einstein – it also provided the religious outlook out of which Christianity emerged. Jews believe there is one God, a God who has a covenant relationship with the Jewish people. God's requirements of his people are set out in the *Torah* (what Christians regard as the first five books of the Old Testament) and holiness is obtained by observing its teaching. Jews believe that God acts through history and that in the future God will vindicate his promises through the coming of a Messiah. Many of the teachings of Judaism emphasize kindness towards animals and a general reverence towards nature. Jewish law is strict in its requirement that animals be treated properly. It demands that close attention is paid to pets and domestic animals, indeed the *Talmud* (the source of oral law, coming from the rabbis) states that people must provide for their animals before they themselves sit down to eat or drink. It also states that an animal should not be kept unless it can be cared for and fed. Mediaeval rabbis spoke of the obligation to provide for homeless animals and that beasts of burden should not be overloaded, nor should cats and dogs be tormented. Jewish law disapproves of hunting and other blood sports and one of the Ten Commandments requires that animals be allowed to rest on the sabbath. The part of the tradition concerning animals, which is perhaps regarded as the most controversial today, is that of *kosher* killing (*kosher* is a Hebrew word meaning 'fit for use'). These rituals were originally prescribed in order to minimize animal pain and suffering but are thought by many to be inhumane. The method of ritual slaughter (*shechita*) requires that an animal be tied up and hoisted upside down by a chain wrapped around its hind leg, before having its throat cut by a very sharp knife. Some Jews, and others, feel that more modern methods of killing should now be used and that this would be in keeping with the original spirit of the law.[3]

Christianity

Christianity is the religion of the followers of Jesus, a Palestinian Jew who lived approximately 2000 years ago. Christians believe that this Jesus was the Son of God, sent by God to re-establish the broken link between humankind and God. In this way Jesus is regarded as the Messiah who has overcome the human tendency towards selfishness by living a selfless life and finally dying as an innocent victim on a cross.

Scripture, tradition and reason are given weight within Christianity. Christian Scriptures (the Bible) consist of the Jewish texts, written before Jesus (the Old Testament) and texts written some decades after the life of Jesus (the New Testament). The Jewish texts have a strong theme of kindness towards animals. In the first book of the Bible, God gives humankind dominion over the creatures of the earth. This dominion is a stewardship, which brings responsibilities and duties towards animals and the rest of the natural world. The New Testament has many references to Jesus entreating his followers to protect animals. Jesus uses animal imagery to illustrate his teaching and teaches that God loves even the smallest of creatures, 'Are not two sparrows sold for two pennies? And not one of them is forgotten before God.' Many of the saints of the Christian Church are said to have had a close and loving relationship with animals. St Francis of Assisi (1181–1226) called the animals his 'brothers and sisters'. Other Christians, however, reflected the Aristotelian tradition of not regarding animals as having much worth, because they lacked rational souls. Where kindness towards animals was commended it was often only because it was believed that such acts would pre-dispose humans to be kinder towards one another. Such was the attitude of many in the West for centuries, because for this time Christianity was the dominant, or only, religion represented in the population (see pp. 24–8 'Animals in modern Britain'). An increasing number of contemporary Christians are returning to the example of St Francis and today a number of churches have prayers and services for, or in celebration of, animals.[4]

Buddhism

Buddhism contains many different forms of belief and organization and cannot properly be called a single religion, rather it is a family of religions. Buddhism was founded by Siddartha Gautama (560?-483? BC) who, after entering a grove and meditating, experienced the ecstasy of *Nirvana* – the losing of greed, hatred and delusion. From this point on Gautama became known as the Buddha (the Enlightened One). In the *Dharma* (the teaching) the Buddha tells us that all life forms are interrelated and part of a larger unified life force. Thus, to do harm to any part of this single entity is to harm oneself and all life. One of the injunctions of Buddhist monks and lay associates is 'Refrain from destroying life' (*ahimsa*). The *Dharma* states 'Whoever in seeking happiness inflicts pain on beings which also seek happiness, shall find no happiness after death.' Buddhist teaching frowns on the eating of meat, killing animals for sport, the selling of land where animals may be hunted or killed and the use of animals in medical research. Buddhists may not provide for others anything, such as nets, weapons and poisons, which may be used to inflict injury on other living beings. Indeed the *Dharma* states that humans 'must not hate any being and cannot kill a living creature even in thought'.

Islam

Islam is the fastest growing major religion in the world and has been responsible for one of the truly great civilizations of the world. Islam holds that there is one God (*Allah*) and that idolatry and polytheism are mistaken. Muhammad (born 570 AD) is regarded as the Prophet of God, to whom God has given absolute and final revelation. The revelation is contained in the *Qur'an*. Muslims are required to observe the Five Pillars of Islam: witnessing to the faith, ritual prayer, fasting during the month of Ramadan, charity, pilgrimage to Mecca. Islam has very strict prohibitions against cruelty to animals. The scripture called the *Hadith* contains the traditions of the Prophet. The *Hadith* tells us that 'all creatures are like a family of God; and He loves the most those who are the most beneficent to His family'. Muhammad often spoke of the rewards and punishments which individuals would receive on Judgement Day, according to their treatment of animals. He also spoke of 'Kill not a living creature, which *Allah* has made sacrosanct, except for justifiable reason'. The Prophet also condemned blood sports, inciting animals to fight and the trading of wild animals' pelts. Islam sets clear limits as to what is or is not permissible in regard to animals. Animals may be used by humans for food, clothing, as beasts of burden and as a sacrifice in submission to *Allah*, although unnecessary abuse, overwork or cruelty to animals is forbidden. Islam places strong emphasis on food being *halal* (Arabic for 'that which is permitted'). *Halal* slaughter must be carried out by an approved pious Muslim of sound mind, the act must be done manually using a steel knife which must be cleaned after each kill; the animal's respiratory tract, oesophagus and jugular vein must be severed, and the animal must be dead before skinning takes place. *Halal* killing is exempt from the UK legislation which requires that animals be pre-stunned prior to slaughter.

Hinduism

The term 'Hinduism' is something of a misnomer. It is a term which is a convenient European shorthand for many of the varied religions of India, which are based on the ancient and sacred scriptures called the

Vedas written in approximately 1200 BC. To make generalizations can be misleading but the following beliefs are shared by most of those whom we might term 'Hindu'. The universe is interconnected across time and space. Rocks, plants, animals and humans are all interrelated and all are thought to have kinship with one another and to be worthy of respect and life. People are re-born and the location of the soul and body are determined by *karma* (the moral law of cause and effect where one's future existence is determined by the thoughts and actions of the present life). Hinduism therefore compels kindness to animals so as to aid reincarnation (*samsara*) and because humans and animals are part of the same family. Many Hindu texts teach that all species should be treated as children. The cow has a special place in Hinduism, so much so that Gandhi said 'Protection of the cow means protection of the whole dumb creation of God'. Although many Hindus keep a vegetarian diet, others do eat meat. Some of the Hindu castes permit animal sacrifice and others would, under certain circumstances, allow animals to be used for scientific research if there were no alternatives and if human benefit could clearly be shown to come about.

Philosophical approaches towards animals

Thus far in this chapter's consideration of ethics and the history of animal welfare we have seen how ancient and religious views of animals have informed the thinking of our own culture and context. It is important for us to acknowledge that such discussions are not simply dispassionate observances but part of the process whereby we are able to make sense of history by understanding it better and thus allowing it to inform our present and future. Moral theory has a long, distinguished history and has developed a particular vocabulary in its striving to make itself both clear and open to further discussion. The word 'ethics' comes from the Greek word *ethicos* which in the plural means 'manners' or 'customs'. Ethics are then culture-bound and what one society may feel is acceptable may be regarded as beyond the pale in another. Likewise, if viewed as what is customarily acceptable, ethics will differ from age to age. What is regarded as ethical in the twenty-first century may well have been viewed as immoral centuries before, and vice versa. In the developing histories of ethical theory certain categories or divisions are now customarily made between differing types of ethical theories. These are often labelled consequentialist and deontological theories. Briefly we will examine these so as to understand that moral decisions are influenced and guided by the tradition of ethical theory in which each of us, consciously or otherwise, places ourselves.

Consequentialist ethical theories

Though there are various categories of consequentialism, each has the view that the value of an action stems entirely from the value of its consequences, rather than from any features it may have such as truthfulness or faithfulness. Of course, all plausible moral theories recognize that the consequences of an act are morally relevant but consequentialist theories see these as the dominant moral consideration. According to consequential theories the ultimate moral aim should be that the outcome of the action should be as good as possible. That is to say, an action is right if it produces the best possible outcome. This raises the question 'What is the best possible outcome?' A classic consequentialist doctrine which answers the question clearly was put forward by Jeremy Bentham (1748–1832) – Utilitarianism. Utilitarianism says that the best possible outcome, what is of ultimate value, is happiness and the avoidance of pain.

Deontological ethical theories

The major point of difference between consequentialist and deontological theories is that the latter sees rightness as primary. For consequentialists, what is right does not have any independent standing but is defined in terms of what produces good outcomes. For deontologists certain actions are intrinsically right and their rightness does not depend on any further claim. Indeed, in deontological terms the best outcome is achieved if the right action is performed.

One of the classic statements arguing for a deontological view is the 'categorical imperative' of Immanuel Kant (1724–1804). According to Kant this imperative can be used to answer the question of whether a certain rule, such as one must always tell the truth, was really a duty. Kant argues that an action may only be taken if we are willing for it to become a universal law, applicable to everyone. Kant argues that such actions should only become universal laws if they are not self-contradictory. Kant believed that animals should be regarded as instruments to be used by humans (means to an end – humans being ends in themselves). A Kantian view of deontological theory is just one expression however of this philosophical approach and it is entirely possible to be a deontologist and to regard animals as ends rather than just as means.

Animals in modern Britain

Eighteenth-century Britain was a country in which calls for social reform arose and gained influential support. Parliament was unable to ignore the calls for radical social change which many notable individuals, often with a single issue as an aim, had been proclaiming. William Wilberforce's tireless work for the abolition of slavery finally succeeded in amending the law in 1807 after more than twenty years of campaigning. Other legislation aimed at outlawing, for instance, cruelty to children, also achieved success. Many of those who campaigned for such changes were motivated by a Christian conviction that it was an affront to the God who was made known in the person of Jesus that human beings, made in the image of God and all equally loved, should be treated so shamefully. It occurred, too, to many that this Christian concern for God's creation should also include those non-human creatures, who were also created and loved by the same God. John Wesley (1703–91), a Church of England priest and the founder of the movement which became known as Methodism, was a vegetarian and argued that humans had a duty to be tender towards animals because both humans and animals 'were the offspring of one common father'. Wesley's widespread preaching (he travelled 250,000 miles on horse during his lifetime) and the writing of such people as Bishop Joseph Butler (1692–1752), had a considerable influence on the change of attitude towards animals at this time.

It would be wrong, however, to think that only those inspired by religious allegiance were calling for changes of attitude and practice. One of the most influential campaigners for fairer treatment of animals was the economist and philosopher Jeremy Bentham. As previously mentioned, Bentham is best known for advocating, with J. S. Mill, the idea of Utilitarianism. When faced with deciding which possible action to take, Utilitarianism offers a simple equation for helping decide which action should be made. Simply expressed, according to Bentham, one should ask which action is going to bring about 'the greatest happiness for the greatest number' and pursue this. Whilst Bentham took this equation to mean what will bring about the greatest *human* happiness, a number of philosophers have subsequently widened the scope of the equation to embrace animals too. When talking of animals specifically, Bentham did, however, ask a question which was revolutionary for his day: 'The question is not, Can they reason? nor, Can they talk? but, Can they suffer?'

Towards the end of the eighteenth century two cases of animal cruelty came to public attention which became instrumental in influencing public opinion to such an extent that there were widespread calls for law reform. In 1790 a man was unsuccessfully prosecuted for ripping out a horse's tongue whilst simultaneously beating it on the head. He was acquitted because there were no laws on the statute books at that time which gave any protection to animals from cruelty. In 1793 two butchers in Manchester were fined for cutting off the feet of live sheep and then driving the animals through the streets. The public was outraged, for not only had cruelty clearly taken place but had the butchers owned the sheep themselves they could not have been prosecuted. At that time there was no legislation in place which prohibited cruelty towards animals which one owned oneself and thus prosecution in such cases would only be successful on the grounds that a cruel act towards an animal had harmed someone else's property.

With such cases seizing the public imagination, legislation, or at least attempts at it, followed. In 1800 Sir William Pultney brought a Bill before Parliament to outlaw bull baiting. The Bill failed, as did a similar one two years later. Even at this stage the welfare of the animals was perhaps not paramount, as one of the arguments against the Bills was that 'it would be wrong to deprive the lower orders of their amusements'.[5] Attempts at successfully introducing legislation continued however and in 1809 the Lord Chancellor, Sir Thomas Erskine, introduced a Bill 'Preventing the Wanton and Malicious Cruelty Towards Animals'. Erskine's Bill was passed by the House of Lords but it failed in the Commons. Nevertheless, supporters of laws to protect animals took heart that if such influential people as the Lord Chancellor were concerned about the matter then the tide must be turning in their favour.

The date which is singularly most important in the history of animal welfare legislation in Britain is 22 July 1822. This is the date of the enactment of the first piece of legislation which gave protection to at least some categories of animals. Sponsored by Richard Martin MP (nicknamed 'Humanity Martin'), the 'Act to Prevent the Cruel and Improper Treatment of Cattle' gave the courts power to impose fines of between ten shillings and five pounds, or up to three months imprisonment, for acts of cruelty towards cattle, horses or sheep. Subsequent amendments to what became known as 'Martin's Act' gave increasing protection to large animals and in 1835 a Bill giving protection to domestic animals passed through Parliament with an ease which indicated the extent to which the arguments of Martin and others had been won.

Although the argument in Parliament may have been won, cruelties, nevertheless, continued. It was still not uncommon for cat skinners to practise their trade. Here, the skins of cats were removed while the animals were still alive and then the animals were often thrown into the street. A number of people also made their living by stealing cats in order to provide the skinners with potential pelts. Pigs were routinely whipped to tenderize their flesh, shopkeepers kept squirrels in cages, running on treadmills, in order to attract customers, and animals were taught to perform tricks for people's amusement through acts of torture and deprivation.

We noted earlier in the chapter that some of those most influential in campaigning for animal welfare legislation had also previously worked for improved conditions for humans who lived and worked in misery, notably as slaves or as child labour. At the time that Martin's Act was beginning to have an effect on the living conditions and treatment of animals, an organization was founded by an Anglican priest, the Reverend Arthur Broome, to educate the public in the matter of humane treatment of animals. The first meeting of this Society for the Prevention of Cruelty to Animals (the SPCA, later to become the RSPCA) was held in the appropriately named Old Slaughter's Coffee House in St Martin's Lane, London in 1824. Its first secretary was John Colam, also secretary of the National Society for the Prevention of Cruelty to Children, and one of its founding members was anti-slavery leader, William Wilberforce.

These then were changes in attitude and legislation up to mid-nineteenth-century Britain, but perhaps the greatest influence on the treatment of animals came about through the scientific work of Charles Darwin (1809-82). Although not the first person to put forward a theory of evolution by natural selection, Darwin was the first person to see his theory gain wide acceptance both within the scientific community and wider society. In his two most notable publications *The Origin of Species by Means of Natural Selection* (1859) and *The Descent of Man* (1871) Darwin blew apart the almost universally accepted theory that human beings were set apart biologically from the rest of the natural order. Whilst his views were widely disputed and opposed when he first published them, Darwin's influence now means that human beings cannot easily believe themselves to be entirely separate from all other living organisms on the earth. Twenty years before *The Origin of Species* was published, Darwin put his view thus, 'Man in his arrogance thinks himself a great work worthy the interposition of a deity. More humble and I think truer to consider him created from animals.'[6]

It is not surprising, given his lifelong work of understanding the links between human beings and animals, that Darwin was also one of those who worked hard to promote the introduction of the 1876 Cruelty to Animals Act. This act was drafted as a result of a Royal Commission appointed to examine and make recommendations on the issue and was the first act to regulate animal experimentation in Britain. It was to remain on the statute books for over a hundred years. Although in the intervening time the issue of animal experimentation was considered by various commissions, and changes were recommended, the law was to remain unaltered until the introduction of the Animals (Scientific Procedures) Act in 1986. Change finally came because of a number of factors. The 1960s and 1970s were times of increased public concern for animal experimentation. In the scientific community, too, the mid-Victorian legislation was recognized as being inadequate to control the pain, distress and other suffering which modern experiments were liable to inflict on animals.

The 1986 Act extends the scope of the 1876 Act to include within its remit all vertebrate animals and their embryonic forms from the halfway point of gestation or, in the case of fish and amphibians, from when they are capable of feeding. Subsequently the Act has been amended to also include regulation over the use of the common octopus – *octopus vulgaris*. Not only does the Act regulate animal experimentation but it also covers the production of vaccines and sera, the growth of tumours and other activities which may cause 'pain, suffering, distress or lasting harm'.

It is not only the range of animal species which is regulated in the 1986 Act but also the licensing of the experiments undertaken. Three separate types of licence are required for experimentation on an animal to be carried out. Each investigator must hold a personal licence which is only awarded on successful completion of a Home Office accredited course and each experiment must be granted a specific project licence, detailing the nature and limits of the particular experiment. In addition, premises used for research or the breeding of animals must be certified. To ensure that, once granted, licences are adhered to there are a number of levels of control. A Home Office Inspectorate polices the research. A national Animal Procedures Committee advises the Secretary of State for Home Affairs on experiments on tobacco research, procedures carried out to increase proficiency in microsurgery, some areas of primate work, and cosmetic testing. Each laboratory where research involving animals takes place must have two 'named persons' who help regulate at a local level. The first of these persons (usually a senior animal technician) has responsibility for the day-to-day care of the animals and the second, a veterinary surgeon, oversees the general health and welfare of the animals together with the anaesthesia and analgesia administered. The legislation allows, indeed requires, veterinary surgeons to immediately euthanize any animal in intractable pain or distress that is not the responsibility of a personal licensee. In extreme cases they may also require the project to be terminated forthwith.[7]

Throughout the twentieth century then, as a result of the pioneering scientific work of Darwin, human understanding of the biological world continued in a way that would have been unrecognizable to him. In 1909 W.L. Johannsen wrote of genes (an abbreviation of 'pangene') as the units of inheritance that control the passing of an hereditary characteristic from parent to offspring. This handing on of characteristics is done by controlling the structures of proteins or other genetic material. In the latter half of the same century the discovery that genes are identified with lengths of DNA or RNA was made. As a result, we now know that humans share approximately 98.4 per cent of their genes with chimpanzees. Such information has potentially enormous consequences for humankind. In pre-Darwinian times a crucial distance could be maintained between humans and other animals. However, with the knowledge that genetically we are so close to other species, our attitudes towards and treatment of these species cannot easily remain unquestioned. Indeed, Richard Dawkins, Professor of the Public Understanding of Science at Oxford, has speculated that if in some remote jungle we discovered a species which was a living link between humans and chimpanzees, 'our precious norms and ethics could come crashing about our ears'.

Reviews and alternatives

We have seen that in modern Britain since the seventeenth century there has been increasing concern over the use and treatment of animals by human beings. This concern has been shown through greater public awareness of the issues surrounding human uses and abuses of animals and, in turn, this awareness has been reflected in legislation and other controls. One of the most significant pressures felt in laboratory use of animals has been 'The Three Rs'. Not only were they of use to those who drafted the 1986 Act but they have a continued significance today for all those preparing submissions of proposed experimentation involving animals.

The Three Rs

In 1959 Russell and Burch published a book which suggested that those undertaking and reviewing animal experiments should look at any trial and ask themselves if the experiment could improve animal welfare in any of three ways.[8] The questions to be asked are: Can there be replacement of any animals in the research? Can there be a reduction in the numbers of animals used? Can there be a refinement of the experimental techniques so as to cause less suffering? In Britain approximately

2.8 million animals are used in experiments of one sort or another each year.[9] Until the very recent interest in procedures for the breeding of transgenic animals this figure had been falling for over ten years, in no small part because of the questions posed by Russell and Burch. Indeed, we might say that larger numbers of researchers are now not asking how many animals will be needed to conduct a particular piece of research, but rather are animals necessary at all for this experiment to take place? The Three Rs have allowed those who oppose the use of any animals in testing and those who argue that some testing is necessary, to work together both to see that fewer experiments take place and that when they do that there is less suffering for a fewer number of animals.

The question of replacement is a straightforward one. Those who conduct research involving animals have seen that it has been possible to reduce the numbers of animals used. This has been done in a number of ways. It may not be necessary to carry out a particular experiment at all if other research methods involving, for instance, cell lines or computer models are used. In some trials it may be that human volunteers are able to replace animals. When considering reduction, biometry (medical and veterinary statistics) has been able to assist researchers greatly in assessing the minimum numbers of animals needed for an experiment's results to be statistically relevant. Through sharing of data with other researchers it has also been found unnecessary for identical trials to take place in more than one research centre, and thus through the publication of results the numbers of trials can fall. The refinement of a trial is made by removing some of the pain or distress likely to be felt by any animals being used in an experiment. This may involve lowering the dosages of drugs administered to the animals or improving the conditions in which an experiment is conducted.

The Five Freedoms

Reference was made earlier in this chapter to that fact that the period from the late 1950s has been one of enormous change for animal welfare in Britain. The work of Russell and Burch and the resulting legislative changes have had a tremendous effect on the conditions under which animals are used. Shortly after the Three Rs were first put forward, the Brambell Committee reviewed the issues surrounding the welfare of farm animals used in intensive husbandry systems. The Committee suggested that such farm animals should have the freedom to 'stand up, lie down, turn around, groom themselves and stretch their limbs'. Collectively known as 'The Five Freedoms', these minimum standards of husbandry have undergone a number of subsequent revisions and have now been widely accepted in Britain and the rest of Europe. Whilst it has to be acknowledged that even the original freedoms are by no means universally accepted and implemented, in 1993 the United Kingdom Farm Animal Welfare Council (FAWC) revised the freedoms of the Brambell text, stating that the standards should be set even higher. The five freedoms now stand as:

1   Freedom from thirst, hunger and malnutrition – by ready access to fresh water and a diet to maintain full health and vigour;
2   Freedom from discomfort – by providing a suitable shelter and a comfortable resting area;
3   Freedom from pain, injury and disease – by prevention or rapid diagnosis and treatment;
4   Freedom to express normal behaviour – by providing sufficient space, proper facilities and company of the animal's own kind;
5   Freedom from fear and distress – by ensuring conditions which avoid mental suffering.[10]

These freedoms are, of course, neither definitive nor independent of one another. Whilst some have pointed out that the freedoms hoped for would give better conditions for living than many human animals enjoy, others have argued that absolute attainment is not only unrealistic but that the freedoms are, to some extent, incompatible: 'Complete behavioural freedom, for example, is unhygienic for all us animals!'[11] The five freedoms do however give a set of principles to hold before us in our husbandry of farm animals. They also make a special contribution in attempting to get humans to see the issue of welfare as it may be felt by the animals themselves, rather than see it as a hurdle to be overcome when economic realities of food production are considered.

Local ethical review process

In the UK since 1 April 1999 the Secretary of State for Home Affairs has required that every designated establishment which carries out scientific procedures on animals has in place a local ethical review process. Failure to meet this requirement, made by the Home Secretary on the recommendation of the Animal Procedures Committee, has serious consequences. In extreme cases the establishment may have its designation withdrawn by the Home Office and thus will find itself unable to carry out scientific procedures using animals. The certificate holder of each establishment is responsible for the operation of the process and for the appointment of people to implement its procedures.

The Home Office has outlined its thinking on who should be involved in the process and has proposed a 'pool of participants' rather than a strictly defined membership. In each establishment the Named Veterinary Surgeon together with representatives from among the Named Animal Care and Welfare Officers must be involved. Project and personal licence holders should also be represented and, where possible, the views of those persons with no responsibilities under the Act should also be taken into account (these people might include ethicists, clergy, statisticians, legal representatives, local councillors, etc.). The Home Office Inspector may attend the meetings of the ethical review process at any time and access its records in order to monitor its operation and to advise.

The ethical review process has three specific functions. Firstly, it is to provide independent ethical advice to the certificate holder, particularly with respect to project licence applications and standards of animal care and welfare. Secondly, it is to provide support to named people and advice to licensees regarding animal welfare and ethical issues arising from their work. Thirdly, it is to promote the use of ethical analysis to increase awareness of animal welfare issues and develop new initiatives leading to the widest possible application of the Three Rs. In all this work the Home Office further expects the process to promote its role, educating both users and non-users, as widely as security and commercial or intellectual confidentiality allow.

Conclusion

In this chapter we have seen that the history of human treatment of animals has been both long and varied. Whilst vestiges of Aristotelianism still linger today, there are also, however, real signs of encouragement for those who urge that humans should both moderate their use of animals and where possible remove the need of animals to be used at all, using them only when necessary. Disagreements as to what 'necessary' use might mean are inevitable, but all (or at least almost all) people in the UK agree that the processes of improving welfare for animals that have been put in place in the last 150 years are to be welcomed. There is a common feeling, too, (as evidenced by the public interest in the issues listed in the opening paragraph of the chapter) that these processes can and should be improved and carried forward.

Notes

1. James Rachels, *Created from Animals: The Moral Implications of Darwinism*. Oxford: Oxford University Press, 1991, p. 130.
2. For an excellent introduction to the world's major religions, together with historical background, religious texts and analysis, see, Ian Markham (ed.), *A World Religions Reader*, 2nd edn, Oxford: Blackwell, 2000.
3. Further discussion of the Jewish tradition's treatment of animals may be found in Andrew Linzey and Dan Cohn-Sherbok, *After Noah: Animals and the Liberation of Theology*. London: Mowbray, 1997.
4. Since the late 1970s there has been increasing interest amongst Christians in studying seriously the demands and questions which animal life raises. A comprehensive introduction to the topic is Andrew Linzey and Dorothy Yamamoto (eds), *Animals on the Agenda*. London: SCM Press, 1998.
5. For this and other details concerning the introduction of legislation in Britain see Lewis Regenstein, *Replenish the Earth*. London: SCM Press, 1991, pp. 91-3.
6. James Rachels, *Created from Animals: The Moral Implications of Darwinism*. Oxford: Oxford University Press, 1991, p. 1.
7. Further details of the British situation, together with an account of animal law and policy in the USA, Canada and Australia, are discussed in Bernard Rollin, *The Unheeded Cry: Animal Consciousness, Animal Pain, and Science*. Ames: Iowa State University Press, 1989, pp. 167-87.
8. W.M.S. Russell and R.L. Burch, *The Principles of Humane Experimentation Technique*. London: Methuen, 1959.
9. This figure does not include animals which may have been bred for use in animal experimentation but are not used. These animals may be deemed 'unsuitable' because they are not the right genotype, sex, age, weight, or 'quality' for experiments. Neither does it include animals killed for tissue to be used in research. The Home Office keeps no record of such animals because a licence is not required to kill surplus animals.
10. Farm Animal Welfare Council, *Second Report on Priorities for Research and Development in Farm Animal Welfare*. London: Ministry of Agriculture, Food and Fisheries, 1993.
11. John Webster, *Animal Welfare: A Cool Eye Towards Eden*. Oxford: Blackwell, 1994, p. 11.

3

Towards a better understanding of animal protection legislation: the meaning of 'unnecessary suffering' explained

Mike Radford

Introduction

The purpose of this chapter is simple, although its implications are far-reaching: namely, to argue that it is important for veterinarians to develop an understanding of animal protection law, not just by reference to what the legislation says, but to what it means in practice. This contention will be demonstrated by providing an analysis of the way in which the English and Scottish courts have interpreted the ubiquitous legislative term, 'unnecessary suffering'.

Traditionally in Britain, consideration of animal protection legislation has not featured prominently as part of a veterinarian's training. There may be a number of explanations for this. Until relatively recently, for example, the volume of such legislation was limited, and both the policy it represented and its application may have appeared to be settled and straightforward. Furthermore, the emphasis of veterinary education has been on science, largely to the exclusion of wider issues which arise as a consequence of our relationship with other species. This state of affairs has been exacerbated as an already overloaded syllabus has come under further pressure in the face of continuing technical advances in the treatment of animals.

Such a situation might be defensible if the veterinarian's role were limited to that of a clinician, but this is self-evidently not the case. The profession seeks, and is looked to by the wider community, to be at the forefront of the debate on the proper treatment of animals, whether collectively in advising policy-makers, or as individuals during the course of veterinary practice. An intrinsic part of this debate focuses on the law, which remains the principal social mechanism relied upon to define the nature and extent of our duties to other species, and for which we are ultimately accountable to the courts. The more the profession as a whole knows of the nature, sources, categories and application of the law, the better will be its members' comprehension of the legislation's strengths and weaknesses, and its potential for promoting animal welfare. On this ground alone it is highly desirable that veterinarians should have a developed understanding of the law. There are, however, two further arguments which make the case unanswerable, at least in the eyes of the present writer. First, by means of inspection of premises, examination of animals, and the provision of expert evidence to the courts, veterinarians play a crucial part in contributing to the effectiveness of animal protection law. Second, and perhaps most importantly, by taking account of economic, moral, political and scientific considerations, the law attempts to reflect an albeit crude consensus of the way in which society considers that animals should be treated. In other words, law can be regarded as laying down a social measure of welfare. This being so, is it possible for veterinarians to be confident of fulfilling their obligation to ensure the welfare of the animals committed to their care if they are unaware of the relevant legal standards? Against this background it is inadequate simply to provide them with a rudimentary account of the main statutory provisions and a copy of the current edition of the RCVS *Legislation Affecting the Veterinary Profession in the United Kingdom*. In view of the controversial and difficult issues raised by our relationship with animals, together with the particular nature of a veterinarian's professional and ethical obligations, it is submitted that something rather more sophisticated is now required. By way of support for this argument, let us now consider in some detail the concept of unnecessary suffering. It is a phrase with which every reader will be familiar, but what does it actually *mean*?

The significance of the unnecessary suffering test

Legislation concerning the treatment of animals has no uniform objective and therefore no abiding principle, but a consistent theme is the prevention of unnecessary suffering. For example, the Protection of Animals Act 1911, the Protection of Animals (Scotland) Act 1912, the Abandonment of Animals Act 1960, and the Protection Against Cruel

Tethering Act 1988, together make it an offence of cruelty to cause unnecessary suffering to a domestic or captive animal as a result of:

1. wantonly or unreasonably doing or omitting to do any act;
2. the manner in which it is conveyed or carried;
3. abandoning such an animal;
4. in relation to England or Wales, the conditions or manner in which any horse, ass or mule has been tethered.

In addition, the test of unnecessary suffering has been adopted in relation to the treatment of animals during transit, at market, slaughtered by religious methods, and as the basis for the protection of wild mammals.[1]

The legal nature of the unnecessary suffering test

Causing unnecessary suffering is a criminal offence. Accordingly, in order to secure a conviction the prosecution is required to establish the defendant's guilt beyond reasonable doubt. At first reading the term would seem capable of meaning all things to all people. It is certainly the case that, in the context of a prosecution, determining whether an animal has suffered unnecessarily is a question of fact.[2] In other words, in reaching their decision as to whether the defendant is guilty, the members of the court are required to exercise their individual judgement in the light of the particular circumstances of the case, and the evidence which has been placed before them. Put in these terms it may appear to be a highly subjective exercise. However, while trial courts do enjoy considerable discretion to decide for themselves whether unnecessary suffering has occurred, it is by no means unfettered. By having regard to the way in which the higher courts have interpreted its meaning, it is possible to piece together a body of guidance as to the nature and application of the unnecessary suffering test, starting from the basic proposition laid down more than a century ago by the High Court: 'two things must be proved – first, that pain or suffering has been inflicted in fact', and, secondly, 'that it was inflicted cruelly, that is, without necessity, or, in other words, without good reason'.[3]

Suffering

Except as discussed below, it must be established at the outset that the animal actually suffered. In the most extreme cases this may be inferred from the facts but, generally, the prosecution will put before the court the evidence of an expert witness, most usually that of a veterinary surgeon. It is at this point that developing scientific understanding of the behaviour, psychology and physiology of animals can be crucial in assisting the criminal justice process, and it is therefore essential that any one putting themselves forward as an expert witness is fully cognizant of the current state of knowledge, aware of all the relevant literature, understands its practical significance, and can help the court by relating their scientific expertise to the facts of the case in a way which is intelligible, relevant and credible.

The alleged suffering will most often take the form of pain, but this need not be so: mental and physical suffering are both equally pertinent. Furthermore, there is no requirement to demonstrate that the suffering was either severe or prolonged. The courts have said that the meaning of unnecessary suffering 'imports the idea of the animal undergoing, for however brief a period, unnecessary pain, distress or tribulation'.[4] It *is* essential, however, to establish that the animal has endured *some* degree of suffering. For example, it is not enough to show merely that the defendant was responsible for the death of the animal. If it cannot be demonstrated beyond reasonable doubt that it previously suffered, either because it is impossible to be sure of the cause of death or, alternatively, 'no skilled opinion or direct evidence is available to support the finding that the occurrence of death was or was not instantaneous', the prosecution must fail because 'an essential link in the chain of proof is lacking'.[5]

The situations in which it is *not* necessary to prove suffering are in respect of the protection of wild mammals, where it is enough to show that the defendant intended to inflict unnecessary suffering, regardless of whether this actually occurred,[6] and in relation to abandoned animals, markets, and commercial transport where, in each case, the legislation specifies that it is enough to demonstrate the circumstances were such as to be *likely* to cause the animal unnecessary suffering.[7] At a practical level this avoids difficult decisions for those charged with enforcement in assessing when an animal's situation has crossed the line from inadequate to unlawful, especially in cases of neglect where its condition and environment may deteriorate gradually over a period of time. More significantly, this prospective test meets the principle which underlies the legislation, namely the *protection* of animals. It is ironic that, in most circumstances, the law is powerless to intervene until an animal is actually suffering. Prior to that point prevention is entirely dependent upon persuasion.

Necessity

Once it has been demonstrated that the animal was exposed to some degree of suffering (or, where appropriate, was placed in a situation in which it was likely to suffer), attention turns to the question of necessity. Causing *necessary* suffering does not constitute an offence. Furthermore, it is clear on the basis of judicial authority that the requirement to avoid unnecessary suffering does not amount to a duty to ensure that an animal is caused the least possible suffering. In particular, where a practice or system of husbandry is expressly or implicitly permitted by legislation, the courts will determine the question of necessity in the context of the lawful practice or system which has been adopted, and not by comparison with an alternative method, even though this might cause less suffering for the animals concerned. This caveat is particularly significant in relation to the commercial rearing of livestock. So where, for example, it was alleged (prior to the practice being banned in Britain) that raising veal calves by keeping them continuously tethered individually in stalls amounted to unnecessary suffering, the High Court upheld the magistrates' decision to dismiss the case on the basis that 'the magistrates did not find that suffering was caused to any of the calves in this instance beyond that which was general in animal husbandry'. The court specifically rejected the contention that account should have been taken of other methods of raising veal calves. 'This was a very much wider question than that which the magistrates had to consider', said the judge. It was not part of their function in determining whether an offence had been committed to undertake 'a general comparison of various forms of intensive farming which undoubtedly arouse considerable controversy'.[8]

The issue of necessity depends very much, therefore, on the circumstances in which the animal happens to find itself. According to the courts 'What amounts to a necessity or good reason for inflicting suffering upon animals protected by the statute is hardly capable of satisfactory definition', but they have affirmed that 'the amount of pain caused, the intensity and duration of the suffering, and the object to be attained, must, however, always be essential elements for consideration.'[9] The question is to be decided by a balancing exercise in which different factors will be given varying degrees of importance, depending upon the particular circumstances. Accordingly, treatment which may be lawful in one situation can amount to an offence in another: 'To attain one object,' the courts have observed, 'the infliction of more pain may be justified than would ever be tolerated to secure another'.[10] It follows that determining whether suffering is unnecessary is not a mechanical exercise. Members of the court are called upon to apply their judgement to the facts before them, and it is inevitable that magistrates and, in Scotland, sheriffs may differ in the importance they attach to the relevant factors they are required to take into account. Hence, different courts may come to incompatible decisions on similar facts. They must, however, always exercise their discretion in a way which is compatible with the general principles that have been laid down by the higher courts.

Thus, to cause an animal to suffer in the absence of a legitimate object points to a conclusion that it is unnecessary. However, the pursuit of a legitimate object does not of itself automatically excuse any suffering which results, the courts having held that where it arises in consequence of something which may 'fairly and properly' be done to an animal, such suffering should nevertheless be no more than that which is 'reasonably necessary to effect the result'.[11] Accordingly, on the basis of judicial authority, in order to establish that suffering caused to an animal is necessary, and therefore lawful, two conditions must be met. First, it must be shown that the animal's treatment was to effect an 'adequate and reasonable object'; secondly, there 'must be proportion between the object and the means'.[12] Or, to put it another way, 'the beneficial or useful end sought to be attained must be reasonably proportionate to the extent of the suffering caused, and in no case can substantial suffering be inflicted, unless necessity for its infliction can reasonably be said to exist'.[13]

The meaning of 'unnecessary' in the context of the offence of wantonly or unreasonably doing or omitting to do any act causing any unnecessary suffering

So, once the legitimacy of the object has been established, determining the necessity of any consequential suffering will normally involve applying this proportionality test, by which the purpose is to be weighed against the degree and nature of the suffering. There is, however, one exception to this general principle: the courts have applied a different formula in respect of the offence of wantonly or unreasonably doing or omitting to do any act which causes a domestic or captive animal any unnecessary suffering.[14] The reason for this is the singular wording used to define the offence which, unlike others based on unnecessary suffering, includes the adverbs 'wantonly or unreasonably'. In consequence, it is distinctive in being made up of three separate components:

1. *unreasonable* conduct on the part of the defendant;
2. resulting in *suffering*;
3. *which is unnecessary*.

On this basis the High Court has held in two recent decisions[15] that in this context 'unnecessary' is to be equated with 'not inevitable' or 'could be avoided or terminated'. At first sight this would seem to remove the requirement to consider the proportionality of any suffering, but in practice this is not so. According to the court, factors such as the reason for the suffering, together with its nature, intensity and duration – the balancing exercise – are to be taken into account in determining whether the defendant acted *unreasonably*, and it would be inappropriate to repeat this exercise in deciding whether the suffering was *unnecessary*.

In this particular situation, then, 'unnecessary' is to be interpreted as 'avoidable', or 'not inevitable', but such a meaning cannot be applied in relation to other offences arising from unnecessary suffering, because in none of them is the term prefaced by the word 'unreasonably'. To do so would oust the proportionality test, thereby making *any* suffering which was not avoidable or inevitable potentially illegal, regardless of its purpose, nature, duration or intensity, something which is clearly not intended by the legislation.

The issue of *mens rea*

In respect of most criminal offences it is not enough merely for the prosecution to prove that the defendant committed the proscribed act; it must also demonstrate that he was culpable by reference to his state of mind at the time of the offence. The technical term for this requirement is *mens rea* (literally, 'a guilty mind'); it is indicated in legislation by words such as 'intentionally', 'recklessly', 'wilfully' and 'knowingly'. The principle reflects the importance attached to personal responsibility as a constituent in establishing criminal liability: the onus is on the prosecution to demonstrate beyond reasonable doubt not only that the defendant perpetrated the offence, but also that he knew what he was doing and was aware, or should have been aware, of the likely outcome of his act or omission. If no such mental element is expressly stated in the legislation, the offence may be one of strict liability, meaning that the proscribed act alone constitutes the offence. However, the absence of words relating to the defendant's state of mind does not necessarily mean that it is irrelevant; the courts often take the view that Parliament can be presumed to have intended that *mens rea* should be a constituent of an offence, and they interpret the legislation accordingly.

The issue of *mens rea* is of considerable practical importance because it defines the standard by which the defendant's conduct is to be judged. Criminal offences broadly fall into one of three groups in this regard:

1. those where the defendant's mental state is considered subjectively;
2. those where it is viewed objectively;
3. those where it is irrelevant.

In respect of offences where a *subjective* test is applied the prosecution is required to demonstrate that the particular defendant before the court knew, or, on the basis of the evidence, must be presumed to have known, the likely consequences of his conduct. In contrast, the *objective* test involves comparing the defendant's behaviour against that which might be expected of the reasonable person in the same situation. Accordingly, it is enough for the prosecution to satisfy the court that the defendant *should* have been aware of the implications of his conduct. The third group of offences are those of strict liability. This means that the defendant may be convicted solely on the basis of his conduct, regardless of his intention or knowledge.

Mens rea and unnecessary suffering

There is no single rule concerning *mens rea* which can be applied to offences based on causing an animal unnecessary suffering. Which category any particular offence falls into depends on the wording of the respective legislation.

Offences to which a subjective test is applied

There are two situations in which a subjective test is applied. First, in relation to prosecutions brought under the Wild Mammals (Protection) Act 1996, the legislation stipulates that the defendant must be shown to have intended to inflict unnecessary suffering on the animal. In the absence of such an intention, no offence is committed. Secondly, where the defendant is only indirectly responsible for the cruelty, in that he caused or procured it, the case law points to there being a requirement on the prosecution to establish that he knew, or by inference must have known, that the animal was suffering. In the absence of such evidence, the causation or procurement of the cruelty will not be established.[16]

Offences to which an objective test is applied

Clearly, if the prosecution demonstrates that the perpetrator intended or knew of the animal's suffering, and the court considers it to be unnecessary, he will be guilty of an offence, but if the prosecution were required always to meet the subjective test, it would have three important consequences:

1. an additional evidential burden would be placed upon it;
2. the degree of protection accorded to an animal would vary depending upon the defendant's knowledge of its needs and awareness of the possible consequences arising from his conduct (the less he understands the animal's requirements, the more difficult it would be to show that he was aware of the likely detrimental effect of his behaviour);
3. the defendant's own view (however misguided) of the appropriate manner in which to treat the animal would become relevant.

Fortunately the judiciary have been alert to the inherent drawbacks of requiring a subjective test to establish that an animal has suffered unnecessarily. As long ago as 1889, for example, the High Court pointed out that, in relation to offences of cruelty, if a defendant could excuse himself on the basis that he honestly believed the law justified his action, 'it is difficult to see the limits to which such a principle might not be pushed, and the creatures it is man's duty to protect from abuse, would oftentimes be suffering victims of gross ignorance and cupidity'.[17] Accordingly, where 'a desirable and legitimate object is sought to be attained', the court pronounced, 'the pain caused ... must not so far outbalance the importance of the end as to make it clear to any reasonable person that it is preferable the object should be abandoned rather than that the disproportionate suffering should be inflicted'. Similarly, the Scottish High Court has held that there is no requirement to prove the defendant's deliberate intention to cause unnecessary suffering. The court was mindful that to decide otherwise and impose a subjective test would require the prosecution 'to assume a very difficult and often impossible onus and by perhaps penalizing the intelligent and sensitive, while allowing the callous, indifferent or ignorant to escape'. The appropriate test to be applied is, therefore, to ask 'whether the facts are such as to justify the inference either that the accused actually knew that he was inflicting unnecessary pain and suffering on a dumb animal, or at least that he ought to have known that, because the proved circumstances would have conveyed such knowledge to any normal and reasonable person'.[18] The significance of these judicial dicta lies in the fact that they confirm that the crucial issue in establishing the defendant's culpability is not his intention, knowledge, or view of what constitutes acceptable treatment of an animal, but whether his conduct can be justified by reference to the putative standards of the reasonable person confronted by a similar position.

The application of this objective test is well demonstrated by the cases of *Hall v RSPCA* and *RSPCA v Isaacs*,[19] both of which were prosecutions based on causing unnecessary suffering as a consequence of an unreasonable act or omission.

In *Hall*, it was alleged that the defendants had caused unnecessary suffering to pigs which had septic arthritis in their joints together with associated lesions. Rather than obtaining veterinary advice they had decided to treat the pigs themselves over the course of three weeks, during which time the animals reached the optimum slaughter weight. Considering the meaning of the legislation, the High Court held that the word unreasonably indicated 'a purely objective test'. Applying this principle to the facts of the particular case the court considered the appropriate objective standard against which to compare the defendants' conduct was that of 'the reasonably competent, reasonably humane, modern pig farmer'.

Taken together with the court's interpretation of 'unnecessary' in the same case as meaning 'not inevitable', the formula for determining whether an offence had been committed was to ask three questions:

1. Had the pigs suffered?
2. If they had, was the suffering necessary 'in the sense of being inevitable'?
3. If it was not, would a reasonably competent, reasonably humane pig farmer have tolerated it? If the answer is again no, the defendant is guilty of the offence.

Applying these questions to the facts of the case the court found that the pigs had suffered as a result of their condition; the suffering was not inevitable because the animals could have been slaughtered sooner; and, as the defendants had failed to put forward any evidence to demonstrate that a reasonably competent, reasonably humane pig farmer would have permitted such suffering to be prolonged for three weeks, they were guilty of the offence.

The following day the court applied the same test in *Isaacs*, a case which arose from the defendant's failure to seek veterinary treatment for her dog. On the basis of the evidence the court decided that the animal had suffered due to a lack of veterinary attention; the suffering was not inevitable since it could have been terminated or alleviated by some reasonably practicable measure, namely, seeking veterinary assistance; and the defendant was guilty because a reasonably caring, reasonably competent owner would not have made the same omission.

There is, then, unequivocal judicial authority for the proposition that an objective test should be applied in relation to unnecessary suffering arising out of an unreasonable act or omission. Logic suggests that the same test is appropriate in respect of the other offences of cruelty based on unnecessary suffering, namely those arising from conveying, carrying, abandoning, or tethering an animal. There is a dearth of judicial authority on this point, but it is clearly desirable that there should be uniformity. Unfortunately the single relevant recent decision by the English High Court points the other way.[20] In a case involving an allegation of abandonment, the court suggested that a defendant could only be convicted if there was some indication that he intended to abandon the animal. However, there is doubt as to whether this reasoning is correct, as it appears to fail to take account of the wording of the statute. This clearly states that a defendant is guilty of the offence when he abandons an animal, whether permanently or not (and it may be the strange concept of temporary abandonment that confused the court), in circumstances likely to cause it unnecessary suffering, *unless* he can show a *reasonable* cause or excuse, suggesting an objective test should be applied. Accordingly, it is submitted that the term 'abandon' would be better interpreted simply as a question of fact: is there sufficient evidence that the defendant has disregarded his duty to care for an animal by leaving it unattended without any reasonable cause or excuse in circumstances where it is likely to be caused any unnecessary suffering?

It must be emphasized that, in applying an objective standard in relation to *mens rea*, the test is whether a reasonable person would have *thought* that the suffering was unnecessary. This is a separate question from that of whether the suffering was *actually* unnecessary. In most circumstances, the answer will be the same, and the distinction will have no practical effect. However, this is not always the case. For example, a failure to seek veterinary attention for an animal might actually cause it unnecessary suffering, but if the court is satisfied that it would not have been apparent to a reasonable person that the animal required professional treatment, then no offence has been committed. Such a situation is to be contrasted with that of a strict liability offence.

Strict liability offences

In respect of strict liability offences the defendant's mental state is irrelevant in determining guilt, to the extent that he may be convicted even though it was his intention that the animal should *not* suffer. For example, the imperative nature of article 4(1) of the Welfare of Animals (Transport) Order 1997, which states that 'no person shall transport any animal in a way which causes or is likely to cause injury or unnecessary suffering to that animal', is characteristic of a strict liability offence. The wording takes the form of a mandatory prohibition, and there is nothing to indicate that the defendant's state of mind is a constituent of the offence. This is not so draconian as it may initially appear, as there is a statutory defence: notwithstanding that the animal was caused unnecessary suffering in transit, the defendant is not guilty of the offence if he can establish, on the balance of probabilities, that he had a lawful authority or excuse for his conduct.[21]

Similarly, in the absence of any direct judicial authority on the point, it is submitted that Article 6(1) of the Welfare of Animals at Markets Order 1990, which provides that 'no person shall cause or permit any injury or unnecessary suffering to an animal in a market', is also a strict liability offence. This view is supported by the decision of the English High Court that, in relation to the similarly worded Article 5(1) ('no person shall permit an unfit animal to be exposed for sale in a market'), 'the prosecution did not have to prove that a person knew or was wilfully blind to the fact that an animal was unfit in order to establish an offence', which was one of strict liability.[22] By analogy, it is argued that the same principle can be applied to article 6(1).

Article 6(2) of the same Order also falls into this group. This states that 'it shall be the duty of any person in charge of an animal in a market to ensure that the animal is not, or is not likely to be, caused injury or unnecessary suffering' by reason, for example, of, exposure to weather, inadequate ventilation, or being hit or prodded. The meaning of this wording is such that, according to the English High Court, it is an offence 'about which there could be no controversy at all as to whether strict liability is imposed'.[23]

Summary

On the basis of the foregoing discussion it will be appreciated that unnecessary suffering is a flexible concept. What constitutes 'unnecessary' depends upon the wording of the particular legislative provision which is being applied, the nature of the suffering, and the circumstances in which it occurs. It ultimately falls to the courts to decide whether an animal's suffering amounts to a criminal offence, but both the English and Scottish High Courts have laid down valuable guidance on how such a decision should be reached. This may be summarized as follows:

- except for the specific situations that have been identified, some degree of mental or physical suffering must be established;
- any suffering which arises in the absence of a legitimate object may be regarded as unnecessary;
- where the suffering is caused as a result of something which, in the words of the courts, may 'fairly and properly' be done to an animal or is to effect an 'adequate and reasonable object', necessity is to be determined by weighing the purpose for which the suffering is caused against its degree, intensity and duration. To quote the courts again, to be lawful 'the beneficial or useful end sought to be attained must be reasonably proportionate to the extent of the suffering caused, and in no case can substantial suffering be inflicted, unless necessity for its infliction can reasonably be said to exist';
- once it has been shown that the suffering was necessary, attention turns to whether the defendant's mental state is relevant and, if so, whether a subjective or objective test should be applied. This will depend on the particular offence which is being considered.

However, in relation to the particular offence of causing unnecessary suffering as a result of wantonly or unreasonably doing or omitting to do any act as laid down in section 1(1)(a) of the Protection of Animals Act 1911, the English High Court has laid down a specific test. Put simply, an offence will have been committed if the court is satisfied that each of these criteria is met:

- the animal has suffered;
- the suffering was not inevitable in the sense that it could reasonably have been avoided or terminated;
- placed in the same situation, a reasonably caring, competent and humane person of the same status as the defendant (for example, a farmer or pet owner) would have taken appropriate measures to avoid or terminate the suffering.

This formula is especially significant for four reasons. First, the offence applies to all domestic and captive animals (except those being used lawfully under the terms of the Animals (Scientific Procedures) Act 1986), regardless of the circumstances in which the suffering arises, or its cause. Because of its general nature, this is the provision which is relied on as the basis for the vast majority of cruelty prosecutions.

Second, as it emanates from decisions of the High Court the formula is binding on all magistrates' courts in England and Wales. Whenever a prosecution is brought under section 1(1)(a) it should be cited to the court, which is then required to apply it.

Third, although not binding in Scotland it is of persuasive authority because the wording of section 1(1)(a) of the Protection of Animals (Scotland) Act 1912 is identical to that of the 1911 Act.

Finally, and most importantly, the formula effectively defines the nature of our legal obligation to domestic and captive animals by implying that suffering is unlawful whenever it arises as a result of the accused's failure to fulfil his or her responsibilities towards such an animal, the nature of those responsibilities to be determined by reference to the standards of the reasonably caring, competent and humane person. In other words, suffering in this context will be regarded as unnecessary if it arises from an unreasonable disregard, ignorance, indifference, or neglect for an animal's needs and interests. In consequence, while the social, financial, and personal circumstances of the accused may be relevant in deciding whether to bring a prosecution, or the severity of the penalty upon conviction, they are not factors to be taken into account in considering whether he or she has caused unnecessary suffering. Similarly, neither oversight nor even a benign intention of itself provides an excuse; application of the court's formula suggests that if, for example, a person keeps an exotic animal in inappropriate conditions, allows their dog to roam the streets, or even permits their cat to become grossly obese out of misguided affection, any consequential suffering may be regarded as unnecessary. Although such a person may not be as culpable as the one who callously allows his animal to starve, they are nevertheless potentially guilty of a criminal offence. It is not suggested that they should all be brought before the courts and prosecuted, but it might concentrate at least some minds if the nature and extent of their legal obligations towards their animals were known to them.

Conclusion

As interpreted by the courts the concept of unnecessary suffering therefore extends beyond traditional notions of gratuitous cruelty to include any unreasonable failure to meet an animal's needs. In the case of its owner this is a continuing, non-delegable responsibility for as long as the animal belongs to them.[24]

It is recognized that the analysis presented in this chapter is of a technical nature, but that does not lessen its importance. It is desirable that every veterinarian should appreciate the extent of the duties imposed by the law on those who assume responsibility for animals. Happily, there is growing evidence of a recognition that this is the case. The introduction by the RCVS of a Certificate and, latterly, a Diploma in Animal Welfare Science, Ethics and Law is, perhaps, the most significant development in this field. At the same time, the establishment of organizations such as the Veterinary Association of Arbitration and Jurisprudence, the Animal Welfare Science, Ethics and Law Veterinary Association, and Lawyers for Animal Welfare, all point to a growing interest in, and appreciation of the benefit of developing a greater understanding of animal protection legislation.

Abbreviations

JP	Justice of the Peace
QBD	Queen's Bench Division (of the High Court)
SLT	Scots Law Times
Crim LR	Criminal Law Reports
Coup	Couper's Justiciary Reports (Scotland)
JC	Justiciary Cases (Scotland)
Unreported	Denotes cases which have not been formally reported in any of the sets of published law reports. Given the volume of cases in the higher courts only a proportion can be selected to be reported. The fact that a case is unreported has no effect on its status as legal authority.

Notes

1. Animal Health Act 1981, s. 37: Welfare of Animals (Transport) Order 1997, S.I. 1997/1480; Welfare of Animals at Markets Order 1990, S.I. 1990/2628; Welfare of Animals (Slaughter or Killing) Regulations 1995, S.I. 1995/731; Wild Mammals (Protection) Act 1996, s.1.
2. *Dee v Yorke* (1914) 78 JP 359.
3. *Ford v Wiley* (1889) 23 QBD 203.
4. *Patchett v Macdougall* 1984 SLT 152.
5. *Ibid.* The English High Court has recently confirmed that a person cannot be convicted for causing unnecessary suffering if an animal is killed outright. *Isted v Crown Prosecution Service* [1998] Crim LR 194.
6. Wild Mammals (Protection) Act 1996, s. 1.
7. Abandonment of Animals Act 1960; Welfare of Animals at Markets Order 1990; Welfare of Animals (Transport) Order 1997.

8. *Roberts v Ruggiero*, unreported; 3 April, 1985. This system of raising veal calves was subsequently prohibited by the Welfare of Calves Regulations 1987, S.I. 1987/2021, now superseded by the Welfare of Livestock Regulations 1994, S.I. 1994/2126, Sch. 2. (These Regulations are, at the time of going to press (March 2000), under review and are due for replacement by the summer of 2000.)
9. *Ford v Wiley*, n. 3.
10. *Ibid.*
11. *Ibid.*
12. *Ibid.*
13. *Ibid.*
14. Protection of Animals Act 1911, s. 1(1)(a); Protection of Animals (Scotland) Act 1912, s. 1(1)(a).
15. *Hall v RSPCA*, unreported (QBD, 11 November 1993); *RSPCA v Isaacs* [1994] Crim LR 517.
16. *Sharp v Mitchell* (1872) 2 Coup 273; *Small v Warr* (1882) 47 JP 20; *Elliot v Osborn* (1891) 56 JP 38; *Greenwood v Backhouse* (1902) 66 JP 519.
17. *Ford v Wiley*, n. 3.
18. *Easton v Anderson* 1949 JC 1.
19. *Hall v RSPCA* n. 15.
20. *Hunt v. Duckering* [1993] Crim LR 678.
21. Animal Health Act 1981, ss 72 and 73; Welfare of Animals (Transport) Order 1997, art. 21.
22. *Davidson v Strong,* unreported (QBD, 29 January, 1997).
23. *Ibid.*
24. By virtue of section 1(2) of both the 1911 and 1912 Acts, an owner is deemed to have permitted unnecessary suffering if it is caused as a consequence of their failure to exercise reasonable care and supervision of the animal: Animal Health Act 1981, s. 37; Welfare of Animals (Transport) Order 1997*, S.I. 1997/1480; Welfare of Animals at Markets Order 1990*, S.I. 1990/2628; Welfare of Animals (Slaughter or Killing) Regulations 1995, S.I. 1995/731; Wild Mammals (Protection) Act 1996, s.1.

* At the time of going to press (March 2000) both these Orders are due for replacement. MAFF circulated a consultation paper in the summer of 1999 and new legislation is likely by the end of 2000.

4

How to deal with animals[1]

Stephen R.L. Clark

Formerly agreed principles

The Farm Animal Welfare Council, a body which exists to advise the Minister of Agriculture, Farms and Fisheries on matters to do with the welfare of farm animals (hereafter, FAWC), has had to formulate the principles that lie behind its reports. Its 'Philosophy of Approach', as described in the opening parts of many of those reports, has been founded on the declaration that 'the welfare of an animal includes its physical and mental state, and . . . that good animal welfare implies both *fitness* and a *sense of well-being*'. FAWC further requires that the welfare of an animal should be considered 'with reference to "The Five Freedoms"', which are taken to identify 'ideal states rather than standards of acceptable welfare'. These five freedoms are, notoriously, freedom from thirst, hunger and malnutrition, from discomfort, from pain, injury and disease, to express normal behaviour, and from fear and distress.

The 1993 Report on Priorities for Animal Welfare Research and Development identifies a number of 'indices of welfare', and recommends that research be carried out to establish the relationships between these indices, and their relative significance. It is not clear whether any absolute or unchanging relationship is discoverable even in principle: few of us think, for example, that freedom from hunger must always be chosen over freedom to express normal behaviour. In practice, more detailed evidence of distress will vary from species to species, even breed to breed.

More recently FAWC has adopted the three guiding principles agreed by the Banner Committee:[2] that there are some things which should not be done to any animal; that there are other things (principally, 'harms') which may be done only if there is sufficient justification; and that any such harms should nonetheless be moderated or mitigated as much as possible, compatible with making it possible to achieve the results that are held to justify the harm. These are also the working principles of the Home Office Inspectorate when considering work on animals under the Act of 1986. The Inspectorate's Notes for Guidance offer a longer list of procedures which are regulated under that Act: namely, any which 'may have the effect of causing a protected animal [i.e. a living non-human vertebrate such as the *Octopus vulgaris*] pain, suffering, distress or lasting harm, [including] death, disease, injury, physiological or psychological stress, significant discomfort or any disturbance to normal health, whether immediately or in the long term'.[3] It is worth noting that *death* is itself reckoned to be something which should be taken into account when judging the harm done to animals. It is not absolutely forbidden to kill an animal: on the contrary, the Inspectorate is empowered to require that an animal suffering severe or lasting pain in the course of an experiment should be killed, and most experimental animals will, in due course, be 'sacrificed'. But such killing itself requires justification. Commonsensically, the deliberate ending of a life before its natural term is almost always a denial of the fourth freedom, and death is usually to be reckoned a worse calamity than many non-lethal injuries. There would, obviously, be some difficulty if FAWC were to judge it a bad thing (something requiring special and serious justification) to kill farm animals. It may still be worth considering whether death should be accepted so unthinkingly as the easiest method of disposing of stock 'surplus to requirements' (for example, 'surplus' males), as if it did the animals no harm at all to kill them.

Finally, earlier discussions of the issue, seemingly acceptable to the Council, speak of animals' 'intrinsic value', and their 'rightful place in the natural order of our world'. It is possible that what was intended by these phrases was that animal species ought not to be driven to extinction, but rather maintained as the kinds they 'naturally' are. It is also possible that the 'intrinsic value' (of individual animals) is here to be contrasted with 'market value' (on which, more below).

Rational priorities and lives well lived

There are at least two contentious premisses in FAWC's avowed philosophy: that an animal's own 'mental state', its own sense of its situation, is relevant to questions about its well-being; that its mental state is not all that is relevant. On the one hand an animal may be less than well off because it is bored, stressed or fearful, whether or not it has an identifiable physical injury. On the other hand, it may be less than well off because it is denied the chance to 'express normal behaviour', whether or not it actually wishes to do so, or realizes its own deprivation. Both premises rest upon some notion of what a 'life well lived' amounts to for creatures of that particular kind.

If it is accepted that animals may be less than well off in so wide a variety of ways, we may have to weigh one harm against another: is mutilation or solitary confinement a greater harm? Is it better to eat less and live longer? At what level of harm is a life just not worth living? In our decisions about our own, human, life we may have idiosyncratic preferences which others find it difficult to understand; we value different things, and accept different losses. One way of discovering our own priorities is to calculate what in the long run we actually pay to do.[4] Similar techniques are open to us in the case of animals: what will they 'pay' to do? How much effort will they expend to have time in the fresh air, or in particular kinds of cage, or with particular company, or to receive particular foods? Experiments to ascertain animals' preferences may assume too readily that *all* animals of one particular breed will have identical priorities, but we can at least be fairly certain what, in general, is *not* preferred. We are in any case aware that individuals' 'subjective' choices are not wholly reliable: how much will an addict pay to feed an addiction? How much *should* the addict pay? Are the animals we test actually capable of acting out their underlying preferences, or have they in effect given up any hope of making any difference to their world? A caged rabbit which ignores an open door is not necessarily expressing a preference for caged life; it simply has no notion that it could secure a life outside, perhaps with good reason. In addition to the individual choices, in short, we recognize – partly by considering what, under 'natural conditions', most animals of that particular type do do – what would be *rational* choices, and draw some line to protect ourselves and others from the penalties of unreason. When required to choose on behalf of infants or the incapacitated we attempt to imagine what they *would* choose if they were capable of choice, and exercised that power rationally. So also with regard to animals: we need to know not only what individuals, or even the mass of individuals, in fact prefer, but also what they *should*, if they were rational, prefer.[5]

That judgement turns on our conception of a 'life well lived according to the kind in question', the life, perhaps, which best makes sense of the creature's inherited structure and proclivities, or which is most in tune with the larger structure of terrestrial life. In appealing, overtly or covertly, to some idea of Nature (whether that creature's 'nature', or terrestrial Nature as a whole) we may be relying, implicitly, on a traditional sense that Nature broadly so-called is what God wills; those who reject this backing have some difficulty rationalizing an appeal to Nature (or to normality), which might be only an ragbag of inherited tendencies and past successes. Some theorists respond by suggesting that the desired form of Nature may not be what, irrespective of human contrivance, actually *is*, but rather what 'we' have decided it shall be. Such utopians have usually looked forward to a world entirely under 'our' control, in which a humanly acceptable order has been created out of chaos. There are also other utopian visions, less dedicated to the dream of *human* (or Western or Enlightenment) domination. Other theorists, conservative in their bias, have doubted the possibility or the desirability of any such rational order; the world as it is is the result of mutual adjustments and occasional changes, and is far more elegant and reliable than any consciously devised order. Recent work in political and especially in environmental theory perhaps suggests that both utopians and conservatives *could* come to agree that the best outcome, the best image of the whole terrestrial order, would be one that allowed as many kinds of creature as possible as much liberty as possible compatible with an equal liberty for all. We should, on this account, attempt to live according to such laws as all would agree upon, to allow as many as possible to live lives that they could reasonably think well lived (not necessarily lives without risk or discomfort, and certainly not ones that last forever).

Doubts about what exactly a life well lived or a biosphere well ordered might be may not, in practice, be especially significant. We may, for example, disagree about the level of[6] 'excitement' that should be expected in a life well lived (and so disagree about the level we require ourselves or the extent we think a creature injured that demands much more or less than ourselves). But no one could sensibly suppose that, for example, deliberate and repeated self-mutilation could be rationally desirable. Terminal masochism must be a mark of derangement. So, for a social species, must be deliberate cruelty. Both obsessive states prevent the victim from living what anyone but the obsessive could consider a life well lived. We may wonder whether a domestic dog, deprived of any chance of a pack-life with its kind, is living (subjectively or objectively) a life well lived. We have no doubt (or no one who is worth listening to has any doubt) that there are better or worse ways even of being a domestic dog. Common sense may sometimes be misled, but it is not too bad a guide. After all, the doubts about domesticity can also surface for humans, without our thereby surrendering the right to notice ordinary hardship, loss or clinical depression.

Counting up the cost

When we have decided what is to count as a more or less serious harm, and what is required for a life more or less worth living, for a particular creature, we must also decide how great an effort (and what kind) is therefore required of *us*. What should we go without to prevent some injury to another? What requirements does 'a life well lived' impose on us? Are we better off, all things considered, if we let no one prosper at our expense, or if we forgo some present advantages so as to allow advantages to others? How many advantages should we forgo, and for whose sake? Is a life well lived, for example, only if it creates as much 'value' (in lives well lived) as possible? That is the implication of some ethical appeals to the overall consequences of action: that act is right, so utilitarian consequentialists[6] declare, which is most likely to result in the greatest satisfaction of serious (subjective or rational?) preferences for all those affected. For consequentialists there is always a best option and anything less than that is wrong. Nor, for consequentialists, is there any ethical difference between 'acts' and 'omissions'; failing to secure the best outcome is just as bad as engineering a worse one (and those who fail to give as much as they can, without risking their own serious deprivation, to save the sick and starving are as culpable as those who take more positive steps to kill them – and may indeed be more at fault).

Pure utilitarianism (in addition to being as morally strenuous an ethic as can easily be imagined[7]) has counter-intuitive results. If what matters (as is sometimes said) is only the maximum satisfaction of whatever preferences affected creatures have, we might conclude that gang-rape, pederasty and enforced lobotomies are all not just permissible but obligatory. If, to avoid such horrors, we insist that there are limits to what could *rationally* be preferred, or to the costs that might decently be imposed on individuals, then we admit that more matters to us than outcomes. We also mind about motives: even actions that would, in the abstract, be permissible, are often condemned when undertaken for objectionable reasons. For strict utilitarians an ailing tramp must be of less consequence than a tax-paying citizen, and should accordingly be left to die – or hygienically disposed of – for 'the greater good', that is, the good of those best able to increase 'value' further. For strict utilitarians it wouldn't even matter if those who left the tramp to die did so for their own private reasons. Those (including professed utilitarians) who reject the implication implicitly rely upon a conception of 'intrinsic value', or importance, that transcends the market (on which more below). On utilitarianist terms we cannot tell what rationally we *should* prefer until we know what everyone affected actually *does* prefer: a community of utilitarians will either reach no decision, or a monstrous one, or else they will be guided by other, non-utilitarian, judgements. How many votes have chickens? What level of injury would it be fair to impose on any single creature, for an imagined 'greater good'? All attempts to calculate the 'right' answer by quantifying consequences rely on hidden premisses about the importance of those affected, and the limits of a life well lived. Since the calculation is in any case almost always quite impossible, the policies which utilitarians (variously) advocate are actually grounded on other more direct and fluid choices.

Rejecting utilitarianism, FAWC – and the Home Office Inspectorate – insist that there are some things that are not to be done to any animal at all. There are those – there were indeed some at the meeting of AWSELVA – who question the claim, usually by instancing horrendous situations of a kind familiar to philosophers: what if the world could only be saved by flaying one's mother alive? Even utilitarians, in practice, would be loath to conclude that flaying one's mother could be an ordinary or easy choice. Such dreadful fancies are better kept apart. A society in which we simply don't entertain that option would be better, on any plausible utilitarian calculation, than one in which we have to wonder whether now is the time. Act utilitarians, busily calculating the odds for any given act, are often going to be mistaken, and will always be vulnerable to tyrannical manipulation, eagerly choosing the lesser supposed evil to avert a greater threat. Sophisticated utilitarians are likely to conclude – though the argument is no more conclusive than any such calculation – that it is better for us all if we are not utilitarians. Fortunately the truth is that we are not. Few of us would doubt that there are some things that we must not do to children, say: we must not rape, sodomize, burn or mutilate them. Other things we might legitimately do, if there is acceptable reason, even if the children themselves object. And even such things as we may do we should seek to mitigate and may have to compensate them for. Speculation about what we would or might do were the fate of the world to hang upon our act is bound to be irrelevant to simple, practical distinctions.

Market and intrinsic values

In short, the whole idea of engineering 'the best outcome' (judged in terms of the number and weight of satisfied preferences) is no more than rhetoric. We cannot literally 'weigh' the costs (to animals) against the benefits (mostly to us), because there is no available unit of measurement, because some things are 'beyond price', and because we usually cannot even identify what the likely consequences of any particular act might be. The apparatus of ethical decision-making is more complex, and more commonsensical. This does not necessarily make it easy. Whose interests should count with us, and how much? Would it be compatible with a life well lived, if we were to disregard the interests of our children, of our neighbours, or human strangers, or domesticated cattle, or the wild things in our country? 'The righteous man has a care for his beast', according to the Book of Proverbs (12:10; see 27:23ff), and it is 'a mark of a civilized society' (according to the Conservative Party Manifesto for 1997) 'to respect animals'. But how much, and why? What does it mean to 'respect' them?

At least two evolutionary arguments are possible: human beings have depended for millennia on their ready understanding of what other creatures – human and non-human – think and want; and their appreciation of healthy and contented animals amongst their herds. As hunters and as pastoralists our ancestors, to live at all, needed to get 'inside the skin' of those they preyed upon, precisely so as to prey on them. They have needed to relish 'health' in those they farm because unhealthy beasts don't pay as well. Some of us have come to appreciate the integrity of any living thing, and regret its violation. Understandably the tensions created resulted, all across the world, in rationalizations about the willingness of animals to be killed, or milked, or shorn, for us, and the advantages we gave them in return. The history of religion is, in large part, the history of the rationalizations our ancestors engaged in so that they could feel they were behaving as the victims wished, or as the Creator and Owner of all things would allow. It is still surprisingly common for people to contend that animals were 'given' to us, even if they have no knowledge of the Giver.

Our ancestors, of course, internalized similar defences for warfare, patriarchalism, slavery and the caste system (including ritual humiliation and jokes about the victims[8]). Ethical humanism, as it arose in Greece, Palestine, India and China during the so-called Axial Era, has – very slowly – eroded our conviction that we have a right to conquer and enslave. Human beings, it was said, are to be valued irrespective of their market value; we should not use other human beings simply as means to our own ends, but rather recognize that they have ends as well (or even that they *are* ends), that they have as great a claim on the forbearance or the aid of others as ourselves. Unfortunately for the non-human, by elevating human beings we depressed all others; the slogan has, precisely,

been that humans should not be treated like animals – and by implication animals may be – that is, they may be starved, evicted, imprisoned,
tortured, killed whenever it is convenient to 'us'. That thesis, however
ill-argued, at least made sense as long as we supposed that 'human' and
'non-human' named essentially different sorts of creature. The spread of
neo-Darwinian theory must cast doubt on the hardness of the boundary:
if all of us alike are products of genes almost all of which we share with
the non-human, and species boundaries do not reflect essential differences but only limits on successful interbreeding (till the genetic
engineers take a hand), then it is hard to see why all and only humans
merit that respect.

There will be those who insist that only (though not all) humans have
any long-term plans, or life preferences, and that the importance to us of
taking account of all such serious, long-term plans only requires us to
attend to humans. It may still be important to treat our cattle well, but
only because we need them, and only to the extent that such care is cost-
effective. Some theorists have accepted that human infants, and the
incapacitated, have a similarly marginal claim on our attention: only
'persons' have any definite 'rights' apart from local legislation. Some
conclude that the State should not give any legal weight to the interests
of animals, since this would be to contravene the rightful liberty of
human citizens to make their own decisions as long as they don't violate
the equal liberty of others.[9] Others prefer to retain such customary or
legislative barriers to ill-treating the defenceless as we have managed to
create, while still denying that we would be really wrong (wrong in the
eyes of God, or any other unbiased moral agent) to treat them badly. In
declaring that animals have their own intrinsic value FAWC demands a
higher level of attention, approaching that demanded by those who
reckon animals have rights of the same, non-legislated kind as human
beings.

Those philosophers who speak most readily of intrinsic values usually
mean that what has such value has it irrespective of any human, or other
finite judgement. Some things demand respect even if no one offers it,
just as some propositions are true even if no one believes them (or even
articulates them). This is to embark upon a lengthy argument: whether
there are moral facts, like other facts in being so, whether or nor they are
recognized as such, and whether some moral judgements are, objectively,
mistaken. Commonsensically, we all suppose that this is so: paedophiles
are simply *wrong* to think that they have any right in what they do, and
so are animal abusers. But FAWC needs to make no final judgement on
that matter, any more than the Banner Committee – or Parliament itself
– has any corporate view about the metaphysics of morals. It is enough

that animals are judged to have non-market or inherent values: we value them for what they are whether or not they give us further profit. It may be that some moral judgements are really true; if none are (but all such judgements merely define our own priorities), we are at liberty to say that what we wish to exist are happy and healthy animals.

Cattle are to be valued for more than commercial ends and even when they afford us no return. A sheep farmer who reckons it not worth calling in a vet to see to a sick lamb (since the price of the lamb would be far less than the cost of the vet's visit) is at fault: the farmer has a *duty* to care for his beast, because the life well lived (as a human being) demands that he be alert to the lamb's condition. Anything less is willed self-blindness and a failure to assign priorities correctly. A similar judgement may be made of the dog owner who would rather see the dog dead than pay to board it out, or the horse owner who repays a lifetime of service by sending the horse to the knackers, or the farming nation which deals with suspected sickness by slaughtering whole herds. The implicit bargain of domestication is that humans care for animals in return for an advantage: that bargain is no bargain at all if each animal is cared for only as long as it offers a direct advantage (Lloyd's Names do not invest money in order to lose it, but are at fault if they refuse to pay up). How many of these reasonable responsibilities should the State enforce, whether by prosecuting offenders or by denying them financial subsidies?

One further gloss on 'intrinsic value': in considering the well-being of human creatures we are also concerned for human dignity. To treat the human form with contempt, to hold it up for ridicule, is reckoned wrong irrespective of the subjective state of the victim. We may reckon that such victims *would* mind, if they knew, but think that such contempt is symptomatic of a moral flaw even if the victim, imaginably, managed not to mind. Attempted humiliation is an evil, even if the victim, being a saint or sage or holy fool, or dead, does not feel humiliated. Those who willingly or eagerly humiliate others, or hold them up to ridicule, offend human dignity. There may be similar occasions even in our relations with the non-human: sometimes the victim itself experiences humiliation (a formerly dominant male, for example, who loses his place in the group when experimenters make him look ridiculous or foreign); sometimes, we may suppose, the victim does not realize (for example, the chimpanzee dressed up in chintz to advertise a tea bag). Those who aim to make an animal ridiculous offend even if they fail to convince the animal. Maybe we should look more carefully at farming practices that deny the animals dignity whether or not they also injure them more openly.

Thought experiments and moral frameworks

So what ethical framework might suggest itself? What form of social life will in the end allow us to see straight and not demand a larger presence in the world than we have any right to conceive? Even those who don't believe in God[10] may sometimes find it helpful to enquire what would be required of us by an all-knowing and benevolent creator (who 'hates nothing that He has made: why else would He have made it?', as the *Wisdom of Solomon* has it). Those who *do* believe, of course, whether from a Christian, Jewish or Islamic background, have definite reasons to act as such a God would wish; even if they suppose that 'animals were given to us', they must also reckon that 'nothing was given to man to waste or destroy', but always on condition of decent treatment. Our Hindu and Buddhist fellow citizens have similar reasons to regret ill-treatment. Equivalently, what sort of world would all of us agree to constitute if we did not know what part we'd play ourselves? What sort of world would be worth constituting? Cooperative life, as distinct from the merely and self-destructively predatory, has always been an option: domestication, civilization, are only recent forms of that cooperative nisus. Maybe in some utopian future we will all learn to live together in ways that allow each creature liberty, and necessary help, to live a life well lived: 'the cow and the bear make friends, their young lie down together; the lion eats straw like the ox' (*Isa.* 11:6ff.). Until that time we make such bargains as we can, and try not to demand more of others than we would think it reasonable, in their position, to give. The social contract is a useful story, requiring us to reason calmly about the perceived costs of different strategies. In many cases part of the bargain is that human beings should provide companionship: not only, as one interpretation of the fourth freedom suggests, companionship of the animal's own kind, but also of the human beings that such cattle have been bred to welcome. It is imaginable that, say, sheep would prefer a predator that cared (a little) for them to one that did not; shepherds may be better for the sheep than wolves – but only on condition that the shepherd does preserve a decent life for sheep. Without that the shepherd's claim is as spurious as any tyrant's wish to be praised as 'Shepherd, or even Father, of the People'.[11] It is worth adding that wolves characteristically pull down the weak and old: we characteristically kill animals with every natural prospect of a long and healthy life. It is not as obvious as some suppose that the bargain is a good one for the sheep, even if they *did* receive the medical and other care we promise.[12]

The life well lived, for creatures such as ourselves, traditionally demands that we appreciate existing beauties (including those displayed in lives well lived), and acknowledge the real costs of what we do. Self-deceit is an evil, and so is any claim to be objectively of more importance than others with whom we share the world; different creatures are not equally important *to us*, but that judgement is relative. The liberal agenda for a humane, human society is that we should, as far as possible, live by such rules and institutions as allow everyone a reasonable chance of living well. That same agenda can be extended to the creatures with whom we share the world, both the wild and the tame. Our relations with the wild may mostly be defined by duties of non-maleficence. Towards the tame we have additional duties of beneficence. In both cases we should respect the real being and autonomy of the creatures we affect.[13] Both duties require us to respect the would-be rational preferences of others, as best they can be judged, and not seize a greater advantage from them than we are willing to repay.

The notion of a natural order, and associated respect for the different sorts of creature that make up that order, may have one further relevant effect: the production (by selective breeding or genetic engineering) of animals which are better adapted to factory farming (as a limiting case, as anencephalic lumps) might have definite welfare advantages. It would not be absurd to wonder whether the creation of such deeply damaged creatures might not be just such an offence against nature as opponents sometimes suppose. The notion of a natural order, and of a normal life, combine to suggest that we ought not wholly to remake that order. It is a bad thing to deprive creatures of a normal life, and also bad to create creatures whose life is bound to be abnormal.

Since one of the philosophical slogans that has spread like a mental microbe through the educated public is 'You Can't Get an Ought from an Is' (an attempt sometimes labelled 'the naturalistic fallacy'), I must pause to comment. Neither David Hume nor G.E. Moore (the chief begetters of the slogan) ever supposed that moral reasoning was impossible, or that our respect for an existing beauty was irrelevant. That something strikes us as 'natural' or 'normal' is bound to be an element in our moral reasoning – our reasoning, that is, about what we should allow or do. Those who describe such responses, disparagingly, as 'the yuk factor', while continuing to give disproportionate credit to 'the yum factor' (our sensual pleasure at particular outcomes), are guilty of confusion. The question remains, what world is it that we actually want, for ourselves and those we care about? Maybe that world is also one that God (the supreme, objective standard) demands: if it is, it is not unreasonable to suppose that He has written some of His requirements into our hearts; if it is not (because He is not) we can still only trust in those heartfelt convictions. As above, the metaphysics of morals need not be our present and most pressing concern.

FAWC, in identifying what counts as an injury to individual animals, and in acknowledging the intrinsic (non-market) value of such animals, must attempt to moderate the bargain of domestication. If that bargain is to be a serious ethical defence of domestication there must be someone willing and able to speak for the weaker partners. There remains a more utopian vision, of a time when we no longer think it any more right or reasonable to exploit our fellow mammals than to keep human slaves. Even now, more matters to us than the provision of cheap food: we wish to believe that we are no great burden to those that support us, and that we are part of a community, a land, in which everything has some chance of having a good life. It follows that the demands we make on farmers are not simply that the animals in their care should be protected, as far as possible, from the injuries identified in the other freedoms, but that they should have as good an opportunity to live well, according to their kinds, as others.

The minimal standard of concern for animal welfare is that farmers should take account of their stock's freedoms (as described above), and not diminish them more than is absolutely essential if they are to make a profit. The stronger standard is that they should take action to give their stock as good a chance of profiting from the implicit bargain of domestication as do they themselves. The bargain is a fair one if both sides stand to gain from it. The strongest standard of all is identified by asking whether the parties to the bargain might reasonably agree to change places. The application of *that* standard would probably put an end to farming (and many other) practices.

Acceptance of the second version may allow farming to continue; it does so on the understanding that farm animals are not merely 'not treated too badly', but that they actually stand to gain, in positive terms, from being farmed. FAWC's goal is not just to balance the harms inflicted on animals against the profits made by farmers and others, as though there were some common currency of benefit (to us) and loss (to them), but to identify as fair a bargain as we can. There are some advantages that cannot be justly won, some costs that no reasonable being would pay, nor any impartial judge allow.

It follows that reports upon the conditions under which this or that variety of farm animal is kept must go further than identifying welfare problems, to be dealt with at the least expense compatible with continuing the practices that cause the problem. We must also enquire whether a just bargain is possible, and whether the animals in question have, or have not, been betrayed. As long as farm animals are valued only at their market price they will often be left without food, comfort, medical care, freedom (that is, the chance of living as creatures of their kind would prefer to live), and consolation. Once we admit that they have some intrinsic value it must be admitted that such neglect is wrong. We should not only *not inflict such harms* upon farm animals but also seek to amend them, and offer such compensation for the inescapable ills of farming practice (the animal's imprisonment, frustration and death) as we can manage.

The question is: what harms (as identified under the heading of the Five Freedoms) are caused, or bound to be caused, the animals, and are these harms that they could reasonably accept for the sake of receiving the advantages of domestication? The goal must not be simply to minimize such harms compatible with making an acceptable profit, but to provide such advantages to the animals as might give them reason to accept their role.

Notes

1. This chapter was originally written as a submission for a sub-committee of the Farm Animal Welfare Council. While certain of its principles have been accepted by that Council, the whole is solely my own responsibility. A later version was delivered to a meeting of AWSELVA at the annual meeting of the British Veterinary Association in Nottingham on 26 September 1998.
2. *Ethical Implications of Emergent Technologies in the Breeding of Farm Animals.* London: HMSO, 1996.
3. *Guidance on the Operation of the Animals (Scientific Procedures) Act 1986.* 1.10, London: HMSO, 1990.
4. What we will pay to acquire a good is usually less than the sum that would be needed to induce us to give it up; nor is it easy to discover what individuals would pay as their share of the price of a communal good. And of course there are some things that are not for sale. For my present purposes, I shall ignore these complications.
5. Since such animals are thought incapable of reason, it may seem absurd to wonder what they would do if this were not so; but even creatures that cannot reason intellectually are still capable of making more or less sensible choices, ones which do or do not have some chance of achieving outcomes appropriate to their kind. One test will often be, as before, what creatures of that kind generally do under natural conditions, and when not constrained.
6. Other consequentialists prefer to reckon up the outcome only for themselves, or for the group to which they are loyal; utilitarians count the cost for *all* those whom they affect.
7. Which is why consequentialism is not, *pace* some accounts, 'the antithesis of deontology'. Utilitarians identify one single, absolute duty – to do whatever has the best chance of achieving the highest ratio of satisfactions to dissatisfactions; other moral theorists doubt that this duty can be satisfactorily defined, and rely instead

upon more local, achievable duties. There is an extensive literature on the subject: see, amongst others, David Oderberg and Jacqueline Laing, (eds), *Human Lives*. London: Macmillan, 1996.

8. Jokes are often a convenient way of releasing emotional tensions, by trivializing the acts and demeaning the victims: 'boys throw stones at frogs in fun, but the frogs die in earnest'.

9. The claim would be more convincing if such freedom-loving citizens did not require financial subsidies from their compatriots' taxes.

10. Belief in God, in this context, is the belief that there is an objective moral order which our moral judgements, generally, 'track'.

11. 'These were the words of the Lord to me: Prophesy, man, against the shepherds of Israel; prophesy and say to them, You shepherds, these are the words of the Lord God: How I hate the shepherds of Israel who care only for themselves! Should not the shepherd care for the sheep? You consume the milk, wear the wool, and slaughter the fat beasts, but you do not feed the sheep. You have not encouraged the weary, tended the sick, bandaged the hurt, recovered the straggler, or searched for the lost; and even the strong you have driven with ruthless severity ... I will dismiss those shepherds; they shall care only for themselves no longer; I will rescue my sheep from their jaws, and they shall feed on them no longer' (*Ezek.* 34:1ff.).

12. A point entertainingly made by Martin Young (1995), The sheep–wolf press conference. *Between the Species*, 11: 74–80.

13. See S.R.L. Clark, *Animals and their Moral Standing*. London: Routledge, 1997.

5

Professional conduct and self-regulation

Jane C. Hern

What constitutes a profession?

The Shorter Oxford Dictionary defines a profession as 'the occupation in which one professes to be skilled in and to follow; a vocation in which a professed knowledge of some department of learning is used in its application to the affairs of others'. In other words a profession is some sort of higher calling than a trade or mere pastime.

According to George Bernard Shaw, writing about a hundred years ago, 'All professions are conspiracies against the laity.' This suggests that professions have access to something not accessible or very comprehensible to lay people. A profession is thus seen as a group with its own language and mystique – capable of taking advantage over the lesser mortals who are not members of the élite.

Features of a profession

There are a number of characteristic features of a profession:

- a high level of education and training in an extensive range of knowledge and skills – leading to a qualification. Most professions now require a degree, together with post-graduate study and further post-qualification continuous professional development (CPD);

- a deliberate career choice rather than just a job – suggesting long-term commitment;
- some detachment and integrity in exercising professional judgement on behalf of clients;
- a relationship with clients based on faith and trust;
- a collective responsibility for the competence and integrity of the profession as a whole. This might be expressed in both a professional code of ethics and a regulatory structure to handle complaints and discipline.

What privileges do members of a profession have?

The Shorter Oxford Dictionary definition of privilege is 'a right, advantage or immunity granted to or enjoyed by a person or class of persons, beyond the common advantages of others'. We might say, in other words, that privilege is some sort of superior status. The privileges enjoyed by professional people include:

- a licence to practise (an unqualified person who practises is committing a criminal offence – according to the rules of most professions);
- letters after your name, often coupled with a certain standing in the community;
- independence of professional judgement;
- the ability to make some worthwhile contribution to society – to make a difference;
- the potential for a life-long career;
- a professional qualification has a 'transfer' value into other fields of employment;
- membership of the body which governs and regulates the profession.

As compared to the privileges enjoyed by individual members of a profession, the fundamental privilege enjoyed by most of the professions in this country is that of self-regulation. This means essentially the right to govern themselves, to decide the standards for entry into the profession and to decide the conduct to be expected of members of the profession.

History of the veterinary profession

In the early 1800s veterinarians wanted to distinguish themselves from the quacks or charlatans who also used to treat animals in those days.

They wanted some means of recognizing their qualification and superior status and also a means of ensuring that they could exclude from membership those who were not prepared to abide by the rules. To exercise this sort of collective power over others they needed government or statutory authority.

Traditionally the State would award bodies of professionals this statutory authority – the privilege of self-regulation – but only in return for an assurance that its members would set standards of competence and an ethical code of conduct that would protect consumers. Professions therefore gained status in exchange for a commitment to good behaviour. This early form of social contract was usually granted by Royal Charter and/or an Act of Parliament.

The Royal College of Veterinary Surgeons (RCVS) was established by Royal Charter in 1844. The Charter was originally granted to the graduates of the two veterinary schools then in existence (at London and Edinburgh) and formed them into a body corporate known as the Royal College of Veterinary Surgeons. The Charter declared the practice of veterinary medicine to be a 'profession' and that members of the College had the sole and exclusive right to be known as 'veterinary surgeons'. The Charter also provided for the governance of the profession, the election of a Council and Officers, the examination of students, the affiliation of new veterinary schools and for graduates to be admitted as members.

Further Royal Charters extended the powers of the College and these powers are now consolidated in the Supplemental Charter of 1967. There have also been various Acts of Parliament, the most significant being the Veterinary Surgeons Act 1948, which made unqualified practice a criminal offence. The current statutory powers are contained in the Veterinary Surgeons' Act 1966, which deals with all aspects of regulating the profession.

Those eligible to become members of the College (in effect signing up to the social contract) and thus to become part of this self-regulatory structure, include all graduates from the six veterinary schools in the UK, nationals from EU member states with recognized qualifications and veterinary graduates from nine other veterinary schools overseas. In addition, those veterinarians with other foreign qualifications who pass the Royal College's membership examination are also entitled be admitted. At the Admission Ceremony to the Royal College new members recite a declaration which involves promising loyalty to the College: 'to do all in my power to maintain and promote its interests'. In other words members agree to abide by the rules laid down by the RCVS in return for the privilege of being able to practise as a veterinary surgeon.

The declaration also requires a promise 'that my constant endeavour will be to ensure the welfare of animals committed to my care' – the equivalent of the doctors' Hippocratic Oath to put the welfare of patients first. Again, this is part of the commitment to the public, consumers or clients (and, in particular, their animals), in return for which the privileged status is granted.

Why is regulation necessary?

The question of why regulation is necessary needs to be answered explicitly, because there is sometimes the temptation to say 'Professional people are responsible aren't they?' What, in effect, is being regulated by the Royal College is the interface between the members of the profession and their clients. Regulation is the means of providing consumer protection and of maintaining the standards and credibility of the profession, i.e. quality assurance. It is also the means of making sure that professionals do not abuse their privilege. The rationale for regulation is based on the following:

- most clients cannot make informed judgements about a professional's work. The range of knowledge and skill encompassed by a profession is vast and although some regular clients will acquire some means of judging whether or not the professional is doing a good job, most have to rely on trust and this can involve literally 'putting your life in their hands'! Animals are even more vulnerable than most humans, as they have no capacity to evaluate the skills of a veterinary surgeon or to consent to treatment;
- there are dangers to clients (or their animals) from incompetent or unethical practice;
- considerable expense may be involved in veterinary treatment and this may be difficult to estimate when clients first seek professional help;
- some treatment which is given cannot always be undone, for example, surgery;
- most professions have a conscience and realize that it is in the profession's interest to maintain its reputation for competence and integrity by disciplining those who bring it into disrepute;
- the public, clients, consumers (and on their behalf, government, Parliament and other bodies, including the media) will insist on some means of protecting their interests.

Who should do the regulating?

In a number of other countries, particularly in Europe, regulation of the professions is carried out directly by government departments. In the UK there is an increasing amount of regulation by a government agency – for example, Ofgas, Oftel, Ofwat, the Financial Services Authority, etc. Such regulatory agencies are relatively new, as traditionally the professions in the UK have been self-regulating.

The professions usually fund these regulatory processes and many feel that this is to be preferred to a situation where external agencies provide the funding and thus call a different tune. Members of a self-regulating profession will have the technical knowledge to make the necessary judgements of what is acceptable and members are also more likely to respect the peer review process. There is, however, increasingly pressure on all the professions to involve more lay people or representatives of consumers or clients in the review process to improve the accountability and transparency of regulation.

What are the essential elements of self-regulation?

- a public register of members – to identify those who have satisfied the necessary requirements to practise;
- a set of criteria to control entry on to the register;
- the ability to take action against those who might falsely present themselves as qualified;
- procedures for regulating education and training;
- a code of professional conduct. This will encompass such things as: the interests of clients; competence; dignity/reputation/integrity; independence; confidentiality; conflicts of interest; publicity/promotion;
- machinery for handling complaints and disciplining members;
- a proper process for removing names from the register.

Changes over the years

In the nineteenth century professions were small, élite, groups where self-regulation often took the form of self-protection, with professions acting a bit like a closed shop to ward off competition. In this way they maintained the ancient monopolies and operated a sort of price-fixing cartel to earn a good and secure income. Of course, they were also effectively gentlemen's clubs. Women were not allowed into the professions until 1919 – and even then they were not always welcomed!

The first woman's name added to the RCVS Register was that of Aleen Cust in 1922.

Traditionally the relationship between client and professional was based on trust. The client would accept the work produced by the professional, on the terms set by the professional, and the professional would honour that trust by producing work of the highest standard. In this relationship it was clearly the professional who called all the shots. However, a survey carried out by the Society of Practising Veterinary Surgeons (SPVS) in 1994 on the *Image and Profile of the Veterinary Profession* noted that respect for the profession is no longer automatic but that it now has to be earned. The privileges can not now be assumed and to a large extent will now depend on public opinion. The survey also showed that what clients look for most are care, compassion and value for money (though this does not necessarily mean the lowest fees).

Today, the average client is less trusting, more informed, articulate and often assertive, particularly when a large sum of hard-earned money is involved. Clients are less inclined to be blinded by science and are more likely to complain if they feel that the case has not been fully explained to them. The trust placed in a professional is no longer blind: clients are demanding more openness and shared information. The current emphasis is on accountability and transparency.

Clients are no longer impressed by professional mystique. They want to see what they get for their money. This means that they expect to have the knowledge which separates them from the professional (the science, the law or whatever) explained to them in plain English, not in technical jargon. They want to understand what the deal is, what their rights are, what the professional can and should do, what they, as clients, can do if they are dissatisfied.

It has to be said that some of the professions have been slow to appreciate that this consumer pressure (or people power) was anything that they needed to take any account of. The professions have traditionally thought they were above things like customer care, communicating in plain English, putting a clear price tag on their services, competition, advertising, etc. However, the days when clients, competition and fees could be controlled by the profession alone have gone. The relationship today is, or should be, more of two-way process. The relationship involves the professional seeking to understand a client's needs and the client needing to understand the limitations of what a professional can do.

For veterinary surgeons as professionals things are even more difficult. Unlike most other professions veterinary surgeons have, in effect, two clients. Primarily, animals are their clients, but they need to keep an eye on the human client too. Human clients can pay the veterinary surgeons' bills with a smile, or alternatively disparage them to friends and neighbours, or even complain to the Royal College of Veterinary Surgeons. To avoid this confusion of terminology of having two clients most veterinary surgeons refer to the animal as the patient and the owner of the animal as the client.

Veterinary surgeons may have to balance what the human client wants, and is prepared to pay for, and what they think is in the animals' best interests. The human client is entitled to reject advice and a veterinary surgeon must respect that – just as they themselves deserve respect for exercising their professional judgement independently of financial or other pressures. No professional person should say just what the client wants to hear. Whilst all professionals are engaged to provide a service they are distinguishable from other service providers in that the very essence of a professional service is the independent advice on which it rests. The 'customer is *not* always right' in this instance, and professionals can be seriously negligent if they do not adhere strictly to this approach.

Indeed, if veterinary surgeons are ever put under pressure by a client or an employer to do something they feel would be unprofessional, they can turn to their professional body, the RCVS for support. The RCVS produces a *Guide to Professional Conduct* which does not exist just to restrict veterinary surgeons (to tell them what they may not do), it is also there to support and guide the profession, and in doing so to tell others what the veterinary profession considers to be unethical and unacceptable. In this way the Royal College sets the standards in accordance with its self-regulatory responsibilities.

The future

The Conservative government, which was in power until 1997, was keen to remove restrictive practices (what it saw as barriers to competition and efficiency). It started with the trade unions but moved on to the professions – seeking to retain similar long-standing practices to those of the miners and print workers in, for example, the solicitors' monopoly of conveyancing and the opticians' provision of spectacles as well as eye tests. There is no reason to suppose that the existing administration takes a different attitude. Indeed the Secretary of State for Health has been publicly critical of decisions made by the General Medical Council and the government has brought forward legislation to enable it to revise the powers of human healthcare professional bodies by Statutory Instrument (Health Act 1999). In effect this gives ministers powers to intervene in the self-regulation of many professions. It remains to be seen if this may erode the independence of the regulatory bodies and the process of self-regulation.

It should be noted, however, that this would not be the first time that government has clipped the wings of a profession in relation to its self-regulation. Following repeated criticism of the solicitors' governing body, The Law Society, in 1990 the government introduced a statutorily appointed ombudsman to oversee the handling of complaints about solicitors and required that all changes to rules relating to education and conduct must be approved by a government appointed independent advisory committee before they can take effect. The accountants are also now facing the creation of a new supervisory board to oversee the regulatory functions of the various accountancy professional bodies, which will have 60 per cent of its members drawn from outside the profession.

All the indications are that self-regulation will need to be more transparent and less self-serving in the twenty-first century. Regulatory bodies will increasingly need to involve lay people in handling complaints and in the disciplinary process. Professions which appear to look after their own will be looked on less favourably by government and the public generally.

It might be said that the laity are striking back against the conspiracy which they perceived the professions to be guilty of. Unquestioning or reluctant respect for the professional has, regrettably, given way to cynicism and suspicion. This change in attitude towards the professions is regrettable, because it was abuses of privilege by some professionals which were instrumental in this change. Not surprisingly, some of those who were taken advantage of now want to get even. Consumers, government and other organizations will continue to put pressure on the professions to improve standards and at the same time to reduce costs. Education, training and career development must become a continuous lifelong process if the professional is to keep up to the mark.

Current concerns are more about competence than ethical misconduct. The professions are all likely to come under increasing pressure to assess and regulate competence. This will not just be at the point of entry into the profession, but throughout the professional career. In addition, there is little public tolerance for professions which allow their members to continue in practice when they are unfit to do so because of mental or physical disability or problems of addiction. In the future, therefore, the licence to practise, issued by professional bodies, might be issued only for five years or even one year at a time, thereafter requiring some re-accreditation or re-registration. Here the argument is similar to that which is applied to the driving licence. The skills which persons may be competent to perform in their late teens or early twenties, they may no longer be competent to do aged fifty or sixty. For professionals to retain the public's trust it is necessary to show that they have kept their knowledge and skill up to date.

In the late 1990s the General Medical Council introduced a scheme which required all doctors to report on the competence of colleagues, senior and junior. This is a serious system of peer review involving downwards, upwards and sideways appraisal. The General Dental Council is considering a form of compulsory Continuing Professional Development (CPD) scheme whereby dentists would be required to undertake a specified number of hours of CPD each year and submit formal evidence of this every five years in order to stay in practice.

Management and entrepreneurial skills, traditionally eschewed by professionals, will be needed to survive in an increasingly commercial environment. Whilst this may not be welcomed by all professionals, particularly those dedicated to practise in their chosen profession, there is good news in the extent to which information technology can free professionals from much routine work, to concentrate on the more complex and interesting aspects of their chosen career.

Another development is that of the para-professionals, increasingly common in most professions. In the veterinary world the most established para-professional is the veterinary nurse, but there are increasing numbers of others (for example, artificial inseminators, ultra-sound scanners, equine dentists). Veterinary nurses have been around since 1963 when they were originally called Registered Animal Nursing Auxiliaries (RANA). Their qualification is awarded by the Royal College of Veterinary Surgeons and currently nearly 3000 are on a list maintained by the College. This list is not as formal as the Register of Veterinary Surgeons (there are no powers to 'strike off'), but only those on the list may carry out certain limited acts of veterinary surgery as defined by the Veterinary Surgeons' Act.

In the past, and to an extent still today, these people would be regarded as unwelcome competition, a reason to exert the collective muscle to maintain the profession's exclusive position. Now it is seen as beneficial to incorporate these new groups within the regulatory structure, recognizing that many acts of veterinary surgery can be carried out by others if they are properly trained and supervised. In this way the profession can delegate a number of its more routine and less demanding tasks and at the same time protect the public and animals from incompetence by overseeing the activities of the para-professionals. Thus the self-regulating approach is maintained, and indeed driven by, what is in the best interests of those seeking to engage the services of the profession.

What does the Royal College of Veterinary Surgeons do?

Under the terms of its Charter the RCVS is a corporate body, that is to say made up of all its members. It is a body consisting of those whose names are on its Register. Members can all vote in elections, stand for Council, attend the Annual General Meeting and place the letters MRCVS after their name. Decisions about who should be registered or not, taken off the Register or not, are all taken by members. Those who determine the educational requirements, consider complaints and judge the disciplinary cases are similarly fellow members. Self-regulation is in effect a form of peer review.

Statutory functions – as set out in the Veterinary Surgeons Act 1966:

- management of the veterinary profession – through a Council of elected and appointed members;
- registration of veterinary surgeons:
  - gives a qualification to practise throughout the EU and other parts of the world;
  - provides a means of ensuring that those qualified abroad are trained to a similarly high standard;
- regulation of professional education involving regular checks on course content and facilities at the UK veterinary schools.
- regulation of professional conduct:
  - provides ethical guidance in the *Guide to Professional Conduct* and in response to individual enquiries
  - deals with complaints – both justifiable and otherwise – and takes action against those members who would bring the profession into disrepute;
- cancellation or suspension of registration in cases of misconduct (this operates in accordance with due disciplinary process).
- Connected purposes:
  - as specified in the Royal Charter – to confer certificates, diplomas, fellowships, etc., and other prizes and awards;
  - provides a forum in which members can be elected to participate in the governance of the profession;

- organizes regional meetings at which members may attend and raise issues with the College Officers (President, two Vice-Presidents, Treasurer and Registrar);
- provides information in an Annual Report and a newsletter published three times a year.

In essence the RCVS strives to ensure that members of the public and their animals are able to obtain veterinary services from veterinary surgeons who are properly qualified and regulated and who conduct themselves in a professional manner.

The benefits for the profession are a clearly defined professional status, independence and a licence to practise supported by self-imposed ethical rules policed by peers.

The RCVS Trust

Established in 1958 as the charitable arm of the College, the Trust exists to:

- promote, encourage and advance the study and practice of the art and science of veterinary surgery;
- advance education in connection with the art and science of veterinary surgery and medicine. To this end the Trust provides an extensive library facility at the RCVS headquarters in central London and on the Internet and provides funds for projects and posts.

6

Ethical dilemmas and the RCVS

Diane Sinclair

In this chapter I propose to consider first the general responsibility of the RCVS in relation to the provision of ethical guidance to the veterinary profession in the United Kingdom, then to concentrate upon those dilemmas which arise out of specific relationships between veterinary surgeons and others, and finally to look at the dilemmas directly related to particular procedures or activities.

At the six UK university veterinary schools the conferment of degrees in veterinary science is immediately followed by a further ceremony during which the new graduates are admitted to membership of the Royal College of Veterinary Surgeons. Under section 19 of the Veterinary Surgeons Act 1966 membership is a legal requirement to practise veterinary surgery in the United Kingdom. An integral part of this ceremony is the making of the following declaration:

'Inasmuch as the privilege of membership of the Royal College of Veterinary Surgeons is about to be conferred upon me, I PROMISE AND SOLEMNLY DECLARE that I will abide in all due loyalty to the Royal College of Veterinary surgeons and will do all in my power to maintain and promote its interests.

'I PROMISE ABOVE ALL that I will pursue the work of my profession with uprightness of conduct and that my constant endeavour will be to ensure the welfare of animals committed to my care.'

This declaration is made by all veterinary surgeons on admission to membership of the RCVS, wherever they originally qualified, and encapsulates the social contract which they are making as members of the veterinary profession in the UK.

Membership of any profession confers special rights and privileges which inevitably go hand in hand with responsibilities. The latter involve acceptance of a collective responsibility for the integrity of the whole profession through a code of ethics and a regulatory structure for complaints and discipline. The full range of statutory/regulatory functions of the RCVS is dealt with in the previous chapter of this book. This chapter concentrates on the dilemmas inherent in the formulation of the College's ethical guidance to the profession as a whole, and in its advice to individual members on specific ethical problems which they may be facing.

The general ethical advice is embodied in the RCVS *Guide to Professional Conduct* which must, therefore, cover a number of crucial relationships, particularly those between veterinary surgeons and clients, between veterinary surgeons and other professionals or lay persons associated with or employed by a practice and involved in the treatment of animals, and between colleagues within the veterinary profession. The task is to formulate a broad basis of advice setting out a common professional ethical standard acceptable to all members, and also to provide individual advice when required to members faced with individual problems. This is done by discussing the issues involved and assisting members in exercising their own professional judgement in a proper manner by applying the general principles to the particular set of circumstances.

In one sense the veterinary profession is unique among health professions in that the legitimate interests of the animal owner – legal, psychological or even economic – may apparently conflict with the emphasis on animal welfare in the veterinary surgeon's declaration. It is the responsibility of the RCVS to recognize this additional dilemma, and to guide its members appropriately.

No longer can any profession or its regulatory body maintain a paternalistic attitude to those who may question its activities, the sort of attitude which enabled George Bernard Shaw for example to suggest that all professions were 'conspiracies against the laity'. In the new millennium professional codes of ethics must be accessible equally to the profession and to clients, and, in the case of veterinary surgeons, to the animal owners whose interests the RCVS is there to protect. They must be sufficiently flexible so as to reflect an awareness of continuing advances in science or technology, of new pressures and problems affecting the profession, and of associated ethical issues which may arise.

Dilemmas arising out of the relationship between veterinary surgeon and client

The relationship between veterinary surgeon and client, in common with that between any professional person and client, must be founded upon faith and trust. Animal owners are reliant upon veterinary surgeons to help them in making informed decisions about the treatment of their animals in the light of all the relevant circumstances. The Royal College's guidance must in turn help veterinary surgeons balance their responsibilities to the animals entrusted to their care with their responsibilities to their clients. They may need to reconcile their ability and desire to make use of the latest diagnostic techniques and advances in treatment, and often a client's expressed wish to 'do everything you can', with an awareness that finances may be severely limited. The RCVS therefore requires veterinary surgeons to take the time to explain and discuss fully with their clients the treatment options available, their likely cost and the effect of each on the overall prognosis. The option of euthanasia should never be excluded.

The RCVS must support veterinary surgeons in situations where they may need to help clients, in cases where cost is a serious consideration, to select a more conservative form of treatment, with a poorer prognosis or even euthanasia, without any associated sense of guilt. The other side of this ethical coin can occur when a client may seek to insist upon treatment being continued against the advice of the veterinary surgeon, where the animal is suffering and the prognosis is hopeless. The veterinary surgeon is then at risk of breaking his promise to make it his constant endeavour to ensure the welfare of animals committed to his care.

Equally problematic may be the conflict between scientific and clinical capability and welfare, when a client demands a procedure – organ transplantation for example – which while not illegal, still raises as yet unresolved ethical issues, particularly in relation to the source animal. Can the removal of an organ from a healthy animal with the attendant risk to that animal be justified? It is for the RCVS to support its members when they face such dilemmas and are reluctant to accede to such requests on ethical grounds. It is also for the RCVS to keep all such issues under review and to maintain a position based upon current knowledge and ethical considerations upon which veterinary surgeons may rely.

Confidentiality is a vital part of any relationship based on trust. Clients therefore do not expect any information about themselves or their animals to be passed on to a third party without their knowledge and agreement. The RCVS emphasizes this expectation while identifying a number of exceptional circumstances when disclosure may be justified. Some of these are straightforward: for example, in the case of notifiable diseases or when a criminal offence is known to have been committed. Others are much more difficult and involve veterinary surgeons in making a decision as to whether animal welfare or the public interest are so compromised as to override any duty of confidentiality to their client. Decisions of this nature inevitably involve complex ethical considerations.

Should cases of suspected cruelty or neglect always be reported, particularly in the light of recent research which links abuse of animals to child abuse? Indeed the researchers advocate obligatory reporting by veterinary surgeons of any suspected cruelty to animals. In this context it may be relevant to recall a case which occurred some years ago when, after several lengthy discussions with the RCVS, a member decided to alert the local social services department to a particular case where post-mortem examination of several puppies over a period of about eighteen months had confirmed abuse leading to their death. This resulted in the discovery of a case of Münchausen syndrome by proxy with animals, putting at risk the children of the family concerned.

But then what about the elderly widow or widower whose pet, albeit suffering, with a terminal condition and with a severely impaired quality of life, is the last link with the deceased partner? Should one report a case of suspected organized fighting between animals when this raises the possibility that treatment will no longer be sought for animals injured in this way if the organizers are brought to the notice of the authorities? Although not obliged to do so should veterinary surgeons exercise their right to report to the Kennel Club any surgery which alters the natural conformation of a Kennel Club registered dog, when issues of both welfare and public interest are involved? An example of this might be the repair of an umbilical hernia or the surgical correction of entropion which if not reported could result in an hereditary defect being perpetuated.

Some of the most difficult decisions in recent years have been those associated with the flawed dangerous dogs' legislation. Although the legislation does not place an obligation on veterinary surgeons to report the possession by a client of an unregistered dog bearing a resemblance to the so-called 'pit bull type', many veterinary surgeons are concerned as to whether they should do so, bearing in mind the likely seizure of the dog followed by a lengthy period of captivity before a Court decides upon its future. Others, once they are satisfied that the animal is temperamentally sound, have taken the view that the dog is of the 'type known as a mongrel'.

It is for the RCVS in all cases where a breach of confidentiality is being considered to accept the responsibility for resolving jointly with veterinary surgeons the ethical dilemmas involved, in order to enable them to exercise their clinical judgement so as to reach a properly considered decision.

Dilemmas arising out of the relationship between veterinary surgeons and other professionals or lay persons involved in the treatment of animals

Although in terms of the Veterinary Surgeons Act 1966 the practice of veterinary surgery is essentially restricted to registered members of the RCVS, giving veterinary surgeons a near monopoly in the treatment of animals, the legislation does allow other significant groups (principally veterinary students, listed veterinary nurses, farriers, physiotherapists, osteopaths and chiropractors) to be involved subject to certain conditions. Ethical dilemmas do arise over ensuring the observance of the conditions affecting treatment by members of these groups, and the RCVS has a significant part to play in the resolution of these dilemmas. Veterinary surgery is defined within the Act as encompassing the 'art and science of veterinary surgery' which includes the diagnosis of diseases and injuries in animals, diagnostic tests, advice on diagnosis and the medical and surgical treatment of animals, the key word being 'diagnosis'.

Monitoring the training of the largest of these groups – veterinary nurses – is one of the responsibilities of the RCVS, which, on satisfactory completion of the qualifying examination, will place a veterinary nurse's name on the list of qualified nurses maintained by the College. The Veterinary Surgeons Act 1966 (Schedule 3 Amendment Order) 1991 extended the exemptions of those permitted to treat animals to listed veterinary nurses, but only under the direction of their veterinarian employer in relation to companion animals under the veterinarian's care. No veterinary nurse is otherwise entitled to treat any animal or in any event to make a diagnosis. Since the 1991 Amendment Order makes no reference to specific procedures, it falls to the RCVS to guide veterinary surgeons on the matters to be taken into consideration before directing any listed nurse to carry out the medical treatment or minor surgery which the Order allows them to perform under direction. In so doing the College must ensure that veterinary surgeons have regard to the balance between the expectations, confidence and ability of the veterinary nurse and those of the animal owner, who should certainly be made aware if any procedure is to be carried out by a nurse rather than by a veterinary surgeon.

Veterinary surgeons and farriers are both involved in the treatment of horses' feet. Ethical problems do arise, however, in that there is no clear demarcation line in the exercise of their respective responsibilities. Much depends on individual responsibility and the relationship between them. Decisions as to whether a particular procedure is to be performed by one or the other is a matter for consultation and co-operation between them. It is for the RCVS to assist in the avoidance of conflict on ethical grounds by fostering co-operation between veterinary surgeons and farriers, and to discourage its members from making derogatory comments about the work of farriers except where these may form part of a formal complaint to the regulatory body.

The Veterinary Surgery (Exemptions) Order 1962 allows for the treatment of an animal 'by physiotherapy' under the direction of a veterinary surgeon, provided that the animal has first been seen by the veterinary surgeon who has diagnosed the condition and referred it for treatment by physiotherapy. Physiotherapy has been defined by the RCVS as including 'all kinds of manipulative therapy' thereby including both osteopathy and chiropractic in addition to physiotherapy itself.

Diagnosis and/or treatment by any of the above, except on referral by a veterinary surgeon, would be both illegal and unethical since all three bodies recognize the restrictions in relation to the treatment of animals, and emphasize these in their respective codes of practice. Whereas clients may wish for a variety of reasons to bypass the veterinary surgeon and call in a manipulative therapist directly, it is for the RCVS to fulfil its function by collaborating with the other professional bodies to ensure as far as possible that this does not occur.

All other kinds of complementary therapy may only be administered by veterinary surgeons. It is, however, very difficult for owners who themselves choose to be treated by some form of complementary medicine, to understand that they may not entrust the care of their animals to, for example, the same lay homoeopath whom they trust to treat themselves. The perception is simply of protectionism on the part of the veterinary profession. The RCVS is in a position to redress the ethical balance and must do so by emphasizing that it is incumbent on any veterinary surgeon who offers any form of complementary therapy to be adequately trained in its application.

Dilemmas arising out of the relationship between veterinary surgeons and their colleagues

Veterinary surgeons who have reason to be critical of a colleague face an ethical dilemma in terms of voicing that criticism openly. There is an obvious danger of destroying the bond of confidence and trust which must exist between the individual veterinary surgeon and his client, and also of undermining the reputation of the veterinary profession generally. For this reason the RCVS advises veterinary surgeons not to write or speak critically or disparagingly about colleagues, and wherever possible to settle disputes between colleagues within the profession by means of mediation, conciliation or arbitration. It encourages veterinary surgeons to be aware of, and acknowledge the limits of their own competence by referring cases when necessary to a colleague with more skill or expertise in the particular area. Second opinion veterinary surgeons are in turn discouraged from making openly adverse comments about the first veterinary surgeon's ability or clinical handling of the case.

Nevertheless, there are two occasions when veterinary surgeons may need to overcome any reluctance to be critical of colleagues – both are in the interests of justice. The first of these occurs when the RCVS calls for comments on a case in the course of an investigation which it is carrying out in response to a complaint against a veterinary surgeon. In such a case consideration for a professional colleague could inhibit the RCVS in its statutory function. The second arises during a court hearing when one veterinary surgeon appearing as an expert witness may need to challenge the opinion put forward by the veterinary expert for the other party, or even to question his professional standing. The resulting discomfort does sometimes provoke a complaint to the RCVS by the aggrieved expert. The RCVS must then emphasize that the function of an expert witness is always to assist the court in reaching the truth even when to the extent of casting genuine doubts on the ability of a colleague.

Dilemmas arising out of particular veterinary procedures or activities

Any procedure which in effect alters the natural conformation of an animal and is not necessary to its welfare may fall into the category of a mutilation. Veterinary surgeons asked to perform such procedures are then faced with the dilemma of balancing the wishes of the animal owner with their duty to ensure the welfare of the animal, and also to follow RCVS guidance on such matters.

Can it ever be ethical, for example, to declaw a cat and thus destroy its natural defence mechanism? Initially the answer may seem simple, but the request may be made for a number of different reasons. Whereas most veterinary surgeons have no problem in accepting RCVS advice that declawing cannot be acceptable merely for the convenience of the owner (because, for example, the cat is tearing up expensive curtains), other situations may be more difficult to resolve. Would it still be wrong if the cat never went outside, or if the alternative were euthanasia? What about the owner in a physically fragile state through illness or disability, whose cat is their only companion, and who develops a severe reaction to cat scratches? All these situations can and do arise from time to time, and the RCVS must be prepared to help its members to resolve the ethical problems involved.

The docking of dogs' tails raises even more complex problems in terms of what is classified as prophylactic docking – to guard against the risk of injury to the tail of an adult working dog. The RCVS, in formulating its advice on docking, had to recognize that whenever there is a body of opinion suggesting that a particular form of treatment is valid, clinical judgement must not be fettered. Its guidance on prophylactic docking therefore creates for the veterinary surgeon the difficulty of justifying a 'true belief' that docking is necessary in the case of a puppy whose future lifestyle may not be by any means certain. Even in the case of docking for purely cosmetic reasons, which the RCVS has declared unethical, the veterinary surgeon may still face problems in following that advice. What about the possibility that if he refuses to dock a litter of puppies it will be docked elsewhere illegally with the associated welfare risk, or when he may be faced with the loss of a good breeder client who claims that it is impossible to sell puppies unless they are docked?

Apart from veterinary services provided by the animal charities for those who could not otherwise afford treatment, it must be acknowledged that whilst the practice of veterinary surgery may be a vocation, a veterinary practice is also a business. Economic fees must therefore be charged if the business is to remain in being and to meet its overheads. Although the RCVS has no specific jurisdiction over fees, some related issues do raise ethical concerns.

All veterinary surgeons are expected to provide emergency first aid and pain relief for any animal in an emergency, irrespective of its owner's financial circumstances. This applies equally to the emergency treatment of wildlife and strays. How far, however, does the obligation extend? Should complicated orthopaedic surgery be undertaken, for example, in the case of a young animal injured in a road traffic accident when the prognosis is good but with little likelihood of payment? Most veterinary surgeons undertake a substantial amount of 'charity' work of this nature, and re-home the animal once it has recovered. However, they may need to reconcile their professional conscience in terms of treating the patient with their responsibilities to the practice when escalating bad debts may threaten the livelihood of all those employed in the practice or even, in some extreme cases, the continued provision of veterinary services in an area. In helping veterinary surgeons to resolve such conflicts, the RCVS must help them to accept that on humane grounds euthanasia may sometimes be appropriate.

As more and more animal orientated programmes are shown on TV, more and more veterinary surgeons are faced with dilemmas over the treatment of injured wildlife presented to them by members of the public. The latter expect this to be a free service provided automatically by a caring profession, without having any regard to the cost to the veterinary surgeon of providing the service. Should they be charged? Or should the veterinary surgeon gently agree to 'take care of it' and destroy the animal once the member of the public has left the surgery? In this event, how should he respond to a subsequent request for a progress report? The RCVS must support its members in deciding on the honest and ethical approach to these problems. It must equally encourage and support veterinary surgeons in attempting to take a realistic approach to treatment options and in trying not to raise false hopes, by enquiring in a sensitive manner into the client's ability to pay. In this way a client may be enabled to come to terms with a decision to opt for euthanasia where the prognosis is poor. In other cases it may be possible to obtain charitable assistance towards treatment where the prognosis is good, or to arrange for payment by instalments at a rate which the client can afford and is therefore likely to meet.

In an increasing number of cases when an animal has been hospitalized and substantial treatment given, it may become obvious that the owner intends to collect the animal without paying the fees already incurred. Veterinary surgeons are then faced with either exercising their legal right to hold the animal until payment is made in full, which may not be in the best interests of the animal, or following RCVS advice to release the animal whether or not payment is forthcoming. In giving this advice the RCVS must acknowledge that it is concerned as much with the possible effect on the profession of adverse publicity generated by a sometimes unscrupulous owner as with the interests of the animal, which may not always be endangered.

Euthanasia, or humane destruction, presents perhaps the most diffi-cult issues faced regularly by all veterinary surgeons. The worst of these probably arises when a client requests the destruction of a healthy animal. Veterinary surgeons by the very nature of their vocation and training are dedicated to the saving of life, and no veterinary surgeon is ever obliged to destroy a healthy animal. A refusal to do so is not, however, a simple decision in that there are two important factors which must be taken into account. The first is that in law animals are the property of their owners who have the right of disposal, and the second is that euthanasia is not an act of veterinary surgery. The practical significance of this is that it may be carried out by the owner or anyone else on his behalf, subject only to the requirement that it be done humanely. Veterinary surgeons must, therefore, consider whether it may be better to accede to the owner's request (after first trying to persuade them to consider all the possible alternative such as re-homing), so as to ensure that the procedure is carried out in a peaceful and dignified manner for the animal, or whether to take the risk of the owner arranging for destruction in some other way. The RCVS must always be prepared to discuss the issues with veterinary surgeons and help them to reach a decision in accordance with their conscience.

The dangerous dogs' legislation creates problems for some veterinary surgeons who may be expected to carry out a destruction order. There is, however, no obligation on them to do so, even in cases where the veterinary surgeon is named in the order, and the RCVS must support veterinary surgeons whose conscience does not permit them to do so.

In the case of large animals difficulties may arise when the most efficient method of euthanasia may not be aesthetically acceptable to the owner. In such cases, should the veterinary surgeon seek to insist on shooting a horse, for example, rather than accede to the owner's request for destruction by lethal injection which may not always be immediately effective?

The one instance in which the RCVS must not support a veterinary surgeon is if he accepts an animal for euthanasia with the intention of re-homing the animal without the owner's knowledge. This amounts to dishonesty which the RCVS, whatever the motives, can never condone. Similarly, honesty is essential to uphold the integrity of veterinary certification. The RCVS will never support any veterinary surgeon who backdates an insurance certificate so that treatment for a pre-existing condition will be covered which the owner could not otherwise afford, or who alters the date of birth of a cow destined for slaughter so as to enable a farmer to claim a higher sum in compensation. There can be no ethical considerations which justify a dishonest act.

Finally, the RCVS faces its own dilemma, as both the advisory and the regulatory body for the profession, in being obliged to investigate all complaints against veterinary surgeons which fall within its jurisdiction, however trivial they may at first appear. In so doing its staff are inevitably conscious of the anxiety caused to veterinary surgeons by the formal investigation process, the length of time involved, and the ultimate fear of disciplinary action which could threaten their livelihood.

To ensure that the process is conducted in an impartial manner which takes account of the legitimate interests of both parties, this procedure is followed:

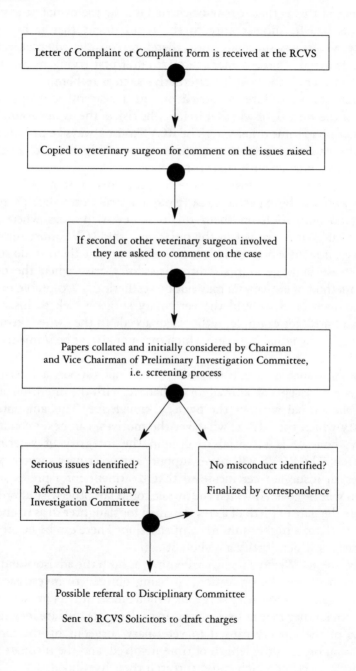

The price of freedom is indeed eternal vigilance, and the RCVS must constantly monitor all ethical issues in the light of any new developments in order to ensure that its advice is reliable and up to date.

PART TWO

PART TWO

7

Issues in small animal practice

John Bower

Ethical issues in small animal practice fall into two broad categories – those involving primarily the animal, and those involving people. The overriding responsibility of all veterinarians, however, is as contained in the Declaration of the Royal College of Veterinary Surgeons – ' ... to ensure the welfare of animals committed to my care'. Within this framework of responsibility though, veterinarians must behave in an ethical manner to the people with whom they come in contact in caring for the animal – the owner or agent, other veterinarians, the practice staff, the public, the police, and local animal welfare organizations. In large animal practice ethical issues often arise because of commercial reactions; although this can be the case in small animal practice emotional reaction is more usual.

The reference 'bible' for all ethical matters in the profession is the RCVS *Guide to Professional Conduct*. This covers all forms of veterinary work but small animal practice involves certain issues that are specific because of the nature of the work, not least of which is that in many cases we are dealing with the uninformed owner. This is not usually the case in farm animal and horse practice.

Animals under a veterinarian's care

Issues under this heading would include the supply of PML (Pharmacy Merchants' List) and POM (Prescription-Only Medicine) medicines. The *Guide* is quite specific but, in practice, interpretation is not always easy. Veterinarians can only supply the above categories of medicines to clients who have genuinely, not just nominally, placed the animal under their care, and would have to have seen the animal often enough to have knowledge of its health situation. This becomes an issue in small animal practice when a pet owner calls in for simple medicines such as wormers or flea treatments for their dog or cat which has never been seen by the practice. These may be PML or POM medicines. In summer this is a daily issue and problem in a busy practice which can cause genuine anger and frustration to the owner who cannot understand why the veterinary practice will not sell or prescribe such a product, especially as the selfsame product can be bought over the counter in the chemists' shop!

In the case of PML worm or flea medicines, RCVS guidance has been that if the animal is under the care of another veterinarian, then owners must purchase the product there. If their animal is not under the care of another veterinarian they should genuinely register the pet with the practice and the medicine may then be supplied. A more strict interpretation would be to offer to examine the pet, often at no charge, and then supply the product. With the development of the 'new generation' flea treatments, which are POM, this is indeed the best method of ensuring ethics are not compromised. However, this inconvenience is still incomprehensible to owners and the accompanying explanations take up a lot of receptionist and nursing time and can be stressful.

Provision of emergency services

Covering for a colleague in an emergency

Veterinarians who offer a service to pet owners have an ethical obligation to provide a 24-hour emergency service for their clients' animals. This can be via their own practice, or by prior arrangement, via a neighbouring colleague. It becomes an ethical issue between the two practices, and between the client and the first practice, when practices simply do not answer their calls during anti-social hours leaving neighbouring practices to attend to distraught clients' needs. This is probably the single greatest cause of inter-practice disputes, and one of the simplest to correct by mutual discussion. The single-handed practitioner and others on a frequent on-call rota obviously find it a great strain to be on call every day and night, and cannot give a good service to patients, so an arrangement is strongly advisable, either on a rota basis with neighbouring practices, or by arranging for a nearby large practice to carry out the emergency work.

A particular ethical issue arises where specific tasks only are carried out, such as in neutering clinics. Such a practice must still provide proper

24 hour care – telephone contact, and facilities for hospitalization, intravenous drips, and intensive care. This may be by arrangement with another practice, but there is an ethical duty to provide it and it becomes a real issue when one is called out because the original surgeon is not contactable.

A similar issue occurs following the docking of puppies tails by a veterinarian, possibly a 'travelling' veterinarian, who has chosen to ignore the RCVS guidance that this is an unethical procedure in all but the rarest case. Such puppies can and do need post-operative care – haemorrhage and sepsis are not unheard of – and the original veterinarian is frequently too far away to attend. The puppies' own veterinarian, who is rarely advised of this act of supersession, has no way of determining who the docking veterinarian is, such is the secrecy, and therefore cannot determine what medicine or treatment has previously been given.

One of the dilemmas facing the anti-docking veterinarian is – to dock or not to dock! If the veterinarian believes that cosmetic docking is wrong, and/or wants to follow the RCVS guidance, but having seen dogs damaged for life by incompetent docking he may feel it is better that someone who knows what they are doing carries it out if the owner is insistent. This was a common dilemma prior to the change in the clause in the Veterinary Surgeons Act 1993 which made docking an act of veterinary surgery, and since then lay personnel are not legally allowed to dock. This leads to a new dilemma where the veterinarian now has to intervene where docking, illegally carried out by a non-veterinarian, has gone wrong.

In-surgery or house visit?

In most circumstances the patient is best served by treatment in the surgery and, provided veterinarians agree to see an animal in need, in most circumstances ethics do not require them to pay a house call. It would be difficult ethically to justify a refusal to visit a paralysed Great Dane owned by a single elderly or frail person. This can develop into a problematic issue but it is a responsibility that the practice staff should be trained to recognize and deal with satisfactorily. This can and does become an issue, however, especially during night-time hours for the lone vet, and not necessarily only female vets, where the visit is requested in known dubious areas. Personal safety is paramount.

The other house-call ethical issue is in the case of a request where the owner is known to be unable to afford the fee. The veterinarian must attend the patient (animal) in an emergency, but whether a visit must be made, or whether the veterinarian can agree to see the patient but insist it be transported to the practice, is another dilemma.

Urgent case – can't afford treatment!

This is a real ethical issue for veterinarians in small animal practice and occurs often, and usually during anti-social hours because the owner has been disinclined to seek help at an early stage. The problem usually starts with the phone call and the explanation of fees followed by the owner admitting inability to pay, or being suspected of having no money or no intention of paying. This is an area where training of lay staff is essential, but often (usually) neglected.

The animal must, of course, be seen – but by whom? The correct questioning may reveal that the call should have been made to a charity, if a local one exists, in which case the receptionist can redirect the call, or offer to do it for the owner, or offer to see the animal in an emergency with a view to referring on as soon as sensible for the animal. This is a frequent issue and one for which the practice should have a clearly defined protocol. It is certainly unethical to refuse to see the animal.

A similar dilemma exists for the injured unowned stray, brought in by the finder. Any emergency treatment is covered by the police, local authority, or RSPCA, but for how long? Practices have solved this ethical problem in many ingenious ways from just accepting the loss to earmarking funds raised by 'Friends of the Practice' for this very purpose. It is infinitely more sensible to formulate a strategy so all practice members know how to handle the situation. This could also apply to an injured wild creature but most practices provide treatment for these free of charge, at least during normal working hours.

Large animal and unfamiliar species

All veterinarians must provide at least first aid for any species in distress. If a horse is injured outside a small animal practice the veterinarian must attend or make rapid arrangements for a colleague in large animal practice to do so. It is sensible to anticipate such a situation and make prior arrangements with another practice first and then inform everyone what to do. If this has not been prearranged it could become both an ethical issue and one of real suffering on the part of the animal if the veterinarian does not attend.

Cosmetic surgery

From time to time small animal veterinarians are asked to modify a dog or cat to improve its chances of success at pet shows. This may involve endodontics (the moving of misplaced teeth), removal of nasal folds, entropion or ectropion operations and many more examples. Some cases are clear cut and do not benefit the patient. An example would be a misaligned but non-painful permanent tooth where endodontics to move it would not benefit the dog but would probably enable it to win at shows. It would thus be in demand for breeding during which it may pass on its dental misalignment, if it was an hereditary condition.

With painful conformational problems, such as entropion, surgical correction is necessary on humane grounds, but may also improve the dog's chances of doing well in the show ring. In such cases it is perfectly permissible (and indeed desirable) for the operating veterinarian to inform the Kennel Club of this operation, as the rules of Kennel Club registration absolve veterinary surgeons from the obligation of confidentiality in this specific area. It does become an ethical issue, however, if it is not explained to the owner that this will take place, or in circumstances where an operation has obviously been carried out by a previous veterinarian but the dog continues to be shown.

The docking of dogs' tails

This is probably the commonest ethical issue facing the small animal section of the veterinary profession today. The government decreed in 1993 that it was no longer a lay procedure and could only be carried out by veterinarians. The RCVS then confirmed their declaration that it is unethical to dock puppies' tails unless for therapeutic or truly prophylactic reasons. A British Small Animal Veterinary Association survey revealed that some 92 per cent of veterinarians were opposed to docking, as there was obviously no benefit to the individual puppy to have its tail amputated. Yet on a daily basis a few veterinarians on a list compiled by the Council of Docked Breeds travel to perform this operation. The ethical issue concerned with emergency cover and supersession have already been discussed. The ethical debate as to whether anyone has the right to amputate this useful organ for no good reason except appearance seems to run and run. The same debate occurred for horses many years ago until the government produced legislation in the form of the Docking and Nicking of Horses Act which banned the practice. Unfortunately, governments' lack of conviction and action has plummeted the veterinary profession into this current ongoing ethical debate with breeders, the Kennel Club, and fellow veterinarians, by their failure to ban the practice outright. The same argument applies also to the firing of horses – another dubious procedure against which the RCVS has taken a stance.

Spaying and castration

There are those who are of the opinion that neutering of pet animals is unethical as it deprives them of the right to express themselves normally. However, the many benefits to the pets themselves, even without the benefit to the owners, ensure that neutering is an ethical procedure. Suffice to say that every major animal charity promotes neutering of both cats and dogs – they see the results of non-neutering in the many thousands of unwanted puppies and kittens which are destroyed annually. It is the pet's place in society that determines the need for neutering unless needed for breeding – for example, an unneutered male cat will prowl his territory of two miles by one mile daily whether he is in the country or in an inner city. Little wonder that tom cats are frequently severely injured or killed in road traffic accidents.

Both male and female entire dogs show signs of frustration at not being allowed to mate but usually adapt to the luxurious life of a family pet when neutered. In addition there are many medical benefits to the early removal of, say the uterus and ovaries. Some 80 per cent of female rabbits of four years of age develop mammary cancer if not neutered; surgical removal of their sex organs to prevent this cannot be classed as unethical.

Inherited disease

Many breeds of dog, and some breeds of cat, are known to be prone to various inherited disease conditions. In many of these diseases the method of inheritance is known, and in some, such as hip dysplasia, elbow dysplasia, and various eye diseases, joint British Veterinary Association/Kennel Club Schemes exist to reduce the chances of producing progeny with the problem. Frequently, however, the veterinarian is faced with distraught owners of growing puppies with one of these problems. In some instances it is genuine ignorance of the potential problem by the prospective purchaser and the owner of the bitch. In others the owner of the bitch or dog has deliberately omitted to have the parents tested, leading to a defective pet and a devastated family. This surely is an ethical issue and one that occurs frequently in small animal practice – a classic case of genetic modification.

Obligations arising from the use and sale of veterinary medicinal products

The use of medicinal products is one of the major skills of a veterinarian involving diagnosis and treatment. However, the sale of all medicines except GSL (General Sales List) and unclassified products is restricted in principle to pharmacies in the Medicines Act 1968. Veterinary Surgeons are granted a concession to dispense these medicines to 'animals committed to my care' − it is not a right. Pharmacies and agricultural merchants may, however, sell PML products to anyone. This does become an issue in small animal practice when a neighbouring practice interprets the law somewhat more leniently and retails such products to anyone who calls at the practice. This is becoming more of an issue with the new generation flea treatments, most of which are POM medicines. Even some worming products are PMLs and can only be sold to existing clients whose animals have been seen recently by a veterinarian in that practice. In the summer especially this becomes a daily issue with angry owners who cannot understand the logic. Offering free examinations of their pet to ensure RCVS guidelines are followed usually solves the issue.

By following the ethical rules to the letter animal welfare can sometimes be put at risk, as it is strictly unethical to supply another veterinarian with a veterinary medicinal product for him to use on one of his patients. This can occur in cases such as a dog needing urgently anti-tetanus serum in a practice which is out of stock. The time taken to borrow it from a neighbouring practice would be much less that obtaining it from a wholesaler.

Off-label usage is another ethical issue. Ideally a veterinarian should follow the 'cascade' ruling of the RCVS whereby only medicines with a product licence for use in that species for that condition must be used. This is obviously sensible for large animals destined for the food chain or for human consumption, but not so necessary in the pet small animal which clearly will not be eaten! Residue levels of medicines are not crucial in pet animals. There are several species that we treat that have no licensed medicines available for treatment − many children's pets for instance, and veterinarians have to use their judgement in the use of medicines off-label. Ethically, owners should be warned in all cases, but as this would occur with almost all medications used for children's and exotic pets this seems an unnecessary burden in the vast majority of cases. Where a problem occurs ethics can be involved if a second veterinarian becomes involved in a dispute.

Parrots are almost a special case, as they tend to be very valuable yet only two drugs are licensed for use in this species. RCVS advice is to obtain informed and written owner consent before using other medicines.

The veterinarian–client relationship

Fees

Clients expect veterinarians both to exercise special skills and to treat them with courtesy and respect. It is our ethical duty to so do. This extends to charging the correct level of fee for the task – not too low and not unnecessarily high. However, fees are governed by business considerations and thus ethics are only compromised in certain situations which can and do arise in practice. The RCVS receives an increasing number of complaints about fees, so this issue must be addressed in practice.

Fees are rarely an ethical issue if discussed with the client in advance and the client agrees to the procedure. However, the RCVS also receives many complaints about veterinarians who 'only seem interested in the money'! Thus, although it is important to discuss fees, it must be done in a sympathetic manner and at the right stage of the client contact; not always an easy issue to solve. Ethical issues surrounding fees, if communication has been dealt with, arise around the two extremes. On the one hand are the few practices blatantly overcharging or over-treating and on the other are those who blatantly undercut correct fees, usually by cutting corners that can have ethical and animal welfare implications. Fees charged naturally reflect the work done and medications involved, and so will vary between practices. Thus, advertising of fees is specifically declared unethical as the fees quoted will not necessarily be for the same procedures. For instance, will the spay fee include pain relief?

Inability to afford fees

The emergency case where the client admits to not being able to afford one's fees arises often in practice and is a difficult ethical issue. Veterinarians are bound by the RCVS *Guide to Professional Conduct* to render emergency treatment whether they will receive payment or not, but cases arise where clients take advantage of this and repeatedly abuse the system. Thus it is necessary (and ethically possible) occasionally to give clients written notice informing them that treatment will no longer be available. They should be advised to register with another veterinarian. Even then there are those clients who take advantage of this and repeatedly present emergencies that are either obviously not genuine, or have become so only because the client has delayed contacting the practice to save on fees.

Pet insurance

Insured cases are very desirable to most practices as this usually means that the patient can receive whatever diagnostic test and treatment it needs without the worry of whether the client can afford the treatment. Ethical issues do arise here – it is all too easy to over-treat such cases, to overcharge such cases, or to charge higher fees for insured cases than uninsured cases. All this is highly unethical but insurance companies point out that it does occur to a very minor degree.

Fee splitting or supplementing

Where a second practice or a laboratory has contributed to the treatment of a patient, it is unethical to add a percentage on to that fee when charging the client. It is, however, certainly possible and advisable to charge the client for any administration costs involved in the referral or the collection and interpretation of samples and results. This becomes an issue in small animal practice especially in insured cases and transparency, in the shape of itemized invoices, is essential.

Fee tendering

This is usually contrary to the patient's, the public's, and the profession's interest, and is specifically declared unethical by the RCVS where treatment of animals is involved, except in veterinary work involving meat or dead animals. Yet it does happen, is not prevented by the RCVS and does lead to poor relationships between neighbouring practices. A recent RCVS working party has recommended that tendering is still to be discouraged but, as in all cases, welfare is not to be compromised by cutting corners in treatment. The concept adopted by the RCVS is that while tendering can lead to cost cutting, it should be seen as, and often is, about the value of a package of services of which the likely fees are just a part.

Bona fide clients

Many veterinarians now circulate clients with reminders about many procedures – vaccinations, worming, health checks as age advances, etc. Patients may be out of date with their vaccinations, for instance, and when an epidemic occurs, veterinarians will refer to their databases and circulate clients whose animals' inoculations are out of date. This is obviously in the patients' interest but the RCVS ruling is that only clients seen within two years can be contacted in case they have attended another practice. This is a serious ethical and welfare issue because many clients will have omitted to attend any practice and thus will miss out on the information. It is suspected that most practices ignore this ruling, with some justification, as any client who has changed practices would surely attend the 'new' practice when the reminder arrived. It is a case where patient welfare is not best served.

Confidentiality

All information concerning an animal under a veterinarian's care must remain confidential to the owner. There are only a few exceptions to this ethical obligation:

- with the owner's consent;
- where obliged to divulge information under the law;
- in a court of law;
- where, in an exceptional case, animal welfare or public interest is so endangered as to outweigh the obligation to the owner.

Confidentiality becomes an ethical issue in small animal practice fairly often, when, for instance, neighbours ring up to find out whether an animal has an infectious complaint, whether one has been vaccinated, etc. Usually the owner's consent is not difficult to obtain, but without it divulging any information is unethical. A particular current issue surrounds the greater media focus on the profession. Here it is imperative to obtain owner consent prior to featuring a patient in the surgery in a news item.

Certification

In small animal practice certification only becomes an ethical issue if asked to complete certificates erroneously to fulfil a client's needs, or if papers are signed without due regard to their contents. From time to time a very small minority of owners will want certificates backdated, forward dated, whether these are export certificates, vaccination record cards, insurance claim forms, etc. It is fairly easy to explain tactfully that this is impossible within one's profession and that case histories can be checked, etc., rather than just refuse with no explanation and lose the opportunity to re-educate that owner. Care must also be taken when re-issuing vaccination cards that have become illegible. For instance, veterinarians should not write down and certify histories of which they cannot be certain. This type of ethical issue is likely to become an increasing problem now that the quarantine has been lifted. The RCVS have strict guidelines on certification.

Claims to qualifications

The referral network available to veterinarians is expanding rapidly now, and basically consists of RCVS recognized 'Specialists', RCVS Diploma holders, RCVS Certificate holders, other Diploma and Certificate holders and those with special interests in certain species or disciplines. As advertising of services is now widespread, it is all too easy to claim qualifications not possessed by using loose or inaccurate wording. This becomes an issue between practices when one claims specialisms that are in reality special interests. The public is understandably confused and may well equate *special interest* with *specialist*. Anyone can legally call themselves a specialist provided they can justify such a claim. In the event of non-justification a veterinarian can be sued for misrepresentation and possibly be called before the RCVS Disciplinary Committee. However, this network of referral possibilities is highly valuable and veterinarians should be careful not to use confusing claims.

Canvassing and touting

Canvassing and touting is unethical and cannot be carried out by veterinarians. It does cause problems between practices when clients receive personalized letters from competing practices. However, it is now possible to enclose flyers in newspapers or to cold-drop advertising features through letterboxes provided they are not addressed personally to the occupants. It is likely that at some time the RCVS *Guide* will allow all legal advertising, excluding misrepresentation and comparative advertising, which EU directives will allow professions, but not anyone else, to ban on ethical grounds.

Relationships between veterinarians

In small animal practice, second opinions requested by clients dissatisfied with their previous veterinarian often lead to an expectation by the client of condemnation of the previous vet's treatment. To do so would be unethical and unwise. It is all too easy to agree or at least be non-committal, but if veterinarians fall into this trap it usually rebounds in a court appearance. There is always another expert who will agree with the first veterinarian and this leaves both the second veterinarian and the profession undermined.

Second opinions and supersession

In a busy small animal practice second opinions can occur frequently and if handled correctly will not become an ethical problem. If possible, agreement should be reached on a local basis as to how these should be handled, but in all cases the initial veterinarian should be contacted. Some practices prefer this to be well in advance of the second opinion, others at the time or just after. Some second opinions are in reality a request to change practices permanently, and the client's wishes should be listened to and advice given as to whether a permanent change is necessary.

Postmortems

A request for a postmortem can be a sensitive issue for client and veterinarian, as well as inter-practice relations and can raise ethical issues. When asked by a client for an independent postmortem on an animal the normal rules of supersession do not apply. The original veterinary surgeon must be notified that the postmortem is to take place, but the results communicated only to the client. Another, more common, issue involving postmortems is that a veterinarian must seek the owner's permission to carry out a postmortem on an animal which has died, before carrying out the procedure.

Emerging ethical problems

Organ transplantation is in its infancy, but if past experience is a guide once a technique becomes possible and successful the demand grows. In the USA there are several centres undertaking kidney transplants, mainly in cats but also in dogs. At the time of writing it seems that this is not happening yet in the UK. It would seem that provided certain conditions are met transplantation *per se* is not unethical. In the USA success rates of 80 per cent are achieved, with survival times of three to six years on average.

The British Veterinary Association ethical committee has advised that they see no intrinsic ethical objection to organ transplantation surgery provided that:

- it is subject to strict professional control to prevent the exploitation of the animals involved;
- the primary beneficiary of the operation is the recipient animal, as opposed to the owner or the treating veterinarian;
- the recipient is expected to experience an improved quality and duration of life;
- organs are taken with the consent of the owner only from animals which were destined for euthanasia;
- no animal is specifically bred for the purpose of providing organs for transplantation.

In the USA source animals often come from rescue kennels and are only used if the owner of the recipient agrees to adopt the source animal after surgery, usually in compensation for the animal providing a kidney. It would appear that most ethical issues in transplantation concern the source animal. If the recipient will benefit (as animals benefit following any major surgery) there can be few other ethical considerations. It is the source animal which is the problem area and where potential abuse can happen. At this early stage of this newly emerging field it is essential that these ethical issues are addressed. It is not beyond the realms of possibility that kidney transplants, particularly in cats, will be fairly commonplace in referral centres within a decade. Costs of organ transplant will necessarily be high so there is here yet another ethical issue – will not this new developing field be only available to animals whose owners can afford treatment and thus discriminate against those owned by the poor?

8

Issues in large animal practice

Bob Moore

Introduction

One of the earliest references to the relationship between humans and animals is found in the Old Testament in Genesis, chapter 1, verses 26–28: Then God said, 'And now we will make human beings . . . They will have power over the fish, the birds, and all animals, domestic and wild, large and small.' . . . 'I am putting you in charge of the fish, the birds and all the wild animals.' (Good News Bible)

These principles have operated in respect to the keeping of animals for human benefit for the intervening centuries. Implicit in the words quoted above is the requirement for humans to be responsible for the care of the animals over which they are given charge. In more recent times the end of the nineteenth century saw the introduction of animal welfare legislation. Much remained unchanged until review of the legislation and the introduction of codes of practice for animal keeping were introduced following the Second World War. At the turn of the twenty-first century public interest and concern over the whole question of animal welfare and the ethics of keeping animals for human benefit has been given much more emphasis by the general public.

Farm animals may be kept for one or more of several reasons:

Source of produce

The two main products obtained from animals for human benefit, without slaughter, are milk and wool. Milk from cows, sheep and goats has for centuries been a staple part of the human diet. As soon as humans kept animals in domestication they had a regular source of this food for their own use. Wool and other animal fibres provided and still provides a raw material for the production of cloth for human benefit, as an alternative to the actual hide of the animal. Eggs are another produce humans utilize as a food source.

Source of food

The slaughter of an animal to provide food for humans has forever been part of human existence. Not only does the carcass provide food but also many other useful materials for human benefit, the hide and bones being two examples.

Source of power

The introduction of the internal combustion engine has reduced the use of horses (and bovines) as a source of motive power. However, there are still animals used for draft purposes in a few isolated instances.

There are, therefore, valid reasons for humans to keep animals: to improve human living conditions and to benefit in other ways. The keeping of animals does, however, impose responsibilities on the keeper of those animals. In 1966 the Bramble Report introduced the concept of certain freedoms which must be accorded to animals kept in domestication. Professor Webster and others have reiterated the Five Freedoms and these have now been incorporated into Ministry of Agriculture Fisheries and Food Welfare Codes and RSPCA Freedom Food documents. Although the precise wording varies the concepts of the Five Freedoms is constant:

- freedom from hunger and malnutrition;
- freedom from thermal and physical distress;
- freedom from disease and injury;
- freedom from fear;
- freedom to express natural behaviour patterns.

These freedoms can of course have a profound impact on farm animals. We will consider a number of farm animals in detail, discussing some of the problems farmers have to deal with in keeping animals for profit and human benefit.

Cattle

Five main groups of cattle must be considered: calves, young or rearing stock, dairy cows, beef cows, bulls. Each group has its own specific requirements and associated problems.

Calves

A cow only produces milk for a limited time after producing a calf. This means that most dairy farms will aim to produce a calf per year from each of the milking cows. Calves from dairy cows tend to be removed from their dams at an early age and fed replacement milk products so that the main product of the dairy cow, milk, can be collected and sold. It follows that the calf has to be cared for by the stockperson in separate accommodation. In separating a neonate from its dam, the husbandry provided must be appropriate to avoid problems with welfare and ethical considerations.

It is this separation of the neonate from its dam that raises ethical questions. Do we have the right to interfere at this level with the natural process of rearing that takes place between mother and offspring? Certainly when the separation occurs there is some period of obvious agitation in both mother and offspring. Blaring by the cow and attempting to get near to the calf is often observed. However, if separation of calf and cow takes place at a later age the distress appears to be much more marked and to persist much longer.

If we accept that early separation of calf from cow is going to happen, then the stockperson must make certain that proper care is taken for the welfare of the calf. Adequate colostrum must be provided. Disease control by passive immunity is essential to ensure the health and welfare of the growing calf. Socializing with other calves is considered necessary for the calf. If individual pens are used to control disease spread, then the ability to see other calves is necessary. Free access to water is essential too for all stock. Dry bedding, the absence of draughts, adequate ventilation and adequate floor space and air space all contribute to the creation of an environment that will produce healthy and well cared for calves. Appropriate food must be provided for the successive stages of growth. Fibre and concentrate feeds must supplement the milk ration as the calf grows towards weaning.

Calves that are reared extensively, such as is often found with beef herds, will stay with their dam for a much longer period before weaning, and may never be housed as calves. The rearing of such calves follows more closely that of wild ruminants. Different considerations apply in these instances. Shelter from extremes of climate must be provided. This may take the form of planting suitable trees to form a wind and rain break, or perhaps the provision of open roofed or closed shelters of local materials.

'Mutilations'

One ethical consideration affecting both groups of calves is that concerned with what is sometimes referred to as 'mutilations' carried out for the convenience of the farmer. The two common procedures are disbudding and castration.

Animals with horns invariably manage to damage each other at some time. Often it is no more than bruising and a 'bit of fisticuffs' but the damage which can be done can be very severe and, on occasions, life threatening. Legislation exists which controls the mixing of horned and hornless animals in the same confined space, and this reasons has led to most farmers opting to disbud calves. Are we ethically correct in condoning and encouraging this procedure? Anyone who has seen the damage done by a determined horned cow will have no hesitation in recommending the removal of horn buds from young calves.

Castration of male calves is routinely carried out on most British farms. There are periods of fashion for bull beef when small numbers of entire bulls are reared to killing weight. The reasons for castration are to avoid heifers getting pregnant at an unplanned stage and to avoid the difficulties and dangers of having entire growing bulls on farms either housed or grazing open fields. Health and Safety legislation covering the rearing of bull beef is evidence of the dangers. The ethical considerations of castration can be debated at length, but the practicalities of the situation, and the pragmatic view, is that the benefits of castration will take priority over any negative view.

In carrying out either procedure it is incumbent on the stockperson or veterinary surgeon to observe all codes of practice and laws covering questions of anaesthesia. Fortunately in Britain we do not see tail docking as a routine measure on dairy cattle, although in other parts of the world it has been common practice. However, even in those areas where it has long been a tradition, routine docking is now being brought into question.

Young or rearing stock

This group of animals includes those between calfhood and adult status. Depending on local climate and geography this group of animals may be kept extensively throughout this stage of their growth. Others, particularly dairy replacement heifers, will be housed during the winter months. There are few ethical questions to be raised about this group of cattle. Such concerns as exist will centre on the questions raised by welfare issues. The stockperson must be vigilant in ensuring that the animals are kept humanely and in good condition.

Those youngstock kept outside during winter months can be exposed to severe extremes of weather. Feeding areas can become severely muddied and lead to extensive soiling of the limbs and belly of the animals. Although cattle are stoic animals conditions such as these cannot be considered suitable and should be discouraged by advisers to the farmer. Feeding of extensively reared stock must be given careful consideration, as grazing is often insufficient for maintenance. Housed youngstock usually fare better than extensively reared animals, but this will depend on the stockperson responsible for their care. The requirements listed above for calves are also the basis on which to judge the care for this group of animals. The provision of a suitable environment is entirely in the hands of the stockperson.

Dairy cows

The popular perception of the British dairy cow is a black and white animal with a long swishing tail standing knee deep in a field of green grass dotted with yellow buttercups, a long strand of grass hanging from her mouth and a small calf a few paces behind her. How different from reality is this perception. Modern farming has put ever-increasing demands on the productivity of the dairy cow. Breeding developments and nutritional expertise has enabled the yields of dairy cows to increase two or threefold over the last ten to fifteen years. These developments have put additional pressures on the animals and the stockperson to meet new levels of production, and on the stockperson to fulfil the need to meet the Five Freedoms criteria mentioned above.

The ethical questions to be addressed include some raised earlier concerning the removal of calves from the dam. Other considerations have also to be addressed. Is it right to continue to breed and feed for ever increasing milk yields from our dairy cows? Can we justify keeping cows housed in conditions that lead to high incidences of diseases such as mastitis and lameness? In the furore of the BSE epidemic it was revealed that cows' rations included meat and bone meal; should we feed herbivores and ruminants with plant material alone as nature intended? Should we allow cross-breeding with breeds that produce such big calves that Caesarean operation is required to deliver the calf?

Increasing milk yields

Milk yields have certainly increased by considerable amounts over the last two or three decades, but other features have changed as well. The animals are bigger and have bigger appetites (dry matter intake is a function of body weight and yield). Genetic improvement has been accompanied by improvements in the understanding and practice of feeding high yielding dairy cows. Increasing milking frequency from two to three times a day will mitigate many of the concerns about udder distension. Even when these arguments are taken into consideration some people will still be ill at ease with high yields in dairy cows. Perhaps a final judgement should be based on a visit to a well-managed, well-run high yielding dairy unit where examples of such cows can be seen functioning. Implicit in accepting high yields is the requirement for good management and empathy with the cows.

Disease incidence

The incidence of intensive farming related diseases such as mastitis and lameness is a cause for ethical consideration. Cubicle design, flooring materials, building layouts, bedding material, ventilation quality, frequency of cleaning, overall management and many other factors will all influence the incidence and severity of these two conditions. If intensive farming methods lead to higher incidence of disease it is hard to defend those intensive methods on ethical grounds. As mentioned earlier, the drive for genetic improvement in breeding has produced several effects. Dairy cows are now bigger than they were when many of the cubicles were designed and built. As a result the cubicles are too small for the modern cow. Experience has also shown that some of the design features of earlier buildings can be dramatically improved upon. Management methods have improved and milking machines and procedures have advanced. On farms where all the improvements have been made, or where new buildings incorporate the improved ideas, the incidence of disease has been markedly reduced. There is no excuse for those where improvements are still needed, to avoid taking action.

Feed inclusions

The BSE crisis focused considerable attention on to the constituent parts of the food of cattle and the human population. Many inclusions in processed foods that were formerly undeclared are now being considered in detail. Under current legislation it is illegal to include mammalian tissue in cattle rations. This is one ethical issue that has been scrutinized in detail in recent years and changes made through the heavy hand of legislation. It will probably be a very long time, if ever, before ruminants will be recycled to ruminants.

Obstetrical considerations

The most common reason for carrying out a Caesarean operation on a dairy cow is a disparity between foetal size and the birth canal of the dam. The problem became worse with the introduction of big beef bulls as the cross to use on dairy cows, when the calf was not required as a replacement dairy cow. In the Friesian breed some pedigree bulls can produce oversize calves on a regular basis. The policy of using a large, usually continental breed as the sire, knowing that a Caesarean operation will result, cannot be an ethically correct policy.

Extending the discussion concerning oversize calves will include the comparatively recent technique of embryo transfer. What are the ethical questions to be addressed when a cow is artificially induced to produce a superabundance of follicles and eggs intended for collection and implantation? What considerations should be given to the recipient cows, concerning the synchronization and implantation, and then possible obstetrical difficulties later? There will be many differing views and opinions on these difficult questions. Most discussions will devolve into the welfare aspects of the whole issue rather than the purely ethical questions. Many veterinary surgeons will take the pragmatic view that if welfare is properly protected at all stages of the process, that drug usage is properly controlled, then the process is an acceptable one in modern farming.

Beef cows

The majority of beef cows in Britain are kept on extensive systems, which means grazing fields during the summer months and being housed during the winter months. No two farmers will adopt exactly the same system and some herds may well spend almost all the twelve months out of doors.

Many of the ethical questions raised about dairy cows and calves will apply equally well to the beef cow and calf. It can be difficult to separate the welfare aspects from the ethical questions. The majority of the population which accepts that animals can be kept and reared for food will be happy with the ethical questions provided the welfare of the stock is never compromised. With this being the case most attention will be directed at the provision of shelter from extremes of weather, especially when animals are kept out of doors over prolonged periods, and attention to diet, in particular minimizing the weight loss over the winter months or whilst suckling a strong calf.

Some management systems may give rise to more ethical questions than others. One system is based on the principle of maximizing the grass that is grown on the farm. The dams are expected to put on considerable body condition during periods of prolific grass growth. During the winter months when the cows are housed, minimal conserved feed is provided and the cow is required to use the stored body tissues as energy and protein source. During the twelve months period the cow's body condition score will fluctuate between very fat and very thin. Whilst this maximizes grass use (and farm profitability) it might give rise to some question about the ethics of the system. The Five Freedoms of animal welfare should be examined closely in relation to the system described where management is poor.

Bulls

Fashion changes in farming as in all other industries, and the fashion for keeping a stock bull has seen changes over the years. Recent years have seen an increase in the number of stock bulls kept on farms and a concomitant fall in the use of artificial insemination. Because of safety reasons (Health and Safety legislation) bulls are frequently confined to a small pen from which they are rarely, if ever, released. Some breeds are more docile and can be allowed to run with the herd of cows.

Once again the ethical question runs parallel to the welfare issues involved and it can be difficult to separate the arguments. If it is acceptable that a stock bull may be kept on a farm and is going to be kept on a farm the argument will then follow that this can only be accepted if the welfare of the animal is totally catered for. This will include all those areas previously discussed (management, bedding, food, water, etc.) and further include some provision for exercise. The practical considerations for the safety of operatives must take precedence however. If these conditions cannot be met on the farm, it may be argued that the ethical position would require bulls to be kept at properly managed, dedicated bull holding centres, and artificial insemination to be the preferred method. So the argument comes full circle.

Oxen have long since ceased from being used as draught animals in Britain and will not be considered here. In other parts of the world, however, they are still a valuable draught animal.

Sheep

Sheep are far less frequently managed on fully intensive systems. Most are managed on traditional, extensive systems with occasional periods of housing at specific times of the year. As far as the commercial shepherding of sheep is concerned the ethical questions to be addressed are fewer than for cattle. If it is accepted that sheep are to be farmed for human benefit then many of the ethical issues will develop into welfare questions.

The fecundity of ewes and the survival rate of lambs have a major bearing on the profitability of the particular sheep farm. As fertility-controlling drugs have become available they have been used to modify the breeding policy on some farms. Increased numbers of lambs born, the synchronization of breeding and the modification of the time of year that breeding takes place are all now possible. The question might be asked if this is an acceptable development ethically. Whilst it may be perfectly acceptable for an individual animal to receive treatment to correct a defect in its fertility, is it acceptable to use the same treatment to modify the breeding policy of whole flocks of thousands of sheep? Again, as has been discussed earlier, this discussion can easily run into welfare questions. There is not a definitive answer to these types of question and the individuals will have to look to their own consciences to arrive at an answer.

Looking beyond the commercial flock it is necessary to consider the fact that the small ruminants, and sheep in particular, are very suitable as experimental subjects or for trials. Their small size reduces costs over using the larger species. Recent developments in the manipulation of genetic material have led to the production of Dolly, the cloned sheep. This is a far larger subject than simply the question of the ethics of sheep farming. Should we use sheep (or other species) in this way? It is not proposed to give any answers in this chapter, but merely to draw attention to the questions we as veterinary surgeons should be prepared to consider.

Goats

Much of what has been said of sheep can be said of goat keeping. However, whereas sheep are almost exclusively kept in flocks, it is quite common to encounter a goat kept as an individual, partly as a pet, partly as a lawn mower sometimes. Recently introduced legislation concerning calf rearing requires opportunity for the calf to see or have social contact with other calves. Although considering a different species, it may be a question that should be addressed to owners of single tethered goats.

Horses

The use of horses for motive power (excluding pleasure activities) is a rarity nowadays. However, some owners keep draught horses either as a normal part of the farm economy or, more frequently, as a hobby or for exhibition purposes. The breeds used are those that have for centuries been bred specifically for this one purpose. The ethical considerations are not too complicated and once again any discussion will involve consideration of welfare aspects of keeping these types of horse. Provided the work undertaken by the horse is appropriate to the breed and age of the horse, and any working in harness together are suitable matched, there will be general agreement that this is acceptable.

Pigs

Many of the arguments discussed under cattle and sheep will apply to the keeping of pigs. Once again it is important to exercise caution and avoid confusion between the concept of the ethics of keeping pigs and the welfare of the stock being kept. There are one or two religious groups for whom all swine are considered unclean in a religious sense (see Chapter 2).

Breeding stock

Without breeding stock there would be no other stock to farm so, if pigs are to be farmed at all, breeding stock are essential. Having accepted that pigs are to be kept for human benefit, the remaining arguments relating to breeding stock devolve into welfare discussions. Sow tethering is now banned in the UK and this has addressed the major welfare issue felt by most people. However, sows kept extensively may face stresses of a different nature. Extremes of climate must be mitigated, from sunburn to arctic conditions. The keeping of sows in deep litter yards present similar problems to those encountered in cattle similarly housed. Boars present their own set of problems which mirror those for bulls but mostly to a lesser degree.

Fattening pigs

The ethical considerations of keeping and rearing animals for eventual slaughter for food remain the same, whatever the species being considered. Once having accepted the concept then the questions become those of welfare again. The use of so called 'sweat boxes' to increase growth rates should be carefully considered. The use of various in-feed medications to promote growth rates may have their effect by controlling sub-clinical disease. Some individuals might consider the continued use of production methods that require such medication unethical. Can the economic argument of controlling sub-clinical disease to enhance cheaper food production be justified?

Fighting between members of closely confined groups of pigs is not uncommon. Various 'toys', such as chains or tyres suspended above the pens to provide diversion for the pigs, have been tried with varying success. Removal of tails from baby pigs to prevent tail biting is practised in some pig herds. The question then becomes, are we right to keep pigs in such conditions if these are the consequences?

A further consideration in relation to pigs is that they happen to be the right size for some of their tissues to be used as transplant material for humans. This type of research (xenotransplantation) is in its infancy at the time of writing but will develop in due course. This raises a number of ethical questions for which there will be no definitive answer. Personal attitudes and religious conviction will influence the individual's opinion in this matter. The basic questions are, 'Is the life of a human of more importance that the life of one pig?' or 'Can anyone justify the slaughter of an animal to preserve the life of a human?' The answer to these questions can be debated at length.

Poultry

Developments in poultry breeding, feeding, management and production over the last two or three decades have provided a source of high quality protein at reasonable cost to a vast proportion of the world's population. In similar fashion, egg production has been transformed from the immediate post-war years. In very recent times the methods of production for both broilers and laying hens has been the subject of close inspection by a variety of groups. The welfare of poultry has been the basis of their investigation and changes to legislation have followed reports of various groups. Once again we find that it is questions of welfare rather than ethical considerations that are at the root of people's concerns. The ethics of keeping and farming poultry is acceptable; the welfare of the birds is their major concern.

The situation with turkeys bred specifically for the Christmas trade presents a slightly different situation. It is reported that in the drive to breed heavy birds some turkey cocks are now unable to mate normally, and artificial insemination is the only method to breed them successfully. Artificial insemination is used extensively in other species, such as cattle and pigs, but for entirely different reasons. Extremes of management systems, of which this example may be one, must be considered as marginal in terms of ethical animal farming.

Summary

The ethics of keeping farm animals seen in large animal practice covers several areas. It can sometimes be difficult to separate issues of ethics and welfare. What might be quite acceptable ethically given one set of circumstances could become totally unacceptable if the welfare of the animal or group of animals is compromised in any way. Each individual considering the ethics of keeping farm animals will have a personal view that will be influenced by his own background, education or personal beliefs. This chapter has drawn attention to some of the issues that need to be addressed by all when considering the ethical questions.

9

Meat food safety and public health

Mac Johnston

Animals and consumers

Food is an essential of life and purchases of it are a significant part of the household budget. Food of animal origin not only helps to sustain life but can also be hazardous to health. It is therefore necessary to protect the purchaser from any hazard or from deceit. In recent years the food industry has increasingly become a target for consumers campaigning for changes in animal welfare and husbandry systems, as well as consumer expressions of concern for the environment. In a survey of 30,000 consumers, in the mid-1990s, by one of the large retailers in the UK, more than half surveyed (57 per cent) said they were now more worried about 'ethical history' of the products on sale than five years previously. Three out of four consumers said they wanted more information about the products sold to enable a judgement on whether to purchase a product or not to be made on ethical grounds. These concerns about the food animal production systems and the methods by which animals and birds are slaughtered to produce meat are very relevant to the whole subject of veterinary public health. Unfortunately there has also been considerable pressure on the industry to produce cheap food of animal origin and in purchasing food the consumer will frequently select only on cost. The production of poultry meat, which is one of the cheapest forms of meat, has increased year on year and now occupies the largest share of the UK meat market. The broiler industry is the meat production system which consistently is subject to criticism in the media. On the other hand there is currently much concern about genetically modified foods and with the very high percentage of products which contain soya as an ingredient, including meat look-alike products; will there be a shift to increased meat eating?

Is it right to rear animals and birds with the sole intention that they will be killed to produce food for humans? Certainly, given time they will all die. Death may be due to disease, old age or, in the wild, a predator may kill them. Such dead or dying animals, however, are not fit for human consumption. Animals and birds intended for human consumption are bred and reared to be healthy at the time of slaughter. The animals and birds are also to produce meat that will satisfy the wishes of the consumer. There is the wish that it should have a good texture and taste, is lean and with an appearance which is attractive to the consumer. As a result the animals and birds have had their genetic make-up changed to meet the requirements of the markets and inevitably there have been some other effects. These can range from the very rapidly growing birds producing so much breast muscle that their immature legs can not sustain the weight, through to the fast growing pigs producing lean carcasses which have the inherited trait leading to the pigs being classed as 'stress susceptible'. As a result of these changes the modern food-producing animals and birds would be unlikely to be able to survive as their predecessors did in the wild.

There is also pressure on the industry to use production methods that will deliver the slaughter animal at predetermined weight and conformation in the shortest time and at lowest possible cost. The farmer, therefore, has resorted to using growth promotion techniques which have included the use of antibiotics as growth promoters and steroid hormones during the growing phase. The use of steroid hormones to enhance growth rates and improve the lean to fat ratio has been justified in that it is making use of natural substances and that it is of no danger to public health. The moratorium on their use within the EU followed concerns about the effect of eating meat produced in this manner, with suggestions that the daily intake of hormones could affect human health. The scientific evidence necessary to make a balanced scientific judgement is lacking but it is known that one, 17 beta oestradiol, is a complete carcinogen and as such is able to initiate and promote cancer. The counter argument is that with correct use and appropriate withdrawal periods there is no danger to human health. One of the problems of following this argument of it 'being safe until proven otherwise' is that it is an argument which is no longer acceptable, especially following such widely publicized food scares such as bovine spongiform encephalopathy (BSE).

The use of antibiotics without veterinary prescription for the purposes

of promoting growth in food animal production started in the early
1950s. Resistance to antibiotics by bacteria was initially assumed to be
by mutation but in 1959 it was shown that resistance could be trans-
ferred from one bacterium to another. Following an outbreak of food
poisoning due to multi-drug resistant salmonella, an expert committee
chaired by Professor Swann reviewed the use of antibiotics in agriculture.
Its report in 1969 resulted in significant changes in the use of antibiotics,
including for growth promotion purposes. More recently there has again
been considerable concern about the use of antibiotics, especially for
growth promotion purposes, in animals, and specifically about food
being a vector of antibiotic resistance from animals to humans. This has
led to a number of groups of experts, nationally and internationally,
considering the use of antibiotics in animals, in humans and for plant
protection purposes. The veterinary and medical professions have agreed
that they have to ensure prudent use of antibiotics at all times. The
reduction of the use of antibiotics involves all stakeholders and includes
educating people, whether as patients, owners or keepers of the animals,
in responsible and appropriate use, as well as educating the professions in
prudent use. That animals need antibiotics is certain but the decision to
use antibiotics should only follow the decision that they are necessary and
will work. There is little justification for the uncontrolled use of
antibiotics at subtherapeutic levels. There is evidence of medical equiva-
lence for the antibiotic, either where the same drug is used in humans
and in animals or if there is known antibiotic resistance problems. Of
major concern is where there is a possible impact on the effectiveness of
important antibiotics used in human medicine, especially when the
antibiotic is one of last choice for life-threatening infections. It is easy to
say that there should be no use of these products just to sustain cheap
food production systems by making animals grow faster. However, some
of the very same antibiotic growth promoters have an effect on controlling disease in animals, and stopping their use would require a greater
use of therapeutic antibiotics. There is a balance which can be achieved
between the two schools of thought, which requires the husbandry
systems to be changed to reduce the need for use of antibiotics in any
form. The issue of consumption of residues in food of animal origin is of
less concern with mandatory testing for residues and a requirement only
to use drugs which are licensed in food producing species within EU
member states.

Methods of slaughter

It is necessary to go back into history to find the earliest reports of production of meat for human consumption. In Greek and Roman times it appears that officials supervised the slaughter process, then removed unfit meat for disposal. One of the earliest indications of slaughter and probably meat inspection is found in the Old Testament in *Deuteronomy*. Many of the controls on the slaughter process were based on religious prohibitions and rituals. A major role of the religious leaders of the time would have been to ensure only healthy animals were used for food production.

Accepting that animals are to be slaughtered then how should this be carried out? The methods used have varied between countries and faiths, and over the years the techniques have evolved with advances in technology. There are significant religious requirements, specifically involving the Jewish and Muslim faiths, which have not changed. In controlled conditions in a slaughter plant the aim should be to slaughter as humanely as possible, irrespective of the method used. In developed countries there is a legal requirement to render the animals instantly insensible to pain. This is usually achieved by using mechanical or electrical equipment or by narcosis using gases such as carbon dioxide. There must then be immediate exsanguination, by severance of major blood vessels of the neck to ensure death supervenes before any possible recovery from the stun, whichever method has been used. Slaughter may also be by use of a free bullet, a method that is particularly useful in the field. The mechanical equipment can effect the stun either by penetration of the cranium by a metal bolt or by a concussive blow to the frontal bone without penetration. There is a legal derogation to permit slaughter without a pre-stun for religious reasons.

Are the old methods of slaughter any less humane than the current methods? The legal requirement for the animal or bird to be effectively stunned also requires the animals and birds to be spared any avoidable excitement, pain or suffering during movement, lairaging, restraint, stunning slaughter or killing. It is easy to define an effective stun but often difficult to decide how the animal or bird can be judged as being free from any awareness of pain during the whole process. Identification of the symptoms and signs of stress associated with slaughter has been the subject of study for many years. This has been most relevant in the pig and poultry industries and therefore most of the recent research has been with these species. There is debate over which form of transport and handling methods are the most satisfactory. However, it is not just the actual systems, although the design and construction of the buildings and handling facilities are major factors, that influence the stress. Research has shown, for example, that handling methods on the farm can produce both easy to handle and difficult to handle pigs at time of slaughter. Animals for slaughter are also herd/flock animals and to a varying degree, according to species, can be difficult to separate out as individuals. In the case of more recently farmed species, such as deer and ostrich, there are very specialized requirements for facilities and handling requirements.

One issue must be whether it is acceptable to slaughter an animal in sight of its conspecifics. This would have probably happened in earlier times when an animal was selected and slaughtered there and then in front of others in the group. Certainly there appears to be little problem with killing deer in a field using a rifle even when they are feeding, as the remaining members of the herd only look up and then continue as before. The difficulty is transferring this finding to the abattoir where the animals have already been stressed by being taken from their familiar surroundings, transported and possibly are now in mixed groups before slaughter. From the experience of a working abattoir there does appear to be a difference in reaction to the stunning of a sheep or pig by the other members of the group, from what is expected if a horse were to be slaughtered in sight of other horses. What gives most concern is not the actual stun but the animals then having sight of others being bled out, especially if this is by hanging from a rail. In the modern high throughput abattoir the stunning of individual pigs and sheep from within groups has been replaced by the presentation of the animals one by one using a conveyor system. This system also presents the animal in a manner that makes it easier for there to be an effective stun, as the slaughterer does not have to chase the pig or sheep round the pen. The requirement for pre-stunning does not apply to religious slaughter, but the act of slaughter has still has to be carried out without the infliction of suffering. There has been considerable debate for many years on the rights and wrongs of allowing slaughter without pre-stunning. The defence from the Jewish and Muslim faiths is that their method of slaughter is no less humane and is carried out according to the law of the religion. The *kosher* slaughter is derived from Hebrew traditions, referred to as *shechita* and the animals are killed and bled by one clean stroke of the knife (*chalaf*) struck into the throat by a trained slaughterer (*shotet*). For Islamic slaughter (*halal*) the animal is killed by a severance of the neck vessels by a single slash of a sharp knife. Only Islamic adherents may slaughter for their faith but these slaughterers are also acceptable for many other faiths. Until recently it was possible to carry out religious slaughter outside a licensed abattoir, but that has been stopped in the UK.

There is often debate on whether the animals or birds should slaughtered on the farm rather than be transported for slaughter. If they are to be transported then how far can, and should, animals be transported for slaughter? The debate is easier to resolve for species such as red deer, which are very 'flighty' animals anyway, and traditionally shot in the field. Game birds and other wild game are also shot in the field. For traditional food animals or birds the most obvious answer is that they should be slaughtered as close to the farm of origin as possible. The basis for some of the claims of quality meat producers for traditional meat is that the animals are slaughtered on the farm of origin and suffer no travel stress, thus benefiting the animals and the meat quality. If this is not possible, some farmers visit the abattoir to assess the lairage and handling through to slaughter before deciding on which abattoir to send the animals. There is also the development of a mobile slaughterhouse intended to travel to the farm of origin so that the same standards of hygiene and inspection are applied, but the animals do not have to be transported but only handled within the farm environs. Handling will always raise the level of activity of animals, the extreme being flight from danger. It is always difficult to define stress or distress: it can be from the actual handling or from their ability to cope with the environment. Recognized stressors are people, noise and new surroundings, all of which abound in the abattoir environment. Obviously there will always be some level of noise but the aim is to keep it down to the minimum. However, the level of noise can be a valuable guide to how well the animals are being treated. A high level of shouting by the staff and vocalization by the animals, banging of gates and hitting the metal work with sticks all indicate a poorly managed situation. The converse suggests a well-run operation with the animals and the staff calm and the handling process moving on in a quiet, efficient manner.

Other relevant concerns

Unloading is a time of increased stress for animals, not least at the lairage. Abattoirs are by nature noisy, often with smells foreign to the incoming animals. By having well designed, covered unloading points with correct lighting, non-slip flooring and appropriate use of bedding material, the stress can be significantly reduced. A major factor is the standard of stockmanship by the lairage staff who should all have undergone animal welfare training. In the lairage, the design of passages and pens make a major contribution to the movement of animals. It is particularly important to keep the animals in their social groups with no mixing of stock from different sources. Animals most subject to stress such as calves, cows in milk or entire males of any species should be slaughtered as soon as possible, as should casualty animals. The movement through to the slaughter point should be carried out as smoothly as possible with few hold ups. The use of goads should not be necessary, or only used in very controlled circumstances. For poultry the slaughter process currently requires each bird to be suspended by the legs while still conscious. This undoubtedly is a major stress for the bird both during the act of hanging and in the period while the bird is suspended as the rail moves to the stunner. Currently under development is a technique where the birds are placed in a gas mixture, which stuns them by narcosis while they are still in the transport boxes. This removes the need to physically remove the birds from the transport boxes and hang them on shackles while they are still conscious, a tremendous improvement in welfare terms.

Is there a role for the use of non-traditional species for meat production? World supplies of animal-derived protein are limited and in some parts of the world are under considerable pressure. It is possible to harvest more from the wild, provided care is taken while drawing on wildlife reserves. Many proposals for game farming and fish farming in particular have changed the availability of different types of meat.

Often the concerns about the whole food chain are associated with food scares and presented as a perceived worry about food related issues that have little, if anything, to do with reason for the food scare. On the other hand, if the controls placed on the industry are so stringent there will be an increase in cost of production the effect of which will be increased imports of produce from countries where the standards of husbandry and slaughter are lower than in the UK. How often is the source of this food taken for granted and even influenced by cost?

10

Interventions for the conservation or welfare of wild animals

James K. Kirkwood

Introduction

There are about six billion humans on earth at the time of writing and the population is growing rapidly. Having learned to use fossil fuels and other sources of power we are free from the constraints of energy utilization rates that have hitherto limited the activities of individuals of all other organisms. Not only are there very many of us but we use energy and other resources and produce wastes at biologically unprecedented rates for animals of our size. Whether we know it or not, or like it or not, we are unavoidably in competition with wild animals for food, space and other resources. It has become clear that human changes to the environment threaten extinction of wild fauna at a serious and growing rate and also compromise the welfare of large numbers of individuals of many species. Concerns about the loss of species have led to the development of many responses for conservation such as translocation and reintroduction schemes. There is also growing interest in interventions for the welfare of free-living wild animals, especially those harmed as a result of human activity. Veterinarians are increasingly involved in these efforts: in diagnosing the causes of diseases which threaten the viability of wild populations and the welfare of the individuals, and through responsibility for disease control and welfare aspects of interventions undertaken for conservation or welfare. These are new fields of endeavour and some difficult ethical issues are emerging which deserve careful thought. For example, where a procedure for species conservation has a welfare cost, how should welfare costs be weighed against conservation benefits?

Should conservation interests always, sometimes, or never trump welfare interests? Or vice versa? We are not in a position to be able to avoid these issues. If we do nothing, very many species will be lost but the options for conservation often come with some potential or real costs to animal welfare.

It is not just veterinarians specializing in wildlife work who may be faced with ethical dilemmas concerning responsibilities for wildlife. Other branches of veterinary medicine can have an impact on wild animals. What is good for domestic animals is not always good for wildlife. For example, promoting good health and freedom to roam in domestic cats is good for cat welfare but not for that of their potential prey, and injudicious use of rodenticides for pest control in, say, a dog rescue shelter could do more harm to rodents than good to dogs. Similarly, measures that are good for the health and welfare of production animals, such as draining ponds to reduce the risk of fascioliasis, may be bad for the welfare (and population viability) of the wild residents. During the latter half of the twentieth century it has become apparent that the biosphere is a complex web of interactions. An action here often has a knock-on effect there, and it is a mistake for people to feel confident that their sphere of activity is isolated from potential environmental consequences. Were it written today, those who drafted the declaration that veterinarians make on admission to membership of the Royal College of Veterinary Surgeons (which is a condition of practising in the UK): 'my constant endeavour will be to ensure the welfare of animals committed to my care', might have considered adding as a footnote, 'and, in so doing to take reasonable precautions to guard against unnecessarily harming the welfare of those that are not'.

Human impact on wildlife

Until quite recently it appeared that there was enough space, food and other resources on earth for humans and domestic animals to be able to exist without causing any serious likelihood of irreversible changes to the ecosystem. However, there are now so many of us and our requirements for resources are so voracious that it is now clear that this is not so. It is forecast that the human population will double to some ten to twelve billion within a few decades and having learned to use fossil and other fuel sources, the daily energy utilization of each citizen of the developed countries is roughly equal to that of a pack of forty wolves (Kirkwood, 1994). Threats to the ecosystem are likely to intensify.

We live in a more or less closed system. Not much except radiation energy enters or leaves our world. Most of life is dependent on solar energy – which is trapped by plants through the process of photosynthesis producing organic matter which is food, directly or indirectly, for us and all other animals. There is a finite amount of space and a finite amount of food available on earth. The net annual terrestrial production of the planet is estimated to be about 150 Petagrammes (Pg) (150 million million tonnes) of organic/plant matter (IUCN/UNEP/WWF, 1991). We may be able to increase this to some degree by cultivating deserts and increasing production efficiency in various ways but, generally, the more of us there are, the more domestic animals we maintain and the more habitat we appropriate, the fewer wild animals there can be (at least of the present range of body sizes). World stocks of domestic animals are very large: about 1.3 billion cattle, 0.8 billion pigs, 1.6 billion sheep and goats, and probably tens of billions of domestic poultry. We humans and our domestic animals and the crops we cultivate for ourselves and for our animals occupy large proportions of the available land in many areas. It has been estimated that 58 Petagrammes of primary production, that is 39 per cent of the annual total, is either destroyed, or used, or its use by natural ecosystems is prevented through human agency (Vitousek *et al.*, 1986; IUCN/UNEP/WWF, 1991). We control a great deal of the available food energy and greatly influence which animals get access to it. Human activities, especially those directly or indirectly related to producing or obtaining food, inevitably, therefore, often have an impact on very large numbers of wild animals. We present threats both to the viability of species (or sub-populations) and also to the welfare of individuals.

Threats to population viability (conservation)

Anthropogenic threats to the viability of populations arise through changes in land use, pollution, killing and disturbance, and introduction of non-indigenous species. A number of species have been hunted to extinction in recent history but in the future the most important threats to biodiversity are likely to be indirect effects of changes to the environment, including pollution, changes of habitat for land use and the consequences of introducing non-indigenous species (and combinations of these factors). Estimates of the scale of the anthropogenic threat to biodiversity vary but it is undoubtedly very great (Wilson, 1993).

Threats to wildlife welfare

Human activities and anthropogenic changes to the environment also affect the welfare of very large numbers of individuals of wild animals of many species. It is important to note that whilst factors which threaten species viability often also have an adverse impact on individual welfare, for example, introduced infections may not just cause loss of a population but also considerable suffering in the process; the two things do not always go together. For example, extinction through genetic pollution, as threatens the white-headed duck (*Oxyura leucocephala*) through cross-breeding with the introduced ruddy duck (*Oxyura jamaicensis*), is unlikely to be associated with fear, pain or stress. Conversely, it is very often the case that factors which have a very serious welfare impact present no threat to species viability. A good example is myxomatosis in rabbits. Since this infection was introduced by humans to the European rabbit population in about 1950, it has caused disease, almost certainly associated with severe pain and distress over days or weeks, in millions of rabbits (in excess of 20 million) each year (Sainsbury *et al.*, 1995). There is no danger, however, that this infection will make the rabbit go extinct.

It is difficult to assess the impact of human activities on the welfare of wild animals because data on the problems, their effects on animals, and the numbers affected are scarce and hard to obtain. However, an attempt was made a few years ago to try to identify important current problems in Europe (Kirkwood *et al.*, 1994; Sainsbury *et al.*, 1995). There are many ways that wild animals are harmed, either intentionally or unintentionally. Examples include various methods of pest control, notably the use of anticoagulant rodenticides, the poisoning of wildfowl as a result of their ingestion of spent lead shot, the oiling of seabirds in oil spills, shooting injuries, injuries due to collisions with road traffic and injuries caused by domestic cats. There is good evidence that all of these severely compromise the welfare of large numbers of animals, but there is a long list of other problems that have been recognized as causing harm to wildlife but whose effects are still more difficult to quantify. Sometimes welfare efforts on behalf of wildlife can backfire as when feeding garden birds at high densities appears to increase the risk of disease and mortality incidents due to *Salmonella typhimurium* or *E coli* infections (Kirkwood, 1998; Pennycott *et al.*, 1998).

Veterinarians are increasingly involved in interventions in response to threats to species conservation and wildlife welfare and some of the ethical issues are considered below.

Ethical stances concerning wild animals

It is useful first to briefly outline some ethical stances regarding interactions and interventions with wild animals.

1. *Biocentric environmentalism or holism.* This relates to respect for the environment, for nature as a whole, for ecosystems and the natural processes of evolution. This concern is the basis of endeavours for the conservation of species and of biological diversity for their own sakes. An early proponent of this stance was Aldo Leopold whose 'land ethic' approach (1949) advocated that the right action is that which promotes the integrity, stability and beauty of the biotic community. Advocates of this position attach greater importance to the wholeness of ecosystems than to the interests of individual animals in them and are inclined to give priority to conservation measures when these conflict with animal welfare. Opponents of this stance argue that systems should not be the prime focus of moral concern because systems have no interests and are thus not morally considerable (see for example, Varner, 1998), and that saving a species cannot be a justification for harming sentient animals because, as DeGrazia (1996) wrote 'there is no being corresponding to the words "nature", "biosphere", or "the environment" who would benefit'. However, many people believe that it is right to try to preserve species – to prevent unnecessary extinctions. Is this just some quirky human bias or is there some ultimate rightness in striving to preserve species? 'That decision rests', as Wilson (1993) put it, 'on the most fundamental question of all: whether moral values exist apart from humanity, in the same manner as mathematical laws, or whether they are idiosyncratic constructs that evolved in human mind through natural selection' (see also Norton, 1987).

2. *Anthropocentric environmentalism.* This relates to the importance of preserving biodiversity for actual or potential human benefit, for example, as a source of biological products for use now or by future generations, for nutritional, therapeutic, aesthetic, financial or other reasons. Here the focus of moral concern is human interests. Biocentric environmentalists may see this as a selfish point of view but Varner (1998) has argued that, nevertheless, anthropocentric arguments can provide a stronger ethical underpinning for habitat and species conservation.

3. *Individualism – animal welfare and animal rights.* Concerns for animal welfare and animal rights rest on the belief that some animals have the capacity to experience pleasant and unpleasant feelings and that this should be properly taken into account in our interactions with them. Opinions differ as to what suffices for this. The utilitarian stance allows that harm may be caused to sentient beings providing it is minimized and that it leads to some greater good. This greater good is usually

judged in the currency of pleasure or less suffering but some accept that it can also encompass other 'goods', for example, conservation of species. In contrast, proponents of the philosophy of animal rights take Regan's (1992) position that: 'The rights of the individual are not to be violated in the name of some collective good, whether that good be the good of the ecosystem or the good of sentient life (both human and non-human), and independently of whether these rights are violated "humanely" or otherwise.' This stance, which tends to argue against interventions for conservation, can seriously conflict with the aims of environmentalism as has been discussed by Callicott (1989).

4. *Human moral hygiene.* This is another anthropocentric stance. It is based on the premiss that humans should avoid harming animals, not because of the harm caused to animals *per se* but because it engenders callousness and is thus bad for character development. This has been seen by some, notably Immanuel Kant (1724-1804), as the main reason why cruel behaviour to vertebrate animals is wrong. Kant wrote 'for he who is cruel to animals becomes hard also in his dealings with men'.

Just leave them alone?

All of these stances pull in the same direction, albeit for different reasons, in arguing that we should, as far as possible, avoid harming natural ecosystems and the wild animals in them. With regard to wild animals, 'the general policy recommended by the rights view is: let them be!' (Regan, 1983) and this is a very appealing notion. However, for the reasons outlined above, this is not just very difficult to achieve; not just something that will take some time to perfect, it is impossible. Six billion people cannot simply let all wild animals be, however much they might wish they could. Humans and the wild fauna occupy the same finite space, compete for many of the same finite resources, and have ecologies that are inextricably enmeshed. Although the efficiency of human food production is increasing, to a considerable extent it is true that if we humans or our companion or farm animals stand here and eat *that*, wild animals must stand elsewhere and find some other food – if they can. It is right that great care should be taken to avoid causing harm to wildlife for all the reasons listed above, but is this enough? Because we fail to avoid causing harm and are extremely unlikely to avoid this in the foreseeable future, if ever, there are times when we must either intervene to try to deal with the problems we cause, or risk exacerbating harms to welfare and conservation through neglect.

There is no conflict with the rights argument over interventions such as habitat protection or control of poaching. The problems arise where, in more active interventions to alleviate the problems we have caused, there is often a conflict between what is good for individuals and what is good for ecosystems. The welfare versus conservation dilemma can present itself to veterinarians in many forms: in the use of animals for conservation research, (for example, into diseases or management of endangered species); in deciding whether or not it is justifiable to subject captive-bred animals to the risks inherent in release into the wild; in deciding whether the welfare costs of a translocation are justifiable; and in deciding whether exposure to possible welfare risks associated with assisted-breeding techniques is justifiable for individuals of endangered species that will otherwise not breed in captivity.

Environmentalism and animal welfare?

In their pure forms, environmentalism and individualism lead to opposing views as to whether priority should be given to conservation or animal welfare interests where the two are in conflict. However, there is a consensus that it is right both to try to preserve species and to protect animal welfare. As Petrinovich (1999) puts it,

> As with many differences in the moral sphere, it may not be possible to reach agreement, given the initial premises. It might be possible, however, for welfarists and environmentalists to make some coordinated efforts to deal with the preservation of endangered species at least as far as rescuing the remaining individual animals and restoring crucial habitats are involved.

Norton (1995) advocates moral pluralism – the acceptance of both environmentalism and concern for individuals – recommending that there should be a shift in emphasis from one to the other depending on situation or context. The obligation to sustain biological diversity requires, according to Norton, 'that we shift our sights from individuals and the various elements of biodiversity towards concern for the processes of nature', but that having decided that a certain intervention is necessary towards this end, that we should then examine 'what means are justified' at the individual animal level.

Ethics of interventions for wildlife conservation

The threats to species and the need for conservation measures are widely recognized around the world and during the past two or three decades there has been a dramatic growth in the technology of species conservation. Whilst habitat protection or recovery is the most important component of protecting biodiversity, there are situations where more active interventions may form important components of conservation programmes. Such active interventions include:

- disease control measures in free-living populations;
- translocations of wild caught animals to restock depopulated areas;
- captive breeding, including the use of artificial reproductive technologies;
- reintroductions of captive bred animals;
- treatment and rehabilitation of endangered species casualties.

Although all of these technologies are new, already some are well on the way to becoming well established conservation tools. All of them raise ethical issues and the veterinarians involved have a responsibility to consider these and especially to contribute to the weighing of the welfare costs of such interventions against the conservation benefits and to minimizing any costs to welfare. These benefits and costs can vary greatly. Conservation measures may range from those directed to making a minor contribution towards reducing threats to a sub-population of an otherwise secure sub-species, to those crucial for saving the remaining extant species of an entire order whose loss would, in terms of genetic diversity, be far more significant. Likewise some interventions may have very minor welfare impact whilst in others it might be impossible to avoid major welfare risks.

Disease control measures for conservation of free-living populations

The viability of small populations is at particular risk from infectious diseases for the simple reason that 90 per cent mortality in a population of ten is final, whereas in a population of one thousand it is not. There have been a number of occasions in recent years when the decision has been taken to intervene to control infectious disease risks to small residual populations of endangered species. For example, free-living mountain gorillas *Gorilla gorilla berengei* have been vaccinated against measles (Sholley, 1989), and free-living Florida panthers *Felis concolor coryi* (Rupprecht et al., 1993) and free-living wild dogs *Lycaeon pictus* (Gascoyne et al., 1990) have been vaccinated against rabies. The issues influencing the efficacy of wildlife vaccination programmes have been discussed (for example, Hall and Harwood, 1990) but ethical aspects have received little attention. If the infections are a natural part of the ecology of the animals, should nature be left to take its course? In cases in which anthropogenic changes have resulted, through reducing population size, in increased risk of extinction from infectious disease, intervention to control this risk through vaccination, which may be associated with some pain and stress if animals have to be captured for the purpose, seems a relatively minor infringement of individual animal welfare for conservation benefit. However, such measures should not be undertaken lightly. The conservation reason for the intervention must be clear, and the details of the programme – for example, what proportion of the population need be vaccinated, with what, and how, must be well worked out in advance.

Most wildlife treatment and rehabilitation is undertaken for welfare rather than conservation reasons and these procedures are not, for example, included in any part of the conservation programmes listed by the Biodiversity Steering Group for any UK endangered species. However, individual care of sick or injured animals could have important benefits for the conservation of very small, highly endangered, populations. An example of this is the treatment of free-living Mountain gorillas for sarcoptic mange (Kalema *et al.*, 1998). Ethical aspects of wildlife treatment and rehabilitation for welfare reasons are discussed later.

Translocations to restock former range

The main ethical difficulty with translocations of free-living animals to restock areas from which populations have been lost is that, whilst this may be good for the long-term viability of the species and for the functioning of the ecosystem through the replacement of a missing component, it may not be good for the welfare of the animals used in the programme. These animals will be subject to some or all of the following procedures: capture, transport, health checks, quarantine, release and re-establishment in a new location, and all of these procedures may have welfare costs. The interests of the individuals involved would mostly be better served by leaving them in their native habitats. Should restoring a population to its former range always override welfare considerations? The Dutch Society for the Protection of Animals is one organization that does not think so. Their position regarding the question of whether it is right to re-introduce animals is summed up as 'no, unless'. That is, that reintroduction should not take place unless it has important benefits ('added value') for the animal or the ecosystem (Diederik van Liere, personal communication). One can envisage cases where the argument for translocation is strong: as when creating new sub-populations greatly enhances the chances of species' survival in the long run and when welfare costs to the individuals involved are low. However, in other cases the argument may be weaker, for example if the species is already secure and there is no compelling biological need for restoring another sub-population (perhaps because the animals are likely to spread back to that part of their range of their own accord given time), and when the welfare costs of translocations would be high.

Captive breeding for conservation

Some authors, (for example, Regan, 1995; DeGrazia, 1996) take the view that because of potential harms to welfare, sentient wild animals should not be taken into captivity for entertainment, education, research or species preservation. Others, (for example, Koontz, 1995; Petrinovich, 1999) see no absolute objection to captivity for conservation reasons providing high standards of welfare are maintained. Koontz (1995) listed six considerations 'that should be discussed, and weighed collectively, when zoo biologists propose to collect endangered animals for zoo-based breeding programmes'. These were: conservation impact; likelihood of establishing a successful captive population; long-term commitment and responsibility; communication and documentation; animal welfare; and risk management.

Although knowledge and experience in the husbandry of wild animals in captivity have developed enormously, (for example, see Kleiman *et al.*, 1996), it remains the case that there are few species for which we can confidently claim a full knowledge of their requirements. Animals of some species taken into captivity may be at some risk from sub-optimal management for this reason. Furthermore, at least for some species, it can be very difficult to provide in captivity all the important features of the animals' natural environment. For example, captive gorillas cannot voluntarily leave their native family groups to join others – the decisions about when to move them for breeding, and where to, have to be made for them and our preferences about these things may not coincide with theirs. For some species breeding in captivity in a confined but otherwise largely natural environment, or a suitable artificial alternative to it, may differ very little from breeding in the wild, whereas for other species there may be greater risks to welfare.

In many cases it is possible (although not easy) to provide high standards of welfare for wild animals in captivity and welfare risks should not be over-estimated. It is worth noting that large numbers of wild animals are taken into captivity for reasons much more trivial than species conservation, notably for sale in the pet trade. Captive breeding has already played an essential role in the conservation of some species (Olney *et al.*, 1994) and it is likely to become more important in the future.

Reintroductions of captive-bred animals

Reintroductions of captive-bred animals are a special type of translocation and the problems do not differ in principle. They may, like translocations, be associated with some risks to the recipient populations especially through accidental introduction of infectious disease (Cunningham, 1996; Woodford and Rossiter, 1993). Reintroductions may also impose welfare costs on the animals involved since there may be various threats to welfare associated with adapting to the wild; for example, in finding suitable food, water, and shelter, and through exposure to climatic, infectious stressors, potential toxins and predators and competitors, for example, Beck *et al.* (1994). The veterinarian's responsibility in planning reintroductions is to minimize the risks to the animals involved and to the recipient populations through disease screening and prophylaxis (IUCN Veterinary Group, 2000) and through ensuring that the procedures involved present as little stress as possible (Kirkwood, 1999). However, there are dilemmas here. Kleiman (1996) suggests that the 'real' preparation of animals for release should perhaps include exposure to food shortages, parasites, predators, dramatic climatic fluctuations and dangerous objects. These challenges may not be in the short-term interests of the animals but experiences with them in captivity may be beneficial to welfare after release. Kleiman (1996) also points out that for the success of the reintroduction (in terms of establishing a self-sustaining population) there is often a balance to be struck between too little and too much care and support of individuals following release. This is a difficult area from the ethical perspective also. Reintroduced animals should be monitored so that problems can be detected and protocols modified in response.

Weighing conservation and welfare interests in interventions for wildlife conservation

All the responses and interventions for conservation of endangered species listed above, from disease control measures for conservation of free-living populations to conservation research, can have negative animal welfare aspects. The environmentalist view is that the conservation of species is an imperative that should trump welfare considerations, the animals rights view is vice versa. This issue, as it relates to veterinary medicine, is a relatively new one and it has not been well aired to date. The present consensus in society appears to lie somewhere between these extremes: that conservation measures should be allowed unless the conservation benefit is relatively minor and the welfare costs are relatively major. Individuals differ in the where they draw the line and (following Kirkwood, 1999) the approach advocated here is that, in all cases, the welfare and conservation benefits and costs should be clearly defined and that there should be some process to weigh these against each other before making the decision as to whether to proceed or not. It will be clear by now that weighing of conservation benefits and welfare costs is far from a mathematical procedure, there is no common currency or unit that can be used in the process. It is a process that should involve several individuals, ideally with a spectrum of interests and expertise, to reduce the chance of reaching erratic decisions. Next, that where the plan is made to proceed, careful consideration should be given to the relevant two of the three Rs: Reduction – use of no more animals than necessary and Refinement of techniques to minimize harm (the third of Russell and Burch's (1959) three Rs, Replacement, is not relevant in this context).

Ethics of interventions for wildlife welfare

Interventions for the welfare of wildlife such as feeding animals at times of food shortage, treatment and rehabilitation of wildlife casualties, and treatment of diseases in free-ranging animals (for example, use of ivermectin in bait to treat mange in foxes), are being undertaken on an increasingly large scale in the UK and in many other countries. It has been estimated that well over 20,000 sick and injured vertebrates are taken into temporary captivity in the UK each year (Kirkwood and Best, 1998). Interest in the treatment and rehabilitation of wildlife casualties has arisen partly as a result of growing awareness and concern for the harm caused to wildlife through human agency and partly because, having developed the technology for the successful treatment of diseases and injuries of domestic animals and of wild animals in captivity (in pursuit of the care of zoo animals and exotic pets), there has been growing pressure to apply these technologies for the welfare of free-living animals. But under what circumstances is it right to do this? Do we have a moral obligation to try to attend to the welfare of all wild animals? Or some? (if so which?), or none at all?

Opinions vary on these issues and are influenced by several factors including: the extent to which humans caused the problem; the extent to which the animal is under human stewardship; the severity of the harm and whether it was caused intentionally or accidentally; and the popular appeal of the animal (Kirkwood and Sainsbury, 1996). The latter is an illogical but powerful factor; for example, there is no reason to believe that rats are less capable of suffering than, say, seals, peregrine falcons or hedgehogs but there is far less interest in welfare support measures for sick or injured rats than for these more popular animals.

In practice, veterinarians are often one step removed from the decision about when and where to intervene for wildlife welfare and are presented with animals for which this decision has already been taken by members of the public. These people require, and expect to find readily, centres which are prepared to accept wildlife casualties, and veterinary practices are often the most readily available source of assistance in an emergency (Kirkwood and Best, 1998). The British Veterinary Association has recommended that its members might accept wildlife casualties during normal working hours to administer first aid treatment free of charge to the person presenting the animal. The veterinarian's responsibility 'to ensure the welfare of animals committed to my care' in these circumstances is clear. The more difficult issue, and one about which vets may be expected to provide guidance, is under what circumstances is it right to make interventions for wildlife welfare.

Of course there are a variety of possible benefits (Cooper, 1989). For example, in addition to the restoration to good health and welfare of the animals themselves, the treatment and rehabilitation of wildlife casualties may contribute to understanding of the epidemiology and treatment of diseases and may through providing a focus for public interest, help to promote a caring attitude to wildlife. On the other hand there are arguments, apart from those relating to the impossible enormity of the task, as to why it might be unwise to try to provide a welfare service for all wild animals. As regards intervening for the welfare of wild animals which live out their lives entirely independent of humans and whose diseases and injuries are not anthropogenic in origin, several points (scientific, philosophical and political) have been put forward which argue for a cautious approach.

1. *Intervention could be a potentially harmful interference with natural selection* (Kirkwood and Sainsbury, 1996). The biology of free-living animals is under continual scrutiny by natural selection. For many species the proportion of individuals that survive to breed is small, for example, some 10 per cent for many small birds. Although luck may play some part in this in the short term, over generations only the fittest lines survive. If it were not that some individuals fail to breed as a result of predation, injury or disease there would be no process of evolution. Wild animals are as they are anatomically, physiologically, immunologically

and behaviourally because of challenges faced throughout their evolution from competitors, infections, the climate and other factors. From the conservation viewpoint there is thus an argument that wildlife should not be aided against natural threats (except where necessary to euthanize on humane grounds) since this is an interference with the processes of evolution. Theoretically a population could experience more welfare harm in the long run if animals are treated than if they are not, since treatment may prevent or delay selection for natural defences.

2. *Non-responsibility.* Norton (1995) argued that humans cannot be and are not responsible for the lives of wild animals that live independently of them:

> When individual wild animals live largely undisturbed by human activities in their natural habitat – humans accept no responsibility for animals as individuals. This very general claim of nonresponsibility is not justified by any absolute claim about the intelligence or sensitivity of those individuals. It is rather a manifestation of a decision to respect the animal individuals as wild.

3. *It could be an inefficient method of promoting animal welfare.* DeGrazia (1996) argued that someone

> devoting a certain amount of time, energy, and money trying to contribute to the general animal good would almost certainly accomplish more by contributing to animal protection groups, writing to congress persons, participating in protests, supporting the study of alternatives to animal research, joining action committees, and the like, than by looking for animals in the wild and trying to help them.

There may be something in this argument but it is very difficult to say what actions may, in the long run, turn out to have the greatest benefit for animal welfare.

4. *Diversion of resources from more important endeavours.* Loftin (1985), writing of wildlife rehabilitation, expressed the view that 'the doctoring of sick animals is of extremely limited value and for the most part based on biological illiteracy. It wastes scarce resources and diverts attention from more worthwhile goals.' This is the environmentalist view that the focus of attention should be at the ecosystem level, particularly in view of the intensity of current threats to it.

The case of moral responsibility for intervention becomes stronger where the animals are to some extent under human stewardship and/or where the harm is due to human agency. Animals are harmed, and often in large numbers, as an incidental consequence of human activities, for example, through being caught in oil spills or poisoned by environmental pollutants. Intervention for welfare in these circumstances is to redress the balance – on the face of it, to right a wrong. In these cases there is a strong moral case for such action, providing it does not result in resources being directed away from still more morally important matters. Regarding the stewardship issue, we have a responsibility to carefully attend to the welfare of animals that are directly dependent on us, but most would agree with Norton (see 2, p. 134) that we cannot be, and are not responsible for, the welfare of entirely wild animals living out their lives undisturbed by us in any way. Between the extremes of complete dependence and complete independence there are many intermediate states: cases in which animals' fates are influenced by our actions to some degree and for whose welfare arguably, therefore, we have some responsibility. These might include, for example, animals in reintroduced populations or in populations that we encourage and foster to an extent by supplementary feeding or through habitat management.

Endeavours for the treatment and rehabilitation of wildlife casualties very rapidly run into the problem of scale unless strictly focused. The arguments above suggest that priority should be given to cases where the harm is human induced and to animals which are to some extent under human stewardship. Furthermore, since this work is done for welfare reasons alone (different considerations apply when casualties are treated for conservation reasons – see above), decisions should be based on welfare considerations only, that is on the balance of what is best for the welfare of the animal itself, that of any dependants it may have, and that of any other animals that may be affected. The right action in this situation is that which leads to greatest welfare benefit. From this perspective, to be ethically consistent priorities should be assigned also on the basis of severity of suffering and regardless of species *per se*. Where treatment and rehabilitation can be accomplished without causing further disproportionate pain and stress in the animal itself or any others there is a case for it. However, euthanasia at an early stage may be the most humane course of action for an animal with little realistic chance of being returned to the wild in a fit state to survive and facing a prolonged period in captivity and possibly stressful handling and treatment (Kirkwood and Best (1998) and in cases where release might put the welfare of others at risk, for example, through accidental introduction of infection or through overloading the carrying capacity of the habitat.

In the long run the key to improving wildlife welfare on a large scale is likely to be through early detection and accurate determination of the causes of diseases of anthropogenic origin (in addition to their 'fire-brigade' work wildlife hospitals have an important role here) and the development, where possible, of methods to prevent or alleviate these problems.

Concluding comments

World-wide, the human population presents serious threats to the viability and welfare of many species of wild animals. Although free-living wild animals are not, in the words of the UK veterinarians' declaration, 'committed to my care', the welfare of these animals and the conservation of species are rightly matters of veterinary concern. Interventions are increasingly being undertaken for species conservation and also to alleviate welfare problems. Actions for conservation may carry welfare costs to the animals involved and it is important that the potential costs and benefits are clearly defined and 'weighed'. The conservation of species is an important principle (the first rule of the tinkerer is never to throw away the pieces (Wilson, 1992) but minor conservation gains do not justify major welfare infringements. Conversely, misguided actions for wildlife welfare could have conservation costs; pursuit of minor welfare gains does not justify actions that put population viability at risk. Veterinarians have an important part to play in these ethical assessments, in developing protocols to minimize welfare costs in conservation programmes, and in determining priorities in interventions for wildlife welfare.

References

Beck, B.B., Rapaport, L.G., Stanley Price, M.R. and Wilson, A.C. (1994) Reintroduction of captive-born animals. In P.J.S. Olney, G.M. Mace, and A.T.C. Feistner, (eds), *Creative Conservation*: London, Chapman and Hall, pp. 265–86.

Callicott, J.B. (1989) *In Defence of the Land Ethic: Essays in Environmental Philosophy*. New York: SUNY Press.

Cooper, J.E. (1989) Care, cure or conservation: developments and dilemmas in wildlife conservation. In Harris, S., and Thomas, T., (eds), *Proceedings of the Inaugural Symposium of the British Wildlife Rehabilitation Council, 19th November 1988*, BWRC, c/o RSPCA, Horsham, UK, pp. 14–23.

Cunningham, A.A. (1996) Disease risks of wildlife translocations. *Conservation Biology* 10: 349–53.

DeGrazia, D. (1996) *Taking Animals Seriously: Mental Life and Moral Status*. Cambridge: Cambridge University Press.

Gascoyne, S.C., Laurenson, M.K., Lelo. S., and Borner, M. (1993) Rabies in African wild dogs (*Lycaon pictus*) in the Serengeti Region, Tanzania. *Journal of Wildlife Diseases*, 29: 396–402.

Hall, A., and Harwood, J. (1990) *The Intervet Guidelines to Vaccinating Wildlife*. Cambridge: Sea Mammal Research Unit.

Hughes, B. (1996) *The Feasibility of Control Measures for North American Ruddy Ducks Oxyura Jamaicensis in the United Kingdom*. Slimbridge: Wildfowl and Wetlands Trust.

IUCN Veterinary Specialist Group (in press) *Quarantine and Disease Screening Protocols for Wildlife Prior to Translocations and Release into the Wild*. Gland, Switerland: IUCN Veterinary Specialist Group.

Kalema. G., Kock, R.A., and Macfie, E. (1998) An outbreak of sarcoptic mange in free-ranging Mountain gorillas (*Gorilla gorilla berengei*) in Bwindi Impenetrable National Park, South Western Uganda. *Proceedings of the American Association of Zoo Veterinarians/American Association of Wildlife Veterinarians Joint Conference*, Omaha, Neb., 17-22 October, p. 438.

Kirkwood, J.K. (1992) Wild animal welfare. In R.R. Ryder, (ed.), *Animal Welfare and the Environment*. London: G. Duckworth & Co, pp. 139–54.

Kirkwood, J.K. (1998) Population density and infectious diseases at bird tables. *Veterinary Record*, 142: 468.

Kirkwood, J.K. (1999) Veterinary considerations and ethical dilemmas in vertebrate reintroduction programmes. In *Bringing Back the Bison: Proceedings of a Symposium on Reintroductions*, 1-2 October 1998, Farnborough.

Kirkwood. J.K., and Best, J.R. (1998) Treatment and rehabilitation of wildlife casualties: legal and ethical aspects. *Practice*, 20: 214–16.

Kirkwood. J.K., and Sainsbury, A.W. (1996) Ethics of interventions for the welfare of free-living wild animals. *Animal Welfare*, 5: 235–43.

Kirkwood, J.K., Sainsbury, A.W. and Bennett, P.M. (1994) The welfare of free-living wild animals: methods of assessment. *Animal Welfare*, 3: 257–73.

Kleiman, D. (1996) Reintroductions. In D. Kleiman, M. Allen, K. Thompson, and S. Lumpkin, (eds), *Wild Mammals in Captivity: Principles and Techniques*. Chicago: University of Chicago Press, pp. 297–305.

Koontz, F. (1995) Wild animal acquisition ethics for zoo biologists. In B.G. Norton, M. Hutchins, E.F. Stevens, and T.L. Maple, (eds), *Ethics on the Ark: Zoos, Animal Welfare, and Wildlife Conservation*. Washington: Smithsonian Institution Press, pp. 127–45.

Leopold, A. (1949) *A Sand County Almanac*. New York: Oxford University Press.

Midgley, M. (1983) *Animals and Why They Matter*. Harmondsworth: Penguin.

Norton, B.G. (1989) *Why Preserve Natural Variety?* Princeton: Princeton University Press.

Norton, B.G., Hutchins, M., Stevens, E.F. and Maple, T. (1995) *Ethics on the Ark: Zoos, Animal Welfare and Wildlife Conservation*. Washington: Smithsonian Institution Press.

Olney, P.J.S., Mace, G.M. and Feistner, A.T.C., (eds) (1994) *Creative Conservation*. London: Chapman and Hall.

Pennycott, T.W., Ross, H.M., McLaren, I.M., Park, A., Hopkins, G.F. and Foster, G. (1998) Causes of death of wild birds of the family Fringillidae in Britain. *Veterinary Record*, 143: 155–58.

Petrinovich, L. (1999) *Darwinian Dominion: Animal Welfare and Human Interests.* Cambridge, MA.: MIT Press.

Regan, T. (1983) *The Case for Animal Rights.* Berkeley: University of California Press.

Regan, T. (1992) Animal rights: what's in a name? In R.D. Ryder, (ed.) *Animal Welfare and the Environment.* London: Duckworth Press, pp. 49–61.

Regan, T. (1995) Are zoos morally defensible? In B.G. Norton, M. Hutchins, E.F. Stevens, and T.L. Maple, (eds), *Ethics on the Ark: Zoos, Animal Welfare, and Wildlife Conservation*, Washington: Smithsonian Institution Press, pp. 38–51.

Rupprecht, C.E., Nuss, J., and Roelke, M. (1990) Vaccination of Florida panthers (*Felis concolor*) against rabies. In *Abstracts of the Sixth International Conference on Wildlife Diseases*, Berlin: Wildlife Disease Association, p. 54.

Russell, W.M.S., and Burch, R.L. (1959) *The Principles of Humane Experimental Technique*, Special Edition, Potters Bar: Universities Federation for Animal Welfare.

Sainsbury, A.W., Bennett, P.M., and Kirkwood, J.K. (1995) The welfare of free-living wild animals in Europe: harm caused by human activities. *Animal Welfare*, 4: 183–206.

Sholley, C.R. 91989) Mountain gorilla update. *Oryx*, 23: 57–8.

Varner, G.E. (1998) *In Nature's Interests? Interests, Animal Rights and Environmental Ethics.* Oxford: Oxford University Press.

Vitousek, P.M., *et al.* (1986) Human appropriation of the products of photosynthesis. *Bioscience*, 36: 368–73.

Wilson, E.O. (1992) *The Diversity of Life.* Cambridge, MA.: Harvard University Press.

Wilson, E.O. (1993) Biophilia and the conservation ethic. In S.R. Kellert, and E.O. Wilson, (eds), *The Biophilia Hypothesis*, Washington DC: Island Press, pp. 31–41.

Woodford, M.H. and Rossiter, P.B. (1993) Disease risks associated with wildlife translocation projects, *Revue scientifique et technique de l'Office International des Epizooties*, 12: 115–35.

11

Zoos

Anna Meredith

Introduction

For the vast majority of people the zoo is the only place where they can come close to wild animals. There is no doubt that zoos are extremely popular. It is estimated that one in five Europeans and one in three North Americans visit a zoo every year. Compared to some other areas of animal use it seems that zoos still have a high degree of public approval. However, there is also criticism and many feel that the keeping of wild animals in captivity cannot be justified. The use of wild animals for entertainment, which is still the primary reason why most people go to the zoo, raises ethical issues that do not arise with domesticated species. The modern zoo community is acutely aware of the need for the continued justification for its existence. The modern zoo is much more than a place of entertainment, and supporters argue that zoos are an essential part of the conservation of endangered species.

History of zoos

Menageries of animals have existed from many thousands of years BC and have been kept by virtually all civilizations. Egyptian priests kept menageries of animals such as cats, baboons, ibises and lions at their temples, Alexander the Great collected parrots from India and brought them back to Greece, and Marco Polo in the thirteenth century saw lions and tigers roaming the palaces of Imperial China. The menagerie (literally 'a show of caged wild animals') was seen as a symbol of wealth and power. Wild animals were kept not for food, sport, or as pets, but purely because their rarity and wildness symbolized the status of their keeper. Wild and rare animals were, and still are, used as gifts to people in power and between governments to foster diplomatic relations. The Emperor Charlemagne was presented with a lion by Pope Leo III at his coronation in AD 800; Emperor Frederick II gave a polar bear to King Henry III and it swam in the Thames in 1251; and Edward Heath received the two famous pandas Ching Ching and Chia Chia at London Zoo as a gift from the Chinese government in 1974. It was not, however, until the Middle Ages that private menageries began to be opened for public entertainment in Europe. Henry III displayed the first elephant in Britain at the Tower of London in 1254, and poorer members of the public could bring along a live cat or dog to feed to the carnivores in lieu of an entrance fee.

The first true public zoological park or garden was established in France in the late eighteenth century. The *Jardin des Plantes* in Paris evolved from a herb garden that was incorporated into the new *Musée Nationale d'Histoire Naturelle*. The animals came mainly from confiscation from travelling circuses and side-shows, plus the King's menagerie from Versailles. It was established as a living natural history museum with scientific research as its stated aim rather than purely a place for entertainment.

In 1826 Sir Stamford Raffles and Sir Humphry Davy founded the Zoological Society of London, whose mission was to be a scientific establishment dedicated to the study of zoology. Animals would be brought in 'as objects of scientific research, not of vulgar admiration'. Initially access was only to members of the Society, but a need for revenue prompted admission for the public along with animal shows, rides and petting exhibits to attract these visitors. Unfortunately, knowledge of dietary requirements of exotic species was extremely poor, as were general husbandry methods, and most animals kept in zoos died soon after captivity, merely to be replaced by another specimen taken from the wild. Mortality was also high during capture and transport. No thought was given to captive breeding to save taking further animals from the wild. Some species went extinct – the last known examples of the passenger pigeon, quagga and thylacine, or Tasmanian wolf, all died in zoos. Cage design was purely to give the spectator the best view of the animals, with no thought for its behavioural needs. Thick bars, pits and spikes shaped the public's perception of wild animals as dangerous and to be feared, rather than to be respected and admired.

Carl Hagenbeck brought about the first real change in the philosophy of exhibiting wild animals to the public. He understood that although people wanted to get close to wild animals, the sight of the means of their confinement made them feel uncomfortable. Hagenbeck opened Stellingen Zoo near Hamburg in 1900, where he pioneered the enclosure without bars – naturalistic settings to display animals as he had seen them in the wild. With clever landscaping he used moats, trees and hedges to give an illusion of freedom and of different species kept together. Stellingen Zoo was, and still is, hugely popular with the zoo-going public, and many other European and North American zoos soon imported its design ideas. Hagenbeck's aim, however, was still that of pure entertainment and he had no scientific ideals. He was a highly successful animal trainer, dealer and entrepreneur who supplied many other European zoos with animals, and he was also well known in the late nineteenth century for his hugely popular exhibitions of foreign people – Eskimos, Nubians and even Buddhist priests. It is incredible to think that as recently as 1906 a human pygmy was exhibited in the Bronx Zoo alongside an orang-utan. The *New York Times* reported one visitor, on seeing this, as saying there is 'something about it I don't like'. Although applied to what was viewed at the time as a 'primitive' human, attitudes to animal welfare have changed dramatically, and this New Yorker's sentiment is often echoed by the modern zoo visitor, especially if he perceives a zoo animal as 'bored' or 'unhappy'.

Zoos continued to evolve during the twentieth century from menageries to scientific institutions that play a vital role in conservation and education. This development of the modern zoo reflects the changing attitudes of the relationship between man and animals, and this relationship is at different stages in different countries around the world. In the Western world most zoos now are forward thinking, scientifically run institutions which place great emphasis on animal welfare, education and conservation issues, whereas in many poorer and third world countries animal welfare standards in zoos are often appalling and the menagerie mentality still exists.

Arks or prisons?

The aims of the modern zoo are seen as recreation, conservation, education and research. Though the last three are emphasized, the recreational role remains vital. We know from studies that most visitors still go to the zoo for a 'good day out'. However, an increasing number are justifying their visit on conservation grounds, and once brought in to the zoo environment the educational and conservation messages can be put across. The paying visitor also funds much of the other zoo roles, and thus zoos are a unique environment where the needs and desires of the visitor have to be carefully balanced against the educational, conservation and research aims, and, most importantly, the welfare of the animals. Are zoos achieving this balance? Mary Midgley (1987) posed the question of cost/benefit analysis, which can be applied to almost any area of man's use of animals. Does the benefit to both humans and future generations of wild animals, such as increased understanding and awareness of conservation issues and preservation of species, outweigh the costs to existing individual zoo animals in terms of their behavioural and psychological needs? This is obviously an extremely complex issue, but nevertheless one which the zoo community must tackle.

Hutchins and Fascione (1991) list the four main ethical issues surrounding modern zoos as the acquisition of animals for captive breeding programmes, the disposal of surplus animals, animal care and husbandry, and the use of animals for research, education and recreation. The conservation role of zoos and captive breeding programmes is increasingly promoted as being the main justification for their existence. Colin Tudge (1992) argues that zoos are now an essential part of modern conservation strategy, and without them mass extinction of species will occur. Extinction of species is nothing new. Ninety-nine per cent of all animals that have ever existed are now extinct. The difference is that until recent times most extinctions have been a purely natural phenomenon, but now most are a direct result of man's destruction of the natural world.

Historically zoos were exploiters of wildlife. Modern zoos, however, seldom take animals from the wild, except in rare cases where it is judged that not to do so would result in rapid extinction. Many populations of highly endangered species are in small isolated pockets with lack of gene flow and loss of genetic diversity which itself can cause extinction. Thus human intervention involving captive breeding, disease control and habitat manipulation are necessary. If a species goes extinct there is less impetus to save its environment, whereas if a viable population still exists, albeit in captivity, it will increase chances that the habitat will be preserved. The conservation successes of the zoo community are very real. Many species would now be extinct without zoos – the Siberian tiger, Père David's deer, Przewalski's horse, the Californian condor and the black-footed ferret to name a few. International breeding programmes and species survival plans allowing maintenance of genetic diversity are scientifically managed and highly co-ordinated. Successful reintroduction programmes have been achieved, such as the golden lion tamarin in Brazil and the Arabian oryx in Oman. It is often argued that there is no point in saving the animals if there is no environment to put them back in to. Saving the whole ecosystem is the ideal, but in the short and medium term it is not always an option. Zoos can act as arks to preserve the animals until there is a safe environment for them to return to. It is impossible to save all species, but the concentration on 'flagship' species, which act as ambassadors for similar rarer species, promotes public support for broader conservation efforts for the whole environment from which that species comes. But why bother? Does it really matter if another species disappears? Some would argue that to gracefully go extinct and 'die with dignity' is better than to face a lifetime of captivity in the hope that one day future generations may return to the wild. But most people have the innate feeling that for an animal to disappear forever as a direct result of man's ravages is wrong. We feel cheated that we can never see a dodo, and do not wish future generations not to be able to see a tiger or a rhinoceros. Utilitarian arguments can be used for conserving wild animals - they can be of benefit to mankind. The International Union for the Conservation of Nature and Natural Resources (IUCN) believes that conservation policies should seek to reconcile the needs of wildlife with those of people. Ecotourism is big business, and can benefit the local population directly, although not always without cost to the environment. It gives local people a reason not to destroy their environment. Animals can also be seen as a huge genetic resource that might yield enormous benefits in the future.

However strong and convincing the conservation argument is, a lot of zoos, even those heavily involved in captive breeding and conservation, still keep species that are not endangered. Zoo visitors often feel that a trip to the zoo is not complete unless they see a lion or a giraffe. Is it justifiable to keep these species as entertainment when there is no conservation requirement?

Disposal of surplus animals can arouse strong feelings. Wherever possible, zoos exchange animals to prevent the need to cull animals, but some culling is an inevitable part of good animal management. Animals may be culled if they are genetically over-represented, if there is a skewed sex ratio, or if they are not healthy. Responsible zoos control breeding very carefully to prevent surplus wherever possible, mainly for good scientific reasons. The health and welfare of the species as a whole takes precedence over the individual, with the goal being the development of self-sustaining captive populations. Modern zoos are now mainly producers and not consumers of animals. Deliberate, irresponsible breeding to produce youngsters that will attract the public is clearly reprehensible, but unfortunately does occur. It is interesting that there is general acceptance even by animal welfare charities that stray domestic dogs need to be put down, whereas the culling of zoo animals is seen as reprehensible. The killing of any animal can generate negative publicity for zoos even if it is done in the best interests of animal welfare. In 1983 the decision at London Zoo to put down the elephant Pole Pole sparked a huge public reaction and the founding by McKenna and Travers of Zoocheck. Organizations such as this are a response to a genuine public concern for zoo animal welfare. One of Zoocheck's aims was to phase out all zoos, and while we may agree or disagree with this view there is no doubt that such organizations do raise public awareness and highlight poor welfare where it exists. Now known as the Born Free Foundation, this organization is more discriminating and does work in co-operation with good zoos and promotes conservation of wildlife in its natural environment. Its aims to abolish bad zoos can only be fully supported by the responsible zoo community.

Welfare protection and legislation

The UK has always been at the forefront of animal welfare protection and legislation. Even Charles Dickens opposed the feeding of live prey to snakes at London Zoo, viewing it as frightening for the prey and demeaning for the spectators. The growing number of zoos in the UK throughout the nineteenth century also led to growing numbers of protests, especially about animals that were trained to perform tricks. Training methods were invariably cruel, and the outcry this caused led to the Cruelty to Wild Animals Act in 1900 which prohibited the teasing, abusing or infuriating of captive animals.

Animal welfare issues really came to the fore in this country with the 1964 Brambell Committee and its investigation into farm animal welfare, from which the now familiar concept of the Five Freedoms developed. Zoo animals are clearly very different from farm animals in some respects – they are neither truly wild nor domesticated; they are in zoos expressly for the purpose of attracting visitors, and a significant part of their environment consists of large numbers of humans. Despite the differing needs of, and demands on zoo animals, the emphasis on psychological well-being is no less applicable. There is no doubt that the physical needs of most zoo species in good zoos are well catered for. Advances in our knowledge of nutritional needs, health care and preventive medicine have resulted in a dramatic reduction in morbidity and mortality over the past decades. However, behavioural and psychological needs are less well understood, and a major problem is our ability to define and assess well-being in these species.

In the UK, zoos are controlled by the Zoo Licensing Act 1981, which is currently under review. The Act places great emphasis on animal welfare and encompasses the concept of the Five Freedoms. It is executed by a system of inspection and licensing and issues standards of modern zoo practice. Inspectors are either senior zoo professionals or veterinary surgeons with specific experience of zoo animals and zoo management. As well as requirements for suitable accommodation, feeding, hygiene and veterinary care, the Act requires that 'animals be provided with space and furniture sufficient to allow such exercise as is needed for the welfare of the particular species' and 'animal enclosures to be equipped, in accordance with the needs of the species in question, with such items as bedding material, branchwork, burrows, nesting boxes and pools, and in the case of aquatic animals, materials such as weed, shingle, etc., to aid and encourage normal behaviour patterns among them'. The veterinary profession plays a vital role in the administration of this legislation, and in advising on zoo animal welfare. There has been some criticism at the lack of consistency between inspectors, and there is clearly a need for more communication, training and consensus amongst the inspectorate in order to promote and maximize animal welfare standards. The EU has recently implemented the Zoo Directive, a British-inspired directive to enforce minimum conditions for the well-being of animals in Europe's 1,000 zoos and wildlife parks. This binding directive, promoted by Britain against the opposition of the EC, will require states to set their own rules for licensing and inspecting zoos by the year 2002. The directive also requires that all zoos have a conservation policy, a commitment to research and education, and will have to satisfy the biological and conservation requirements of species, plus employ environmental enrichment.

Environmental enrichment

In 1993 the International Union of Directors of Zoological Gardens (World Zoo Organisation) issued the World Zoo Conservation Strategy which emphasizes education and captive breeding programmes as crucial aspects of zoo conservation policies. The Strategy states that 'animals that appear to suffer from physical and psychological restraint are counterproductive to education and will spoil the conservation message; conversely, people are attracted to animals that are enabled to explore and display a full variety of natural behaviour'. So-called 'enrichment' measures are therefore a crucial part of modern zoo animal management.

Zoos rely on the exhibition of animals and the attractiveness of the exhibits to the general public in order to survive economically and carry out other areas of conservation work. Promotion of natural behaviours which are interesting and educational, and avoidance of aberrant behaviours are seen as being in the best interests of animal welfare. Enrichment measures which increase the complexity of an animal's environment and make it look more 'natural' are generally perceived to have a positive effect on the welfare of that animal. However, there is still a great deal of ignorance about the real environmental and behavioural needs of zoo animals, and whether many so-called enrichment measures actually do improve animal welfare. Means of assessment are difficult and scientific studies difficult. Preference testing can tell us what an animal does, given a choice, but critics would contend that the animal chooses the lesser of two evils.

With a lack of sound scientific data many enrichment programmes rely on the human perspective of what elements of the environment are important for welfare; for example, little thought is ever given to the olfactory environment, as humans have a relatively poor sense of smell. Naturalistic environments are often an illusion for the benefit of the public. For example, for an animal with no colour vision it is irrelevant whether it is in a green environment reminiscent of the forest or in a grey one, but grey would be unacceptable to the public. Functional substitution may very well satisfy the animals' needs: for example, a wooden platform rather than a natural rocky outcrop, but the appearance of the rock is more pleasing to the public. Unfortunately, architects have designed many zoo exhibits with little input from keepers and veterinary staff, and the emphasis in design is placed on the public's perspective rather than the animal's needs. New zoo enclosures must be designed to maximize both the human and animal aspects. Naturalistic enclosures may actually do very little for animal welfare but can promote habitat awareness amongst the public. It again falls to the educational role of the zoo to inform people of what matters to the animal in situations where exhibits are not so pleasing to the visitor's eye, or where their perception may be that an enrichment device looks unsuitable. Conversely, enrichment measures that would greatly enhance welfare, such as the feeding of live prey to predators, cannot be utilized because of public sensibilities and the law. The small numbers of animals involved, limited facilities and funds mean that trial and error and intuition often still has to be relied on. Inter-zoo communication and comparison can be very useful.

Different species have different needs. Animals can be divided into specialists and non-specialists or generalists. The specialists have relatively simple needs, which, if fulfilled, means it is happy, for example, the big cats. If well fed the zoo lion will spend most of its day sleeping, as it would in the wild. In the confines of the zoo the public perceives this as boredom. Grazing or browsing herbivores which spend most of their time eating or chewing the cud are relatively easy to provide for, and visitors very rarely make complaints about these species. The generalists are opportunists, always investigating and on the move and have much broader needs, and are thus more difficult to keep satisfactorily in captivity. The use of feeding devices, for example, placing insects in a box with a small hole so they emerge at random, or using scatter feeding, are frequently used in zoos to mimic this foraging behaviour, especially for primates.

We should perhaps accept that some species have needs that we can never even approach fulfilling, and therefore they should not be kept in captivity. But what do we do, then, if such a species is critically endangered and will become extinct if not kept in zoos?

Research and education

Research output from zoos is increasing, both in the veterinary and ethological field, and has vital bearing on the evolution and management of animal collections. Research involving zoo animals is invariably non-invasive, except in vital reproductive research. *In situ* research is increasingly being carried out and supported by zoos, and the results fed back into the captive situation.

Most good zoos have an active education department and strong links with local schools. Critics contend that zoos continue to portray a distorted view of animals, and films, lectures and slides would be better. Others maintain that the same wildlife films and the ability of more and more people to travel to countries where they can see wildlife *in situ* actually enhances the appreciation and understanding of good zoos. A 1987 survey in the USA and Canada showed that the public views the zoo as primarily an educational institution and it accomplishes this task well. On the other hand, studies have shown that the time spent actually looking at exhibits or reading factual information by most visitors is very low. Direct interaction with animals, for example, touching a snake rather than looking at a slide of one, does seem to be a very strong learning experience, and few could argue that film footage of a giraffe can portray their size and grace as well as the experience of being a few feet away from a living animal. Public attitudes can be difficult to change. We tend to dislike or find uninteresting small, unattractive, slimy animals but like large intelligent attractive animals with which we can find some similarity in appearance or behaviour to ourselves. Generating public enthusiasm for a charismatic megavertebrate like a rhinoceros is much easier than for a highly endangered partula snail. Education is the key to an understanding of the role of zoos – why there is no lion, why some animals have to be culled, why it is so important to conserve a particular species.

The use of trained, often hand-reared animals in displays or shows can engender criticism. Such circus-like exhibits are seen by some to be demeaning to the animals and not educational. Other criticisms are that training methods are cruel and force them to perform unnatural behaviours. Psittacine birds, cetaceans and elephants are common species utilized in this way. Supporters of this use of animals argue that, if well done, such displays can educate the public and increase appreciation of the animals' capabilities. The animals, in addition, enjoy the opportunity to use their intelligence and find the experience an enriching one.

Conclusion

The keeping of animals in zoos is, and will no doubt remain, a complex ethical area. In the UK we are fortunate to have the legislation and the public attitude that means that at least the spirit of good welfare exists. Obviously some zoos are better than others, and unfortunately some are still very poor. There is no doubt that the welfare of animals in most zoos today has improved dramatically over the past few decades, but continued research and improvement is essential.

Despite their detractors, zoos do have a crucial and legitimate conservation and educational role to play. Whether this role justifies the captivity, perhaps indefinitely, of wild animals, is debatable. The zoo community must continue to strive to develop its role in conservation, and to obtain the optimum balance between attractive, educational exhibits and the maximization of animal welfare.

References and further reading

Bostock, S. (1993) *Zoos and Animal Rights*. London: Routledge.
Cherfas, J. (1984) *Zoo 2000: A Look Beyond the Bars*. London: BBC Publications.
Circus Working Group (1998) *A Report into the Welfare of Circus Animals in England and Wales*. Horsham: RSPCA.
Hutchins, M., and Fascione, N. (1991) Ethical issues facing modern zoos. *Proceedings of the American Association of Zoo Veterinarians*, 56–64.
Kleiman, D.G., *et al.* (ed.) (1996) *Wild Mammals in Captivity: Principles and Techniques*. Chicago: University of Chicago Press.
Midgley, M. (1983) *Animals and Why They Matter*. Athens: University of Georgia Press.

McKenna, V., and Travers, W., (eds) (1987) *Beyond the Bars: the Zoo Dilemma*. San Francisco: Thorsons.

Norton, B., Hutchins, M. *et al.* (1995) *Ethics on the Ark*. Washington, DC: Smithsonian Institution Press.

Tudge, C. (1992) *Last Animals at the Zoo*. Oxford: Oxford University Press.

12

Animals in sport

John Webster

In common with all veterinary surgeons of my generation my professional training was based on a sound education in the principles of
good science but no formal education in ethics. In later life I have
struggled to incorporate into my life principles of ethics that amount to
rather more than the honest desire to 'be a good chap'. Probably because
I was trained as a scientist I have found it useful to consider ethics as 'the
science of morality'. This implies that ethical questions can be addressed
by something closely akin to scientific method, which defines a problem,
selects appropriate tools to study the problem, analyses the elements of
the problem as it stands, poses a series of 'what if?' questions, then, and
then only, frames conclusions and value judgements on the basis of the
evidence. This approach breaks down the ethical problems of animals in
sport as follows:

- Definition of the problem: games people play with animals;
- Methods: principles of ethical analysis;
- Results: application of ethical principles to the different sports;
- Discussion and conclusions.

Games people play with animals

Another piece of baggage that I have carried forward from my classical
veterinary training is the concept of 'animals of veterinary importance', a
morally dubious phrase that refers to those species that we are most likely

to use for our own ends, whether for food, companionship or recreation. We *use* animals for sport. Whether they find the experience distressing or delightful is an important question but it does not alter the fact that they are being used as instruments to give us some form of satisfaction or reward. So far as humans are concerned the primary motivation for taking part in any sport is the thrill of the contest and the more thrilling prospect of winning. The fly fisherman who justifies his pastime with the claim that salmon is good food is, deliberately or otherwise, dodging the issue. There are cheaper and easier ways of acquiring salmon.

Most humans, of course, draw their excitement from animal sports not as participants but as spectators. This applies equally to those who attend a horse-race on foot and those who follow a fox-hunt on horseback. Whatever other arguments are advanced for and against the control of foxes by hunting with hounds, it is an inescapable fact that the riders streaming cross-country in full cry are entirely superfluous to the business at hand. Following the hunt, like fly-fishing, cannot be justified on the grounds that it is necessary. Those who seek to justify these, or any animal sports, must accept at the outset that they do these things because, to them, it is good fun.

Animal sports are based on competition between animals or competition between animals and humans. Where they differ is in the costs (or benefits) to the animals of the contest itself and the penalties of losing. Thus to a racehorse, the race itself may carry little cost (it may indeed be a pleasure) unless it is unlucky enough to be injured, and there would appear (to the horse) to be no immediate penalty for losing. In a fox-hunt, the cost of the event to the fox depends on how hard is the chase and the penalty for losing is death.

The sociobiologist who seeks evolutionary links between the behaviour of humans and animals would argue that the motivation to play is driven by the primitive need to develop life skills and improve evolutionary fitness. Hunting, whether with hounds, rod or gun, has undoubtedly evolved from the primitive human need to ensure fitness by acquiring food and maintaining control over other animal species competing within the same habitat. It would be specious to claim that this is the primary motivation for hunting today, but equally specious to deny that this motivation has been essential to the evolution of the human species and is, by this definition, 'natural'.

Other sports such as sheepdog trials and rodeo have ritualized and celebrated skills essential to farming and ranching. At first sight (to us) sheep-dog trials may appear far more humane than bareback bronc riding. The animals may see things differently. The sheep are always harassed and usually lose – they end up in a pen. The bucking horse is also harassed but (to its mind) always wins, since no cowboy stays on for more than eight seconds.

Undoubtedly the lure that attracts the greatest number of people to animal sports is the lure of gambling. The emotions of gambling, the excitement of the wager, thrill at winning, despair at losing, are the same whatever the contest, be it horse-racing, greyhound racing, cock-fighting or dogfighting. Organizing races between animals to satisfy the punters is legal, organizing fights between animals is not. Dogfighting is prohibited by law because it is deemed to constitute unnecessary suffering according to the Protection of Animals Act 1911. The phrase 'unnecessary suffering' is unhelpfully vague, whether used in a strictly legal or broader ethical sense (see Moss, 1992). It is even worse when read in its original context. Article 1(1)(a) of the 1911 Act states:

> If any person shall cruelly beat, kick, ill-treat, over-ride, over-drive, over-load, torture, infuriate or terrify an animal ... or shall, by wantonly or unreasonably doing or omitting to do any act ... permit any unnecessary suffering to be so caused to any animal ... shall be guilty of an offence of cruelty within the meaning of this Act.

The wording of this Act was clearly designed with the primary purpose of stopping people being nasty to horses in the street. It may be used to prosecute youths torturing a cat or even a wild rat that they have captured. It is not used to prosecute adults who elect to over-ride, terrify and torture the fox. This is, to put it mildly, morally inconsistent.

No use of animals in sport can be strictly described as 'necessary'. By this definition any person who deliberately causes any animal to suffer, or significantly increases the risk that it *might* suffer in the name of sport should be guilty of an act of cruelty. This *reductio ad absurdum* illustrates the inadequacy of the phrase 'unnecessary suffering'. I suggest that it would be better to use the phrase 'unjustified suffering' as a basis for both ethical and legal judgements.

Ethical principles

Most concepts of morality or 'common-sense ethics' are based upon the principles of *right thought* and *right action*. Textbooks of moral philosophy tend to emphasize right thought. However, to quote Thomas Carlyle, 'The end of a man is an action and not a thought, though it were the noblest', and to quote myself, 'what matters to an animal is not what we think or feel, but what we do. If an animal is isolated, without food in a cold box on filthy litter, it will suffer the same whether kept as a pet, run for a bet, killed for food, or sacrificed for science' (Webster, 1994).

Beauchamp and Childress (1994) have identified four principles for right action in the context of medical ethics: *beneficence, non-maleficence, autonomy* and *justice*. The first two principles: 'do good' and 'do no harm' to the patients in your care transpose easily to the treatment of animals in our care. They may be evaluated in strictly utilitarian terms on the basis of the effects of 'doing or omitting to do any act' on animal well-being. Autonomy implies respect for the rights of the patient or animal (both sentient individuals) to exercise control over their own destiny. Justice equates to fairness; in particular, fairness to those, like the animals in sport, who do not volunteer for or stand to gain from the exercise.

Animal well-being

The well-being of an animal or population of animals depends on their ability to sustain fitness and avoid suffering. The words 'suffering' and 'stress' are not synonymous. Some degree of stress is inevitable in the normal life of any sentient animal and is, indeed, a form of education essential for survival of the individual and fitness of the species. Animals suffer when they fail to cope with the stresses of life because they are too severe, too complex and/or too prolonged (McFarland, 1989; Webster, 1994). In assessing the impact of sport on animal well-being, it is necessary to consider (at least) the following:

1. the well-being of each individual during the course of the sporting activity;
2. the risk of suffering to each individual as an indirect consequence of the activity;
3. the impact of the sport on the lifetime well-being of all animals involved in that sport;
4. the implications for the animals of banning the sport.

These principles are all strictly based on utilitarianism, an honourable philosophy but one often diminished by oversimplification to the maxim of 'the greatest good for the greatest number'. Utilitarian principles are most commonly cited in justification of hunting with hounds. The principles selected are usually those which sound honourable, for example, that hunting preserves the habitat and therefore the fitness of the fox population. A more honest utilitarian argument would be that all animals but the fox are having a thoroughly good time: hounds, horses, huntsmen – even the hunt saboteurs. On strictly utilitarian grounds the fox doesn't stand a chance. But I shall not discuss fox-hunting on strictly utilitarian grounds.

Autonomy and justice

The concept of autonomy is based on the notion of 'rights' advanced in the eighteenth century by Immanuel Kant. Whereas Bentham based his concept of utilitarianism on an analysis of costs and benefits for all concerned parties, Kant appealed to our responsibility and duty to treat others as ends in themselves, irrespective of outcome. For those who like to take their philosophy in small sips this equates to 'Do as you would be done by'.

Sociobiologists may argue that the notion of rights is an intellectual device conceived by humans to encourage altruism and so enhance our individual well-being; i.e. it is motivated not so much by morality as by self-interest. Certainly individuals are more likely to sustain fitness and avoid suffering in those human societies which respect individual rights and practise altruism. Extension of the concept of rights to other animals has been argued by many: most persuasively, Peter Singer (1990). On the one hand, it may be seen as truly altruistic, on the other, it may, equally fairly, be argued that the notion of rights as a basis for action has no meaning unless all parties contribute to the debate. We accept that it is wrong for white people to define the rights of black people or for men to define the rights of women. How then can we presume to define the rights of other species?

Respect for autonomy in the context of this chapter implies that animals should have the right not to participate in sport if they don't want to. Hunted animals clearly don't have that option. However, animals appear to participate in many sports as enthusiastic amateurs. No one forces a greyhound to race and there are strict penalties for excessive use of the whip in horse-racing. Moreover, horses have to be trained as amateurs. Unlike human athletes, they cannot be persuaded to run through the pain barrier again and again in the expectation that this will improve their performance in a critical race six months hence.

It is to me an impeccable moral principle that humans should afford respect to each sentient animal as an individual. Beyond that I have difficulty transferring notions of animal rights into principles for right action. I am more comfortable with the concept of justice or fairness (Rawls, 1972). Is it, for example, fair:

1. to kill an animal or directly cause it to suffer simply to obtain personal pleasure?

2. to use an animal for one's own recreational purposes then kill it (humanely) when it has outlived its usefulness?
3. to use an animal for one's own recreational purposes then, when it has outlived its usefulness, sell, or otherwise dispose of it to an unknown fate?
4. to increase the risks of injury or behavioural abnormalities in an animal in the interests of improving its sporting prowess?

These questions may, at first sight, seem to be based on no more than a strictly utilitarian concern for animal well-being. However, I suggest you consider hunting with hounds foxes or deer in the context of question 1 (p. 154) and consideration 1 (p.153) on well-being. Whatever your final opinion on the morality of hunting with hounds, I suggest that the two questions will not evoke the same train of thought.

Ethical analysis: sport by sport

Horse-riding

Horsy sports evolved from the fundamental need of humans to discover and breed from animals deemed superior according to our needs: horses that ran faster, stayed longer or responded better to control. Most sporting events with horses (I except polo and bullfighting) are based simply on exploitation of the animals' natural motivation to run and jump and there is no reason to assume that these natural behaviours are likely to constitute a *direct* source of suffering. I repeat, horses are amateurs who appear to approach riding events with enthusiasm.

Horse-riding is, of course, a risky business for both horse and rider. It is fair to ask the question: 'do horses experience fear during, or in anticipation of events such as a steeplechase? Riders do for certain. This doesn't stop them competing but they do at least have freedom of choice. How is it for the horses? I once heard a very famous event rider refer to the 'Badminton virgins', young horses who took on the entire cross-country course, even in the most appalling conditions, with great enthusiasm, but who sometimes, if their memory of the event was really bad, never again managed to recapture that first fine careless rapture. This implies that they acquired, by experience, an element of fear; not necessarily sufficient to cause suffering but sufficient to introduce an element of caution when next they faced the course.

The main moral issues concerning riding events with horses are likely to arise from consequences of the event rather than from the event itself. These include:

- risks of death and injury incurred during competition;
- risks of injuries attributable to racing thoroughbreds at a very early age (2- to 3-year-old);
- suffering attributable to lack of care in animals that have outlived their usefulness.

Sudden death, for example, a horse that falls and breaks its neck in a steeplechase, is not a cause of suffering – in fact it is about the most humane death possible. But is it fair to submit a horse to increased risk of sudden death? If the horse was fit and running with enthusiasm at the time of the accident I do not see any injustice. If the horse was unfit to start, or clearly needed to be pulled up, that is another matter.

Injuries to horses associated with riding events range from, for example, immediate, severe conditions like bone fractures to chronic states of unsoundness attributable to tendon injuries. The designers of cross-country courses have an obligation not to 'wantonly or unreasonably' incur risk to life and limb of horse and rider but they are also under pressure to make their courses more demanding for the competitors and more thrilling for the spectators. When injury does occur the main welfare problems for the animal are pain and incapacity to behave as normal. It is important to distinguish between acute and chronic pain. Much has been made of the argument that horses (and other athletes) appear to be insensitive to acute pain in the period immediately following a severe injury such as a fracture of the lower limb, for reasons that are usually attributed to secretion of endorphins (the natural opiates). While this may be so, there is overwhelming evidence that horses experience chronic pain in a similar way to humans. Moreover, the chronic pain that accompanies lasting injury does not appear to be eased by endorphins. Indeed, it is often associated with a state of hyperalgesia, or increased sensitivity, which increases the intensity of the conscious sensation (Wall and Melzack, 1994, Webster, 1994). It may be morally acceptable to enter horses for events that carry a significant risk of causing pain through injury. It is not morally acceptable to ignore the long-term painful consequences of any such injury.

If we elect to use any animal for our lasting entertainment then we should, in justice, assume responsibility for its entire life. If we can arrange for our old horse to live out its retirement in comfort and the good company of other horses, then that will not only make us feel good, it will be morally right. If we cannot manage this then we can only guarantee that it will not suffer if we arrange for it to be killed humanely. It is an injustice to sell off a horse that has become surplus to requirements with no thought for the quality of its future life.

Greyhound racing

Most of what I have written about horse racing applies to greyhound racing. I note here only two points of difference. Greyhounds running (without a jockey aboard) are indulging voluntarily in the most natural of behaviour. Retired greyhounds make excellent companions and are therefore worth saving. (Readers should note that there is no respect for either autonomy or justice in that last sentence.)

Bullfighting and rodeo

What these sports have in common is that they both involve violent competition between man and animal. The differences are differences of degree but they are substantial. Consider, for example, contests between man and cattle. These include:

Bullfighting

- Spanish style: the bull is fought and killed, unnecessarily slowly and after incurring both injury and exhaustion;
- Portuguese style: the bull is fought but not killed. It is, however, injured by the banderillas which have to be removed after the contest.

Rodeo

- Bullriding: a bull is goaded out of the shute and spurred by the cowboy, whom it attempts to remove. After eight seconds the bull wins (according to its terms);
- Calf roping: a young calf is lassoed by a cowboy on horseback, pulled over and trussed up;
- Steerwrestling: a cowboy leaps off a horse across the horns of a yearling steer and attempts to wrestle it to the ground;
- Chilean rodeo: two men on horseback first control the movement of a young ox within an arena, then charge it on horseback so that the horse knocks the ox to the ground.

Odberg (1992) has reviewed the welfare implications of bullfighting (for bulls and horses). It is undeniable that both forms of bullfighting cause unnecessary suffering. The legal justification for the suffering differs, of course, in different countries. However, since it is most unlikely that bullfighting will ever be permitted in any society other than those where it is already embedded within the culture, I shall not dwell on it further here.

Most of the events in rodeo are based on skills that were (and often still are) essential to the cowboy managing semi-wild beef cattle on the open range. All the events listed above, plus, of course, riding and spurring bucking broncos (horses) are designed to cause the animals some degree of stress. The first question, as always, is: does this imposition of stress cause the animals to suffer? Calf roping, which is arguably the most functional of events, may be the one most likely to cause suffering. The young calf is isolated, forcibly thrown down and trussed up. Clearly this is an aversive experience. The degree of suffering will depend on how aversive the experience and how often the same calf is used.

Bucking horses and bulls used for riding and spurring events are used again and again. A systematic study of their behaviour would reveal just how aversive this activity was (or was not) for different individuals. My own limited experience would suggest that most broncs stand quietly in the shute before release and leave the arena quietly with other horses after parting company with their rider. Bulls frequently attack their dismounted rider and have to be distracted by the rodeo clowns. What one does not see are signs of reluctance to enter the arena, or learned helplessness. I am satisfied that these animals are stressed during the events but do not suffer. Moreover, they are maintained in a state of high fitness. The rodeo bull, in my opinion, receives a fairer deal from humans than the dairy bull which spends its entire adult life within the confines of a bullpen.

Chilean rodeo, which uses two horses to control the movement of an ox, also celebrates the traditional riding skills of the herdsman. However, the final pass, in which the ox is knocked over twice against a cushioned barrier appears distressing and entirely pointless to me (and most Chileans). This is, in my opinion, only acceptable provided the oxen are used no more than once.

Steerwrestling is just silly. Some of the steers may be hurt sometimes. The cowboys hurt themselves all the time.

Shooting

The nominal reasons for humans to shoot animals are either to provide us with food and clothing, or to control their numbers, or both. These practices are usually justified simply in utilitarian terms. By controlled culling through shooting we obtain valuable commodities and maintain the fitness of the population by managing numbers to match the resources available to the species. However, we blur the moral issues by making a distinction between vermin and game: the former category includes species such as the wild rat which we kill out of necessity by any acceptable means (shooting, poisoning, etc.) for reasons of hygiene, the latter includes species such as the pheasant and red deer, which we shoot for fun.

Most aspects of vermin control (for example, rodents) are outside the scope of this chapter. Suffice to say that killing should be carried out as humanely as possible. However, a gamekeeper may class as vermin any unprotected wild animals that compete with the pheasants being reared. This killing and distortion of natural habitat is done to ensure better 'sport' for the clients.

The simple moral question: is it right to kill an animal merely for our own entertainment? does not have a simple answer. It is ethically valid although practically tricky to sustain the absolute Buddhist argument that it is morally unacceptable deliberately to kill any animal, ever. Most of us, however, including lacto-vegetarians, wielders of fly sprays, etc., are guilty of moral relativism. We permit the killing of some animals according to our own perception of needs. How we rank the needs of ourselves and others for food, hygiene and entertainment is our concern but it is a matter of supreme indifference to the animal that gets sprayed or shot.

I have written elsewhere (in utilitarian mode) that humankind has the moral responsibility to ensure a reasonable quality of life and a gentle death for those animals that come within our dominion (Webster, 1994). In the context of game shooting this defines acceptability according to:

• the humanity of the killing process;
• the quality of life for the animals involved directly or indirectly in the sport.

Stalking wild red deer to achieve a successful shot that kills the animal before it becomes aware that it is being stalked is undoubtedly more humane than rounding up farmed deer and transporting them for slaughter at an abattoir. It appears more natural to allow red deer to range freely over the Scottish Highlands than to farm them in small paddocks in southern England. However, it does not necessarily improve their quality of life. Table 1 compares the welfare of wild and farmed red deer according to the conventions of the Five Freedoms and demonstrates, as always, the danger of simplistic assumptions as to what we think is best for them. Ideally we should ask the animals themselves. Most research in applied ethology is directed towards this end.

Table 1: Welfare comparison of stalking *v.* farming red deer according
to the conventions of the Five Freedoms

	Stalking wild deer	*Farming/abattoir*
Nutrition	chronic hunger in winter	generally good
Thermal comfort	cold stress on open moors	generally good
Physical comfort	generally good	generally good
Pain and injury	no treatment available	treatment available
Infectious disease	low incidence	controllable
Parasitism	external parasites	controllable
Natural behaviour	total freedom	restricted
Fear and stress	natural incidence	transport and slaughter

Most pheasant shooting involves animals that are farmed for the purpose.
Young birds are reared artificially, then turned out into an enriched,
essentially natural woodland environment, before being put up before
the guns by beaters with dogs and given a 'sporting chance' to escape.
Not all shot birds will be killed outright, but the presence of dogs
ensures that badly wounded animals are likely to be retrieved. Once
again, the death, for most birds, is likely to involve less suffering that
that experienced by end-of-lay hens and probably less suffering than
being killed by a fox. Moreover, the quality of life for the birds is
undeniably superior to that of the intensively reared broiler chicken or
battery hen. I believe that no one who eats either chicken or battery eggs
can sustain a moral argument against the practice of rearing and shooting
game birds.

Fishing

It is a common and honestly held belief amongst those who fish that
hooked fish do not feel pain or, at least, do not suffer distress in a way
similar to ourselves or even, perhaps, the fox. The Medway Report (1979)
on welfare aspects of shooting and angling quotes Gathorne-Hardy, 'I do
not believe that salmon . . . feel very acutely, a reassuring theory for the
tender-hearted fisherman. The desperate struggle of the fish to get free
confirms the same view. Not all the instinct of self-preservation would
induce a man to put a strain of even a pound if the hook were attached to
some tender part of his flesh'. This assertion makes an excellent subject
for scientific and ethical debate. Is the violent struggle of the fish to
escape:

- instinctive, involving no element of consciousness whatever?
- consciously deliberate but forceful because the fish feels no pain from the hook?
- genuinely 'desperate' because the fish experiences both fear and pain but the intensity of fear is the greater?

We don't know the answer to these questions and those who claim otherwise are deluding themselves. However, the small amount of research that has been done does indicate that fish which are hooked or stimulated with electric shocks to the mouth display physiological and behavioural signs that we would call fear and pain if we observed them, for example, in a dog (see Webster, 1994). I believe that anyone who elects to fish for sport must accept the fact that it almost certainly does cause some degree of suffering. This forces the question: 'can this suffering be justified?' and *this* creates a distinction between catching fish to be eaten (game fishing and sea fishing), and coarse fishing for species that will not be eaten but stored in a keep net, weighed, maybe photographed and then thrown back to be caught again another day. At first sight, catching without killing may seem the more humane alternative. However, fish can be not only injured by the hook itself but also severely bruised during handling and storage within the confines of the keep net. Such fish are likely to suffer longer.

Hunting with hounds

I repeat: the justification given for hunting the fox, the deer, etc. with hounds is to control population numbers; the *reason* people hunt with hounds and horses is that they find it good fun. The majority of the human participants in a hunt contribute nothing to the object of the exercise, they merely indulge in a hack, followed, with luck, by a mad gallop cross country. The fact remains, however, that hunting is a form of population control which does not seek to exterminate the hunted species but rather to maintain a sufficient population of animals in their natural habitat (in order, of course, to sustain the hunt).

In justice to the hunting community, it is necessary to ask the questions:

- Is hunting an acceptable method for controlling and so preserving a population of wild animals within their natural habitat?
- If hunting with hounds were to be banned, would alternative control methods be more or less humane?

It is undeniable that hunting under strictly controlled conditions tends to preserve the fitness of the overall population of the hunted species by preserving habitat and helping to avoid overpopulation. Indeed, it is fair to conclude that had English country people not enjoyed hunting the fox, the species would have been exterminated as vermin from the English shires and the landscape would be less green and pleasant. The moral debate over hunting with hounds must therefore centre on the degree of cruelty involved in the method of killing, both in absolute terms and relative to the alternatives. The cruelty of the exercise may be taken for granted. The deliberate intention is, in the words of the 1911 Act, to 'ill-treat, over-ride, infuriate or terrify' the hunted animal. By legal definition it is cruel, but not, when the prey is a fox, unlawful.

I have stated already that stress and suffering are not synonymous. Suffering ensues when an animal fails to cope or has extreme difficulty in coping with stress. The key questions are therefore, how much does a hunted deer or fox suffer before it is killed or escapes? If it escapes does the suffering persist?

In deer hunting, the animal is pursued with hounds. The first response of the deer is to run away. Since it can outrun the hounds this strategy works, at first. Eventually, after running for (on average) 10 to 30 km the deer will turn 'at bay' to face the hounds, often having run into water. This enables one of the hunt staff to approach the animal and shoot it with the high probability of ensuring (eventually) a quick kill. The key question is what causes the deer to stop running? Is it because it can run no further through exhaustion or hypothermia or both? Bradshaw and Bateson (1998) addressed this question on behalf of The National Trust and concluded mainly on the basis of blood samples taken at the time of killing that the deer were physically exhausted and some, after long hunts, had they been allowed to escape would have suffered the consequences of exhaustion for days thereafter. Subsequently The Countryside Alliance funded a study led by Professor Roger Harris which yielded very similar data but (surprise!) different conclusions. As one who witnessed the debate between these two groups I think it fair to say that both parties agree that the deer turns at bay when it feels it can no longer outrun the hounds. Where the two groups differ is in their interpretation of whether there is actual clinical damage to muscle and other tissues at this time, and therefore whether there will be prolonged suffering in animals allowed to escape. Neither can say, from their data, how long the deer may have suffered the physical effects of extreme fatigue before it elects to stand at bay. The Harris group, moreover, does not address the more important problem of mounting fear in an animal that becomes progressively aware, over a period that may extend into hours, that its attempts to escape are in vain.

Both groups accept that hunting deer with hounds causes the animals to suffer. Where they differ is in the degree of suffering. The Harris group argues that the degree of suffering is not excessive and the kill is certain. On utilitarian grounds they argue that this form of population control causes less suffering overall than stalking, where 5 to 15 per cent of shot animals may be wounded but not killed. The Bateson group concludes that hunting deer with hounds causes an unjustified degree of suffering, especially when the hunt goes on for a long time, (for example, over 20km). It can be argued that excessive suffering could be avoided if the master of hounds called off the hounds if a deer was still running after a very 'long' hunt (a subjective judgement based on distance and time). This is, however, a dangerous form of moral relativism based on no evidence as to the relative duration of the two phases of the hunt, as perceived by the deer, which are:

1. Coping with the stress of acute fear by escaping from the slower running hounds;
2. Increasing fatigue associated with chronic fear induced by the increasing awareness that the coping strategy is proving unsuccessful.

There has been no comparable study of the physiological stresses incurred by foxes during the course of a hunt. Since foxes are usually caught and killed by the hounds while still in full flight, it is possible that they suffer less than deer from exhaustion and may not experience the same intensity and duration of chronic fear. However, once again, these are questions of degree; questions to which we do not have clear scientific answers, and even if we had would not resolve the moral issues.

It is impossible to escape the conclusion that foxes and deer suffer during the course of prolonged hunts. Any defence of this method of killing must be based on the argument that it is not significantly worse than other killing methods used by humans, for example, shooting and poisoning. This conclusion is based on justice rather than utilitarianism. A utilitarian may argue that the pleasure we get from hunting can be justified if it helps to preserve the health and habitat of the fox population. Justice may decree that it is necessary to kill some animals to control the fox population or otherwise meet our needs, but dictates that we have an absolute responsibility to ensure that the killing is carried out in the most humane possible way.

Conclusions

It is an act of cruelty to cause unnecessary suffering to an animal by 'doing or omitting to do any act'. Since death is the end of suffering what matters most is what we do (or do not do) to animals while they are alive. Although animals do not volunteer they do partake in most competitive sports as enthusiastic amateurs. Some of these sports carry a significant risk of pain and injury. Whenever we choose to use an animal for our own sporting entertainment we must, in justice to that animal, assume the responsibility for its well-being (health and happiness) for life.

Field sports, hunting, shooting and fishing, are based on the deliberate intention to kill or injure another animal. The fact that some humans derive pleasure from killing some animals raises profound questions about the nature of human morality but is of no direct concern to the animals; what concerns them is the manner of their own life and death. A case can be made for field sports on the utilitarian grounds that they help to preserve the habitat and fitness of the hunted species, whatever the means of killing. Justice, however, decrees that whatever other arguments may be in play, each individual animal should be killed by the most humane method possible.

Further reading

Beauchamp, T.L. and Childress J.F. (1994) *Principles of Biomedical Ethics*. Oxford: Oxford University Press.

Bradshaw, E.L. and Bateson, P. (1998) Physiological effects of hunting red deer (*Cervus elaphus*). *Proceedings of the Royal Society, Biological Science*, G24, 1707–14.

Medway Report (1979) *Report of a Committee to investigate welfare aspects of shooting and angling*, RSPCA.

McFarland, D. (1989) *Problems of Animal Behaviour*. Harlow: Longman.

Moss, R. (1992) *Livestock Health and Welfare*. Harlow: Longman, pp. 160–82.

Odberg, F.O. (1992) Bullfighting and animal welfare. *Animal Welfare*, 1: 3–12.

Rawls, J. (1972) *A Theory of Justice*. Oxford: Oxford University Press.

Singer, P. (1990) *Animal Liberation: A New Ethics for our Treatment of Animals*. New York: Avon.

Wall, P.D. and Melzack, R. (1994) *Textbook of Pain*. London: Churchill Livingstone.

Webster, A.J.F. (1994) *Animal Welfare: A Cool Eye towards Eden*. Oxford: Blackwell.

13

Exotic animals

Martin P.C. Lawton

Introduction

The word 'exotic' means, 'brought in from abroad' and may include the rare or unusual, the strange and the bizarre. When applied to animals it usually implies a non-domesticated species that is not usually kept or encountered in this country, being kept as a pet. 'Exotic animal' is therefore a catch-all term which has a different meaning depending on whom one is talking to. To some veterinary surgeons the budgerigar and hamster are considered exotic animals, especially if they may not have much experience with dealing with these species. Indeed, the British Small Animals Veterinary Association includes most children's pets in its definition of exotic animals, as shown by their inclusion in its *Manual of Exotic Pets*. However, to many exotic animal keepers and veterinarians, the term is one that should be reserved and used only for the more unusual type of animal.

Exotic animals can therefore include all examples of non-domesticated species from the animal kingdom. These include both vertebrate and invertebrate animals and number many hundreds of thousands of species. These animals are often the same species as may also be frequently found in organized collections, such as zoological gardens and parks, except they are kept in smaller numbers (sometimes only two or three). Although it is accepted that some of the keepers (owners) of exotic pet animals can be extremely ignorant of the needs of the animals under their care, there are many more that are knowledgeable or may devote much of their spare time, if not their lives, to the keeping of these exotic animals, and studying their needs, breeding and behaviour. Enthusiasts label themselves with titles such as Rodentologists, Herpetologists, Aviculturists, etc., in order to display their knowledge and devotion to these animals.

These exotic animals are frequently imported in the first instance, but this may also continue for long periods of time. The importation of these animals may be a drain on the wild population, but in some circumstances the wild population may be under threat even should there not be capture for export. With development of knowledge and demand for a certain species there will usually be a natural progression to captive breeding which will, in most cases, lead to a reduction in the drain of animals taken from the wild. In some circumstances the breeding may be so successful that it may allow for the reintroduction to the areas where previous wild populations are now extinct.

It will always be disputed whether or not animals of any type should be kept in captivity. These arguments may be more easily stressed when dealing with exotic species as they are seldom domesticated, rarely (in the UK) used as a food source and kept in artificial environments which in most cases are very restricted. They are thus purely being kept for the benefit of humankind. Exotic animals can seldom be allowed the degree of freedom that domestic pets, dogs, cats, etc., or farm animals are afforded. Unless they are caged in a secured environment they are likely to escape, which in itself is a possible offence under the Wildlife and Countryside Act 1981. For many, the secured captivity is, however, essential for their well-being. Many exotic animals would not survive unless they were securely confined; if released in the UK (voluntarily or involuntarily) they would usually die by becoming a victim to natural predators, from the lack of correct or available food, or fall victim to our environment which is so alien to their natural climate. The environmental needs of exotics are of paramount importance when ectothermic animals (reptiles) or poikilothermic animals (amphibian and fish) are kept. Both ectothermic and poikilothermic animals are unable to maintain their normal metabolism and thus their ability to function normally, to grow, breed and fight disease, unless the correct external temperature is provided. There is no doubt that animals are seldom able to live a natural life in captivity and there is no getting away from the fact that they are not being kept just for their own benefit. Despite this, the balance of cost to the animals in captivity has to be weighed against the benefits of pet ownership, of any kind, to humans. It also has to be remembered that in many cases natural lives in the wild may be substantially shorter then those in captivity and often end as a result of disease or natural predation.

Why keep exotic animals?

The interest and ownership of exotic animals has increased substantially over the last fifteen years. This is mainly associated with the increased availability of unusual species to the public. There have always been those who are not just content with seeing these species in the wild or in organized collections but have wanted to own such species or even start their own private collections. These enthusiasts have always been able to find, obtain and accumulate exotic animals. It could be argued that capitalistic reasons are always behind the initial increase and availability of any species. If there was no demand for exotic animals as pets then there would not be the industry of importation or breeding and selling or exchange of these animals. With the increased availability of exotic animals there are inevitably an increasing number of owners, including many who would not previously have considered such animals as pets.

Owners' motives for keeping exotic animals are immensely varied. Much of the increased interest in recent years stems from a desire to learn more about these animals, together with the challenge of successfully keeping and even breeding the various exotic species. Many people are attracted to exotic animals because of their colourful or unusual appearance. Others respond to the intelligence and ability to mimic of some species, as is seen with the parrot family. Indeed it can be argued that some of the intelligent psittacines can provide more entertainment and comfort than a dog or cat. However, there are also those who seek to own exotic animals to make themselves appear unusual or more interesting. These include those who purchase the animal because certain species become fashionable, (for example, terrapins after the popularity of the Mutant Turtle cartoons on television and film); those attracted to the potential of some animals to scare or shock (such as tarantulas); those who like to watch animals eat live food (such as snakes) or even those who think they can dress up animals and treat them as children (the primates). It is these reasons and the people involved that give the genuine enthusiast a bad name and call into question even more the ethics of keeping exotic animals in captivity as pets.

There has now appeared a new type of exotic pet owner. These people may not consider themselves enthusiasts but have decided to keep an exotic animal after much consideration and as part of a well balanced decision. They consider it is far more practical to their life styles to keep an exotic animal than a dog or cat. An exotic animal may be less of a tie or less demanding than a dog or cat, as many animals are kept in their own environment, whether cage, tank, terrarium or vivarium, and can be left safely without risk of damage to their owner's valued home while owners are out all day at work. Food can also often be more easily provided to last for the day, and some species, for example, Burmese pythons, may only need to be offered food every two or more weeks.

Just because an animal is exotic it should not be thought that the owner is not able to form an emotional attachment to or with that animal. The therapeutic effects of some exotics (tropical fish) has been known for a long time and is frequently utilized in potentially stressful environments (such as dentists' waiting rooms). Many of the owners of exotic animals may develop a human/animal bond that may far exceed that seen with the traditional dog or cat. Some of the exotic birds (parrots) and reptiles have a life span that far exceeds traditional pets and, in some circumstances, exceeds that even of the owner. There is no doubt that longevity of life (provided the animals are cared for correctly and kept free of disease and injury) increases human/animal bonding. There is also the dependence of certain species on their owner which further leads to bonding. Some birds are reared to increase the potential for bonding with the owner. Many psittacines' eggs are removed from the parents' nests and artificially hatched and reared by hand feeding. This unnatural rearing causes the bird to imprint (or bond) with the human figure feeding it and this will result in a pet bird that is already acclimatized to humans and may thus be very tame. This is a much sought-after pet and accordingly commands a much higher price than an imported or parentally reared bird.

The attraction of exotic animals for children

The arguments about keeping animals as pets are even more pertinent when the pet belongs to a child. The child should never be allowed to consider the animal another toy, but the concept of caring should be stressed. There are many benefits for children in pet ownership. There is the responsibility, the requirement to feed, water and clean. However, these can be negated unless the parents are firm and insist that the child fulfils its responsibility to the animal, even if the child's interest starts to wane. Care must also be taken to teach the child to handle the animal so as to prevent stress or injury. If the animal is likely to suffer, or the child is able to ignore its responsibility for the animal's care, then this could be counter-productive and build an incorrect attitude to pets which could possibly lead to unnecessary suffering to animals in later life.

The choice of pets is important. Most small rodents do not make suitable pets for children although many do associate them with being a child's pet. Hamsters are a nocturnal species which want to sleep when the child wants them to be active and are active when the parents want the child to sleep. Gerbils are too fast-moving and some are prone to spontaneous epilepsy on handling. Gerbils' tail may come off if grabbed. Mice tend to be too fast-moving for small children and do have a tendency to develop an off-putting odour as far as the parents are concerned. The escape possibility with small rodents is also very high. The rat is by far the most suitable of the small rodents for children. It is large enough to be less likely to be injured on handling or dropping, it is easily tamed and less likely to bite than other rodents. However, there is an in-built fear of rats in most adults (associated with the tails) which prevents their acceptance in most households. The provision of unsuitable rodents to children often results in bites to the handlers or unnecessary injury or stress to the rodent concerned.

In the case of rodents and other exotic animals with short life expectancy there is also the issue of how the death of the pet should be handled by the parents. Parents may have favoured the choice of such a pet, on the grounds that if the child loses interest the parents do not have to continue reluctant care of the animal for too long, but it is not long before the child faces stress and upset when the pet dies. Lies may be told in an attempt to lessen the loss: 'it escaped', 'left home' or a replacement may be made before the death is noticed. Ultra-short lives of pets and their easy replacement may encourage the development of an uncaring or casual attitude towards animals.

The control, importation and sale of exotic animals

The origins of exotic animals inevitably require that they are initially imported. The ethics of the importation have to be carefully considered and weighed against the benefits of importing a new species and the costs to the animals concerned. When animals are to be imported there are many factors that have to be considered. The availability is important and any prospective exportation should never be a drain on the existing population. The method of capture should be humane, and cause as little stress or physical injury to the animal as possible. The storage sites and confines are potential sources of injury, death and transference of parasites and infections. Although there are often calls for the ban on exportation or importation, this can sometimes have a marked effect on humans in the local community. The capture and exportation of many exotic animals is often essential for the local economy, particularly in Third World countries, and a unilateral ban on importation may have substantial effects on the exporting country. There is also the financial incentive of importation. The price of exported animals is often far less than that of captive-bred animals. This imbalance in costs encourages the importation of animals rather than captive breeding and local supply. An exception to this is the hand-reared parrots that are so popular as pets and which carry a premium on their sale. The low cost of some imported wild-caught species makes these exotic animals disposable goods, as far as the importers (wholesalers) are concerned, and importers build in an accepted 'loss' through death prior to, during, or after importation. The low cost of the animal itself makes it less likely that veterinary care or advice is sought and will lead to a culling policy.

The transportation of animals between countries is well controlled by the International Air Transport Association (IATA) regulations. These lay down the requirements for the container construction and method of packing of animals as these relate to size requirements, partitions and compartmental layers. The penalties for breaches of these regulations in the UK are severe, especially as each individual animal concerned could be subject to a separate charge. The days of commonly packaging tortoises one on top of the other, resulting in substantial deaths associated with the importation, are now virtually at an end.

Exotic animals are covered by a variety of legislation. Some is effective but much is not. The importation of exotic animals may be covered by international legislation, such as CITES (Convention on International Trade in Endangered Species of Flora and Fauna) whereby the movement of animals is controlled unless it is licensed. Separate licences may be required from the country of export as well as the country of import. Unfortunately, although the introduction of CITES was meant to control or even prevent trade in certain species, the placement of a species on one of the appendices may increase rarity and thus the demand which can also be reflected in the price. This has led to problems with smuggling or even the theft of existing animals, purely for financial gain. There have also been occasions where an animal, once placed on a CITES appendix, becomes of less concern to its own country. This is especially true in Third World countries where as the loss of trade reduces the possibility of income from the export and there is less of a reason to preserve and encourage breeding.

Animals in the UK are often sold by pet shops. The exceptions to this are those direct from the breeders (who may also be occasional non-commercial sources), who may sell direct to owners or to wholesalers who then supply the pet shops. In order for pet shops to be allowed to sell animals in the UK they have to be licensed annually by the local authority; Environmental Health Officers are responsible for this. The licensing is required under the Pet Animals Act 1951. The licensing is, however, mainly associated with the control of the risk of infection to

humans associated with the animals or their sale. The overall requirement for the welfare of the animals seems to take a second place. The
Environmental Health Officers who are responsible for the inspection
and granting the licences may have little or no knowledge of the exotic
animals (or in some cases domestic animals) that may be involved. There
is no legal requirement for a veterinary surgeon to be involved in the
licensing procedure. Often, however, a local authority will seek guidance
and advice or even request that a veterinary surgeon become directly
involved. The licensing authority may place reasonable restrictions on
the numbers of individual animals or species that may be displayed and
sold. However, unreasonable restrictions are likely to
be challenged in the courts and would very probably be overturned.
Likewise, if a licence is refused, the courts can also be used for the appeal
process and will overturn the decision unless it can be justified.

There are many good pet shops often with knowledgeable staff.
However, there is little requirement under the current legislation for
staff to be fully aware of all the requirements of the exotic animals that
they are prepared to sell. This often leads to incomplete or, worse,
incorrect information being given to the new or prospective owner. This
can often lead to unnecessary suffering to the animals concerned. The
better pet shops will supply information sheets on the animals that they
sell to inform the new owner. Pet shops are businesses which intend to
earn money, therefore they tend to like to display exotic animals
prominently to attract people into their shops and hope that this may
lead to impulse purchases. The majority of the pet shops' profits do not
come from the sale of the animals but from the accessories (cages, lights,
heaters, toys, etc.), bedding and food. A terrapin may be sold for £4.50,
but the tank, filters, gravel, etc. could end up costing £60 and upwards.
There is no doubt that pet shops are not there for the welfare of the
animal, but for the profit that they can bring.

The sale of all animals is covered by the Sales of Goods Act 1979 and
the trading standards. It is illegal to sell an animal wrongly described or
in a condition which is 'unfit for the purpose for which it was sold'.
However, the Sales of Goods Act draws no distinction between an animal
and a pair of shoes and the parties to a sale of an animal are at liberty to
include whatever terms they wish into their agreement. Often this is
to the advantage of the pet shop and to the disadvantage of the buyer and
the animal. This legislation also requires that a sick animal is taken back
to the pet shop to 'offer them the opportunity' to correct any defect. This
is sensible legislation for commodities but not for animals. There is no
requirement for the pet shop to pay (or even arrange) for the treatment of
an animal but legally it just has to offer to replace the animal or

reimburse the customer. This legislation does nothing for the welfare of the animals concerned.

Ownership and legislation

Legislation against cruelty is covered by the Protection of Animals Acts 1911–1964, these apply only to domestic or captive animals and therefore will cover exotic animals but not wildlife that is not captive. The Act places a legal requirement of reasonable care on the owner of an animal to prevent any neglect or suffering. This has led to problems when it comes to establishing the definition of whether an exotic animal is domesticated or captive. Even where obvious acts of cruelty have been performed on non-domestic or non-captive exotic animals, such as kicking or setting fire to a hedgehog, these have failed in an attempt of prosecution. Wildlife is, however, mainly covered by the Wildlife and Countryside Act 1981, although not all species are covered. Those that are covered may only be protected at certain times of the year (usually breeding season). The Wildlife and Countryside Act does, however, also cover captive birds and the legal size of their cages. Section 8 deals with the legal requirement that a cage must allow a bird to be able to stretch its wings freely in all directions. This requirement does not apply when they are being transported, displayed on public exhibition or in competition (providing that this is not for more than seventy-two hours). Nor does it apply to birds that are undergoing examination or treatment by a veterinary surgeon. The size of the cage is therefore critical not only for the welfare of the animal but to prevent possible prosecution.

When an exotic animal is taken as a pet the Abandonment of Animals Act 1960 should prevent the owners from abandonment without reasonable excuse. Some of the exotic reptiles may grow extremely large and/or aggressive. The larger pythons or snapping turtles may be extremely small when they are sold but the true expected size may not always be explained or appreciated. The number of requests for re-housing these large reptiles when they have outgrown the owners' vivaria or tanks seems to increase each year. There is very little realistic hope of finding a new home and this inevitably leads to a request for euthanasia or consideration of release into the wild (the latter being illegal under both the Abandonment of Animals Act 1960 and the Wildlife and Countryside Act 1981).

There has always been a small number of people who are attracted to exotic animals because certain animals are dangerous. Exotics can be divided into those that are of minimum danger, moderate danger or potentially serious danger. Although the Dangerous Wild Animals Act

1976 and Dangerous Wild Animals, 1976 (Modifications) Order 1984 restrict the ownership of a large number of these dangerous animals, not all are covered. Poisonous arrow frogs, if recently imported, can be very toxic and dangerous if handled while there are fresh wounds on human hands. These species, however, are not covered by this legislation as they are regarded as of minimal danger to others. If a poisonous arrow frog were to escape, the chances of it causing harm to others is extremely remote; it would be more likely to die from being stepped on or suffer from the hostile British environment. If an exotic that is covered by the Act is to be kept, a licence is required. In order to obtain the licence at least one inspection has to be undertaken on an annual basis to assess the facilities for keeping the animal, the suitability of proposed or existing husbandry and the owner's suitability to keep a dangerous wild animal. There are also requirements for insurance and for safety features (fire alarms, etc.). Pet shops, as well as zoos, circuses, and premises licensed under the Animal (Scientific Procedures) Act 1986, are exempt from the Dangerous Wild Animals legislation. This leads to the incongruity that a pet shop may keep and offer for sale a dangerous wild animal but as soon as it is sold the new owner needs a licence.

Environment and dietary needs of exotic animals

It has already been mentioned that the environment required for an exotic animal can be expensive, but for many exotic species correct environment is essential for their well-being. This is particularly important for the poikilothermic and ectothermic species where the incorrect environment will lead to failure to thrive, breed and grow, as well as inability to fight infections. It has been suggested that an owner of a reptile has to 'play God' and provide the environment for the reptile's care. A depressingly large number of conditions seen by veterinarians in practice (anorexia, infection, etc.) are associated indirectly with, or directly attributable to incorrect environment. Such conditions could have been prevented if advice had been sought first.

Diets are also varied and are of extreme importance for the well-being of exotic animals. An incorrect diet is a common cause of disease problems in exotic animals. Lack of understanding even by the dietary manufacturers is evident when it comes to exotics. There is often confusion over the natural diet, so it is to be expected that a captive diet is unlikely to be correct. There are attempts to provide an adequate diet composed of what is readily available and this is often adequate. The exact requirement for vitamins and minerals is also, on the whole, poorly understood. However, there is widespread reliance on supplements to balance captive diet for exotics. The provision of inadequate diets will lead to a veterinary surgeon being presented with an exotic animal that is unwell or failing to thrive. Nutritional osteodystropy is a disease that is seldom seen in cats and dogs but is all too frequently seen in exotic pets. This could be avoided if the correct advice is given at the point of sale on the most suitable diet and appropriate vitamin and mineral supplements that should be used. The importance of providing a correct, varied and balanced diet cannot be over-stressed. The diet is very much paramount in the maintaining and establishing of the health of the animal. Until more is known about the basic biology and husbandry of exotic animals there will always be problems with nutritional disease.

In most cases, a breeder should be considered as a better source than a pet shop of both an exotic animal and advice on its care. Breeders usually know more than pet shop workers do, as they have been able to keep and breed the species in captivity and therefore must be doing something right. There is the further major advantage in obtaining one's animals from captive breeders that such sources are not a drain on the wild. The support given to captive breeders by buying their animals can have welfare implications. The continued support of captive breeding in the long term may lead also to the possibility of ultimate release back into the wild and this, in some cases, can even lead to the re-establishment of a population where it used to exist but does no longer. Reintroduction into the wild is not without risk, as there is also the possibility that disease can be translocated back into the natural population. Translocation has to be very carefully considered before reintroduction is undertaken.

There is, of course, the problem that the successful breeding of animals in captivity may result in an increase of animals that are available for sale and thus allow more people to purchase exotics. This in itself can lead to more animals being kept unsuccessfully and may lead to further suffering, but, on the whole, the breeding of animals in captivity is to be applauded.

The cost of ownership to the animal

There is no doubt that there is a heavy cost to an exotic animal which is kept in captivity. In the case of birds, they are often kept in small cages and without association with their own kind. Birds are very social animals and there is much stress involved in being kept in a small cage and with no avian companionship. It is for this reason that a lot of behavioural problems are seen especially in the psittacines (parrots). With their higher intelligence these animals are especially subject to the development of stress, feather plucking and other self-mutilatory behaviours which are all too frequently seen in captivity, but not in the wild. For reptiles that hibernate, the owners have the option of not hibernating them by controlling their environment or allowing them to hibernate, but in many cases for far longer than they would in the wild. The effects on the animal are hard to quantify.

The provision of diets which are readily available is beneficial in that there are seldom periods of shortage or starvation. However, most animals in the wild would forage for a substantial period of the day and the ready availability of food, often of higher nutritional value than that eaten in the wild, frequently leads to obesity and the associated problems this causes.

In the final analysis there is no doubt that most of the benefits derived from the keeping of exotic animals as pets are felt by the humans owning and keeping the animals and very little is felt by the animals which are kept in captivity.

Further Reading

Bellairs, A. (1970) *The Life of Reptiles*. New York: Universe Books.

Benyon, P.H. and Cooper, J.E. (eds) (1991) *Manual of Exotic Pets*. Cheltenham: BSAVA.

Benyon, P.H., Forbes, N.A. and Lawton, M.P.C. (eds) (1996) *Manual of Psittacine Birds*. Cheltenham: BSAVA.

Benyon, P.H., Lawton, M.P.C. and Cooper, J.E. (eds) (1992) *Manual of Reptiles*. Cheltenham: BSAVA.

Coles, B.H. (1985) *Avian Medicine and Surgery*. Oxford: Blackwell.

Cooper, M.E. (1987) *An Introduction to Animal Law*. London: Academic Press.

Cooper, M.E. (1991) Legislation. In *Manual of Exotic Pets*, new edn. (eds P.H. Beynon and J.E. Cooper). Cheltenham: BSAVA.

Cooper, J.E. and Jackson, O.F. (eds) (1981) *Diseases of the Reptilia*, vols. 1 and 2. London: Academic Press.

Fowler, M.E. (ed.) (1978–1997) *Zoo and Wild Animal Medicine Current Therapy 1 to 4*. Philadelphia: Saunders.

Frye, F.L. (1993) *Biomedical and Surgical Aspects of Captive Reptile Husbandry*, 2nd edn. Malabar: Krieger.

Gans, C. (and often guest editors) (1969–1988) *Biology of the Reptilia*, vols. 1–16. New York: Academic Press.

Hare, T. and Woodward, J. (1989) *Illustrated Encyclopaedia of Wildlife*, vols 26–29. London: Orbis.

Hoff, G.L., Frye, F.L. and Jacobson, E.R. (eds) (1984) *Diseases of Amphibians and Reptiles*. New York: Plenum Press.

Marcus, L.C. (1981) *Veterinary Biology and Medicine of Captive Reptiles*. Philadelphia: Lea and Febiger.

Mader, D.R. (1996) *Reptile Medicine and Surgery*, ed. D.R. Mader. New York: Saunders.

Reichenbach-Klinke, H.H. and Elkan, E. (1965) *The Principal Diseases of Lower Vertebrates*. London: Academic Press.

Ritchie, B.W., Harrison, G.J. and Harrison, L.R. (eds) (1994) *Avian Medicine: Principles and Application*. Lake Worth: Wingers.

14

Genetic engineering

Michael C. Appleby

Introduction

The total number of animal experiments performed annually has been declining in a number of countries since the 1970s and in the UK was down to 2.6 million in 1997. However, this number includes one growth sector: the number of animals used in genetic engineering or given mutations in other ways has been increasing for some years and in the UK reached 547,000 in that year (Home Office 1998). This work is controversial and ethical concerns need to be considered carefully, not least by veterinarians. Vets may be involved in Home Office assessment of proposals for animal experiments, in Institutional Animal Care Committees or in the direct care of the animals concerned. This chapter considers some of the ethical issues raised and gives an overview of the lines of work being carried out and their implications for animal welfare.

The term 'genetic engineering' is not wholly satisfactory, because 'engineering' is not an accurate description of the procedure, but will be used as the best available. The main alternative, 'genetic modification' (which produces Genetically Modified Organisms (GMOs)), is not satisfactory either; for example, it could readily include selective breeding. The chapter will be mainly concerned with genetic engineering, but other applications of biotechnology – such as cloning and the modification of hormones and vaccines for use on animals – will also be mentioned where relevant.

It should be noted at the outset that although genetic engineering is a relatively new field it is not being introduced to an ethically acceptable or neutral *status quo*. Indeed, there is no *status quo*: selective breeding and the development of new experimental techniques have been in progress for centuries, and the ethics of such traditional methods are increasingly called into question. Few of the ethical issues raised by genetic engineering are unique to it. However, there do seem to be some special features – such as the production of transgenic animals – which require special consideration. Furthermore, some of the effects produced by genetic engineering, while not necessarily different in kind from those produced by other techniques, may be more rapid, intense and repeatable than hitherto. Others, by contrast, may be minor or almost undetectable, as we shall see.

Motivation and ethics

One ethical issue is the question of why genetic engineering is being done at all. There are three main answers to this question. First there is the scientific interest. This is a major motivation of most scientists in the field, and the main outcome so far has been increase in scientific knowledge. Second, there is perceived to be a genuine need for some areas of work: for example, production of pharmaceuticals. Third, there is the potential for commercial exploitation of the results. In fact commercial considerations are in some ways the most important, because this sort of work is expensive and funding is generally targeted at work with commercial potential. This, therefore, affects the expression of scientific interest and the choice of which needs are addressed. It is not necessarily wrong for technological advances to be driven by financial incentive, but such a motivation does suggest that there should be full consideration of other ethical issues involved.

All those motivations for genetic engineering are in terms of benefit to humans, and therefore suggest (sometimes implicitly) that the work is justified because of its potentially beneficial consequences. This is consistent with the major ethical approach of utilitarianism (see Chapter 2), as long as the balance between likely benefits and likely costs is maximized. Such costs may also be borne by humans; for example, while production of pharmaceuticals is potentially beneficial it could be argued that money should instead be spent on preventive health care. It is difficult, though, to weigh the potential advantages and disadvantages to humans of any specific application of genetic engineering, never mind of genetic engineering as a whole.

Furthermore, our actions affect animals as well as humans. Singer (1975) extended utilitarianism to say that we should reckon up the good and bad consequences of our actions for both animals and humans, an approach which is increasingly widely accepted. This raises the issue of how genetic engineering affects animal welfare – the main topic of the rest of this chapter.

It should also be remembered, though, that utilitarianism is not the only ethical approach. A second major approach (deontology: see Chapter 2) is that there are some things we should do, and some things we should not do, regardless of good or bad consequences. Two main concerns about genetic engineering arise from this approach – although as already mentioned these concerns are not restricted to genetic engineering. First, some people consider that we should not be 'interfering with nature' in this way at all. Second, some people accept the arguments of Regan (1983) that animals have rights, and consider that those rights are violated by genetic engineering, perhaps even more so than by other uses of animals. These concerns are given weight by some authors (for example, Reiss and Straughan, 1996). Others, though, suggest or imply that such concerns will only be widely accepted as important if the technology also causes problems for human or animal welfare. Rollin (1995) suggests that all cogent concerns about genetic engineering of animals come down to arguments about danger to humans, animals or nature. Sandøe and Holtug (1993) perhaps go further in suggesting that animal welfare is the only ethically significant concern in this area, all other concerns either being baseless or turning out really to be about animal welfare, but they may not have considered all the implications for human welfare. Ethical issues other than welfare will be considered below where appropriate.

Procedures

The procedures involved in genetic engineering can themselves cause welfare problems irrespective of the nature of the intended modification, including problems for animals kept in reserve but not used and those on which the techniques are unsuccessful. Some of these problems are associated with husbandry and handling and are similar to those of any other manipulative experimental work. In some countries such problems are being considered more than hitherto under the general licensing procedures for experimental work, but there remains considerable room for improvement.

The main techniques currently used for genetic engineering are pronuclear injection, retroviral infection and introduction of embryonic stem cells in blastocysts, although the field is constantly changing. Each technique involves a number of procedures on a number of animals. For example, Hubrecht (1995) reports that pronuclear injection in mice involves several procedures on females to obtain the fertilized eggs, sterilization of males which mate with foster mothers to produce pseudopregnancy, insertion of embryos into foster mothers and finally several further procedures on the offspring. Other techniques – including cloning to produce and copy genetically modified organisms (Wilmut *et al.*, 1997) – produce embryos by transferring the nucleus of one cell into another without a nucleus. Embryos resulting from nuclear transfer have a high rate of mortality and at least some have been unusually large, so there may be welfare problems for both the offspring and the mother around the time of birth.

With some applications, procedures are only used a limited number of times because once genetically modified lines are established they breed true. With others, procedures are used repeatedly, and in this case it is important that the precise methods and their implications for welfare should not be taken for granted.

For some applications, in which the changes produced are themselves neutral for welfare, effects of procedures may be the most important welfare consideration. None are specific to genetic engineering, so in this respect they are not a cause for especial concern. However, this conclusion must be considered against a background in which the justification of all animal experimentation is increasingly questioned, with increasing pressure for the three Rs of reduction, refinement and replacement.

Genetic modification

If genetic modification is successful it will result in changes to the physiology and perhaps the physical structure of the animal concerned. Many of these will have direct implications for welfare, intended or unintended. Modification is also likely to have indirect effects, with the animal being treated in ways which are different to normal husbandry. This section will consider the types of effects which are possible and the next section will discuss the extent to which they actually occur.

Some modifications appear to have no direct implications for welfare. An example is transgenic sheep which have the gene for human α-1 antitrypsin, a protein of medical value for treating emphysema. The gene is expressed only in the lactating mammary gland and the protein is secreted in the milk. No ill effects are apparent, although complete verification is still proceeding (Hughes *et al.*, 1996).

Some changes may be described as specifically intended to affect welfare. The main potential positive effect considered is increased disease resistance in farm animals. Benefits to welfare could potentially include measures to reduce or prevent other, specific welfare problems such as leg disorders in turkeys. However, the only improvements to welfare likely to be implemented on a voluntary basis are those which are profitable.

Intentional negative effects on welfare exist where transgenics are used to study disease, particularly as models for similar conditions in humans, but potentially also improving the treatment of animals. Mice are most commonly used, for example, which have an increased susceptibility to cancer – including the so-called Oncomouse – but livestock such as pigs are also studied. The appropriateness of the model is a major issue here (Poole, 1995).

Other modifications have effects on welfare which cannot be considered side effects because they are the direct result of the intended change. Transgenics in which normal immunology or development is disrupted, studied for the insight they provide into the normal processes, come into this category. For example, the Legless mouse has major limb and craniofacial abnormalities and dies within twenty-four hours of birth, and is used in embryological and genetic research (McNeish *et al.*, 1988).

The last category of direct effects is side effects, which have probably received more attention than any others. Thus the 'Beltsville transgenic pig' with enhanced growth hormone production had severe arthritis (Pursel *et al.*, 1989) and sheep transgenic for growth hormone genes never attained puberty and died before one year of age (Nancarrow *et al.*, 1991). Work continues to reduce these side effects, but there may be some which cannot be prevented. Some effects arise as side effects but then become subjects for study, as with Legless mice.

Indirect effects of genetic engineering include the fact that many animals are kept or treated in ways which have other implications for welfare. Transgenics are valuable and their health tends to be looked after particularly well, although as with other experimental animals they are often kept in isolation and the importance of hygiene usually means that they are kept in barren conditions. By contrast, one concern which has been raised about the work on disease resistance is that if it is achieved animals may be stocked at higher densities; this also applies to animals treated with vaccines improved by genetic engineering.

Another indirect effect, resulting from the synthesis of growth hormones by genetic engineering, is increased frequency of injections. In addition to the injections themselves, which may be daily, there are also problems with injection site abscesses. Some implants are used, for example, lasting two weeks, but these have to be injected with a thick needle. Work on longer-lasting implants continues.

Numbers of animals kept for different uses will change as a

consequence of genetic engineering. Some uses will be more efficient and need fewer animals while other new uses will increase numbers. The number of animals used in transgenic research is currently increasing rapidly. There is no simple correlation between the numbers of animals involved and the importance of their welfare, but there is probably a consensus that some association does exist.

Lastly, modification of animals is likely to affect attitudes to them and hence other aspects of their treatment; it may also alter attitudes to and treatment of other groups of animals. This applies both to people who have direct influence over animals (such as breeders and producers) and to the public. Attitudes may be affected by new uses of animals, for example, as models for human disease or as suppliers of organs for xenografting, and by changes in their legal status, such as whether particular types of animal can be patented.

Applications

Farm animals used for agricultural products

The main attempts to date to change production characteristics of farm animals by genetic engineering have been insertion of genes for growth hormone into pigs and sheep and of genes which activate growth hormone production in salmon. Salmon modified in this way are now undergoing commercial trials. Attempts to increase growth in mammals have had gross side effects, as described above, but investigations are continuing into whether the worst of these problems can be prevented. For example, it may be possible to have a gene present but 'silent' during early development, then expressed later.

Cloning by nuclear transfer may be used in future to speed up the process of introducing transgenes into breeding stock. It may also be used to copy particularly productive animals. This might seem to give a relative advantage to welfare, because although cloning is associated with welfare problems these are probably less than those of other currently available procedures such as manipulation of growth hormone. However, this does not mean that it is justifiable. Furthermore, improvements in other lines will continue, so such clones are unlikely to be the most productive animals for long.

Some changes in production characteristics being investigated or sought are likely to be neutral or positive for welfare. Work in The Netherlands has produced Herman the transgenic bull whose female progeny are intended to produce milk containing the human protein lactoferrin. This would have the dual effect of making it more suitable for human consumption (particularly for babies and patients on antibiotics) and reducing the risk of mastitis in the cows. Another area of interest is the possibility of producing hens and cows which only have female offspring – for egg production and milk production respectively – obviating the need for killing male chicks or rearing unwanted male calves. This is the sort of application which might have positive effects on welfare but nevertheless raise other ethical concerns, particularly that what is being attempted – and potentially achieved – is unnatural and inappropriate.

Optimism about the prospects of increasing disease resistance in farm animals has abated recently. Some of the approaches being investigated were unsuccessful or restricted to very specific experimental circumstances. In addition, the technology mostly concerns single genes whereas the pathogens concerned are complex, and it is increasingly recognized that any increase in resistance might only be temporary, given the likelihood of change in the pathogens. Furthermore, there are other ethical issues here. Some of the diseases prevalent in current production systems have been exacerbated by intensive selection for production and by the techniques used in those systems, for example, mastitis in dairy cows. Unless genetic modification of dairy cows for resistance to mastitis reduced incidence of the disease to what it was before the increased production, it could be argued that it would be more appropriate to reverse the changes that have caused the problem. This is particularly true if there are other ill effects of increased production on welfare which these techniques help to perpetuate.

Farm animals used for biomedical products

Of all areas of work on genetic engineering this one currently has most commercial potential. As with animal production, the welfare issues are not wholly new; some farm animals are already used for biomedical products, with welfare problems resulting. For example, in North America many thousands of mares are kept in stalls too small for them to turn round for the production of oestrogen from their urine.

The area of work which has received most attention is modification of sheep or goats to produce pharmaceuticals in their milk for human medical use which will be cheaper and safer than those from alternative sources such as human blood. The changes being made – or, at least, those being publicized – appear to be neutral for welfare. Yet vigilance is necessary because certain genes may not be expressed solely in the mammary gland, and because the milk-blood barrier is not complete, so some compounds will be expected to affect the lactating female.

Another major area of activity is the modification of pigs to allow their organs – heart, kidney or pancreas – to be transplanted into humans. This is known as xenografting. One approach is insertion of a gene for human complement regulators into the pig genome; this gene will label the surface of pig cells so that hyperacute rejection does not occur when they are transplanted (White and Wallwork, 1993). Although there are other ethical issues involved there is no reason to believe that the welfare of a pig with such a gene will be compromised in any direct way.

As with farm animals used for agricultural products cloning may be used to copy animals which are particularly appropriate for pharmaceutical production or xenotransplantation. Again, this is likely to involve welfare problems, but these may be less than those caused by repetition of the procedures which are otherwise necessary to produce such animals.

Laboratory animals

Most lines of research are still at the exploratory stage, so in that sense all animals involved are laboratory animals, but the term is used here to mean animals – primarily mice – on which work is being done without immediate application in that species. Indeed, much of this work is not applied but pure science, although potential application may still be given as partial justification, particularly if there are implications for welfare.

Many procedures carried out on laboratory animals are disturbing. As indicated above, some involve intentional production of major welfare problems, as in the Oncomouse, and others require tolerance of such problems, as with the Legless mouse. However, the issues are clearly complex; one point that was made in the public discussion of the Oncomouse (in relation to whether or not it could be patented) was that, in a particular study, use of such a strain would make it possible to use considerably fewer experimental animals. On the other hand, the increasing availability of varied transgenics is rapidly increasing the number of experiments and the number of experimental animals is rising. Only a proportion of those animals suffers, but the absolute number that suffer must also be increasing. A major intention in the production of such animals is prevention or cure of human or animal diseases, but there is necessarily variation in the applicability of such work. This becomes relevant when regulatory bodies decide whether particular research proposals are to be allowed. Laws in the UK and the USA, for example, require consideration of both the likely effects on the animals involved and the likely benefits. However, assessment of the balance between these is clearly difficult.

The issue of patenting has mostly been concerned with this group of animals. Patenting of a whole animal, such as the Oncomouse, is permitted in the USA but is still being debated in the EU, while patenting of DNA sequences is permitted in both. Although patenting does not in itself confer any right to use animals or to condone suffering, it is relevant to welfare for at least three reasons. First, experiments on animals which are restricted by patenting are likely to be done in reputable laboratories, while those on animals which are not so restricted may be carried out in conditions which are less than ideal. Second, however, the patenting process is very slow and meanwhile secrecy is necessary. This hinders full consideration of the ethics of the work concerned, especially open debate. Third, the question of patenting emphasizes the commercial factors involved in exploitation of transgenics.

It is important to note that more transgenic laboratory animals are being produced and are suffering than are needed even for the experiments being carried out, because breeders often keep animals in stock to anticipate demand. It is clear that animals should be bred only for firm orders rather than always being available.

This is also another area where ethical concerns about genetic engineering are not restricted to the question of whether animals are caused to suffer. Many opponents of this technology object particularly strongly to the production of animals that are obviously unnatural, whether or not they obviously suffer. Thus the pressure group Compassion in World Farming (CIWF), which campaigns vigorously for a complete ban on genetic engineering of farm animals, has recently publicized photographs of 'The "geep" – a genetically engineered combination of a sheep and a goat' (CIWF 1997a) – and of a fluorescent green mouse carrying a jellyfish gene as a marker for other gene insertions (CIWF 1997b). It is arguable that naturalness is an aspect of animal welfare, or that it is also relevant to take into account other attributes of animals such as animal dignity. It might alternatively be said that these objections are not primarily concerned with the consequences of our actions but with the rightness of the actions themselves, and that producing animals without regard for their naturalness or dignity is wrong in itself. Either way, such objections are often very strongly held and expressed.

Other animals

Little or no work is being done on genetic modification of sporting animals, companion animals, zoo animals, wild animals or pests. In due course if techniques such as improvement in disease resistance are successful in farm animals, they may also be applied in other groups. Genetic engineering is being applied to vaccines and viruses to be used in wild animals which are dangerous or inconvenient to humans.

Conclusions

Some genetic modifications of animals are detrimental for welfare, some are neutral and some may prove to be beneficial. The two main current applications are modification of farm animals for biomedical products, which appears to be largely neutral for welfare, and modification of mice as models for human disease, which results in suffering, often severe, for large numbers of animals. Genetic modification has few effects on welfare which could not also be produced by selective breeding or other procedures. However, in no country does current legislation avoid welfare problems from selective breeding. Furthermore, the fact that changes can be produced rapidly and repeatedly by new technologies means that additional safeguards are needed. The same arguments apply to use of recombinant hormones, vaccines and viruses.

Procedures for ethical evaluation of genetic technologies are in place in some countries but need to be strengthened even in such countries and established in those which have no such procedures. It is also important that such procedures include an element of public accountability, whereby the public can have confidence that such evaluation is being properly carried out.

Attitudes to animal biotechnology have tended to become polarized, partly because people adopt different ethical approaches and often do not recognize or acknowledge this to be so. An improved dialogue, in which people attempt to understand each other's viewpoints, should enable common principles to be established and practical measures to be taken that enable more co-operation in attempts to improve both human and animal welfare. For example, proponents might accept that opponents are concerned about animal dignity and unnaturalness, and call a voluntary moratorium on work likely to provoke such concern. Conversely, opponents might accept that potential beneficial consequences of genetic engineering are at least a valid component of ethical debate, and, therefore, that some applications of genetic engineering may be more acceptable than others. Veterinarians can make an important contribution to this area because of their expertise in animal care, but they will also need to be well informed in the particular issues involved.

Acknowledgements

My involvement in this area developed in a working group on Ethics of Genetic Engineering in NonHuman Life Forms, organized by the Society, Religion and Technology Project of the Church of Scotland (see Bruce and Bruce, 1998). Much of the material in this chapter has also been published in fuller form elsewhere (Appleby, 1998).

References

Appleby, M.C. (1998) Genetic engineering, welfare and accountability, *Journal of Applied Animal Welfare Science*, 1: 255–73.

Bruce, D.M., and Bruce, A., (eds) (1998) *Engineering Genesis: Ethics of Genetic Engineering in Non-Human Species*. London: Earthscan.

CIWF (Compassion in World Farming) (1997a) Genetic engineering: through the smoke-screen, *Agscene* 125: 20, 1997a.

CIWF (Compassion in World Farming) (1997b) Fluorescent mice: a green light for farm animal experiments, *Agscene*, 127: 18.

Home Office (1998) *Statistics of Scientific Procedures on Living Animals, Great Britain 1997*. London: Stationery Office.

Hubrecht, R. (1995) Genetically modified animals, welfare and UK legislation. *Animal Welfare*, 4: 163–70.

Hughes, B.O., Hughes, G.S., Waddington, D., and Appleby, M.C. (1996) Behavioural comparison of transgenic and control sheep: movement order and behaviour on pasture and in covered pens. *Animal Science*, 63: 91-101.

McNeish, J.D., Scott, W.J. Jr., and Potter, S.S. (1988) Legless: a novel mutation found in PHT1-1 transgenic mice. *Science*, 241: 837–9.

Nancarrow, C.D., Marshall, J.T.A., Clarkson, J.L., Murray, J.D., Millard, R.M., Shanahan, C.M., Wynn, P.C., and Ward, K.A. (1991) Expression and physiology of performance regulating genes in transgenic sheep. *Journal of Reproduction and Fertility*, Supplement 43: 277–91.

Poole, T.B. (1995) Welfare considerations with regard to transgenic animals. *Animal Welfare*, 4: 81–5.

Pursel, V.G., Pinkert, C.A., Miller, K.F., Bolt, D.J., Campbell, R.G., Palmiter, R.D., Brinster, R.L., and Hammer, R.E. (1989) Genetic engineering of livestock. *Science*, 244: 1281–8.

Regan, T. (1983) *The Case for Animal Rights*. Berkeley: University of California Press.

Reiss, M.J., and Straughan, R. (1996) *Improving Nature? The Science and Ethics of Genetic Engineering*. Cambridge: Cambridge University Press.

Rollin, B.E. (1995) *The Frankenstein Syndrome: Ethical and Social Issues in the Genetic Engineering of Animals*. Cambridge: Cambridge University Press.

Sandøe, P., and Holtug, N. (1993) Transgenic animals –which worries are ethically significant? *Livestock Production Science*, 36: 113–16.

Singer, P. (1975) *Animal Liberation*. New York: New York Review of Books.

White, D.J.G., and Wallwork, J. (1993) Xenografting: probability, possibility or pipe dream? *Lancet*, 342: 879–81.

Wilmut, I., Schnieke, A.E., McWhir, J., Kind, A.J., and Campbell, K.H.S. (1997) Viable offspring derived from fetal and adult mammalian cells. *Nature*, 385: 810–13.

15

The use of animals in science

Paul Townsend

Introduction

No other area of animal use raises more immediate and profound questions than the use of animals for scientific purposes, commonly referred to as vivisection. This is the debate over the use of animals by humans in clear definition. On one side there is the view that performing scientific procedures on animals will cause them to suffer, is unadulterated cruelty and that people who use animals in this way are no better than those who beat, neglect or otherwise abuse them. On the other side, the view that the use of animals for the benefit of other animals and humans is a justifiable, even noble use, even where that use may involve pain, suffering, distress or some other long term harm on the part of the animals used, is equally vigorously supported. The two views are diametrically opposed and incompatible. What is a veterinary surgeon to do? As usual a good place to start is by understanding the ideas behind both sides of the argument.

The anti-vivisectionist viewpoint

Anti-vivisectionists are characterized in the extreme by those people who wish to abolish the use of animals for scientific purposes. Other anti-vivisectionists may be more welfarist in their views, in that whilst opposing the use of animals in this way they also recognize that this use is going on and is likely to continue for the foreseeable future. Therefore they see constructive engagement with those carrying out or supporting animal research as a more beneficial way of advancing the cause towards eventual abolition. Both are representatives of a long established tradition in the UK going back at least to the 1860s and the passing of the Cruelty to Animals Act of 1876, which was the world's first legislation to attempt some control over the use of animals for experimental purposes.

One may argue that the combined efforts of both groups have been successful in achieving many of the changes in the laws controlling animal research, especially since the late 1980s in the last decade. This would include the *de facto* banning of cosmetic products testing in the UK in November 1997 (Home Office).

Whilst anti-vivisectionists are generally lumped together as a group, they come from different and differing views on animals. Some will subscribe to the idea of 'animal rights', espoused especially by Tom Regan (1983). This view regards any use or exploitation of any animal by or for humans as a breach of the animal's 'right' not to have its general state of existence and well-being interfered with. This is a view which most commonly presents itself in everyday life as veganism (the refusal to eat or make use of any animal-derived products).

Alternatively, the ideas espoused by Peter Singer in his book *Animal Liberation* (1983) are used by anti-vivisectionists to argue their case. Based on the principles of Utilitarianism first expounded by Jeremy Bentham in 1789, Singer argues that the performance of any painful procedure on a sentient animal can only be justified if the harm done to that animal is outweighed by the benefits which flow from its performance. Singer argues that sentience begins somewhere just above the level of biological development exhibited by a prawn, therefore making it acceptable to pull the legs off flies but not frogs. However, Kantians might argue that pulling the legs off flies could encourage the person to treat higher animals or humans with similar disdain and therefore even this should not be allowed. In Singer's view there is never (or almost never) any sufficient justification or benefit to be derived from using animals for scientific purposes which would warrant even the smallest amount of suffering to be caused to a sentient creature. Thus Singer has adopted Utilitarianism to support an anti-vivisectionist viewpoint.

Arguments for the use of animals in science

The main argument in favour of the use of animals for scientific purposes rather oddly draws on the same tradition as does Singer's argument for its abolition, namely Utilitarianism. However, this time the strength given to the benefits derived from the use of animals in this way is given much more weight in the performance of the harm-benefit analysis carried out when assessing the rights or wrongs of any particular use of animals. This argument gives human beings a much heavier moral weight and, whilst not excluding other animals from consideration, it does say that in properly justified circumstances harm to a sentient animal can be justified if the benefits arising from the use of that animal outweigh the effect of those harms. Incidentally, a similar argument is used in the case of research on humans providing they give their consent.

Control of animal use in science in the UK

The view that, in these special circumstances, animal use can be justified is the basis of the permissive legislation in place in the UK. The Animals (Scientific Procedures) Act 1986 (A(SP)A) draws also on the work of Russell and Burch (1959) who, whilst accepting the use of animals in this way, laid down three other additional principles. These are replacement, reduction and refinement, commonly known as Russell and Burch's Three Rs.

Russell and Burch's Three Rs

Writing many years before the increased general public awareness of animal research, Russell and Burch's first idea was that where possible animals should be replaced, either by less sentient creatures or, ideally, by non-sentient systems. This principle is reflected in the current legislation where applicants for a licence to use animals must give a signed assurance that they have attempted to find such alternatives. They must also demonstrate that in vitro methods have been used in the development of the research programme up to the stage at which living animals are a required and necessary part of the programme of work.

The reduction principle put simply is that all use of animals must employ only the minimum number of animals consistent with obtaining valid scientific results. This must be based on a sound understanding of experimental design. This principle often seems to conflict with another basic tenet of A(SP)A where, in every procedure, the amount of suffering undergone by a single animal is of primary importance and must be the minimum consistent with achieving a valid result. Thus, if an answer can be obtained by using ten animals but each animal will suffer to level 10 on some notional pain scale of 1 to 10, or, alternatively, the same result can be obtained by using 100 mice each suffering to level 1 on a scale, the preferred option is to use more animals, each of which suffers less. This is obviously in apparent contradiction of the reduction principle and illustrates some of the difficulties inherent in making judgements in this area.

The third R defined by Russell and Burch is refinement and this is the area in which the veterinary surgeon involved in research can have a major influence. Refinement is the reduction in suffering by the application of modern veterinary and animal husbandry techniques. Refinement can therefore be applied in all circumstances in any research establishment and at any stage of any animal's life, not simply those times during which the animal is the subject of a scientific intervention. A refinement may be as simple as providing pregnant mice with sufficient bedding and nesting material to allow them to perform their natural behaviours at the time of parturition. It might be the availability and use of high-health status animals to ensure that intercurrent disease does not affect the validity of the science, which otherwise might cause an uninterpretable or false result, leading to a potential waste of animals due to having to repeat the work.

Another significant area of veterinary contribution has been in the introduction of safer and more effective techniques for anaesthesia of animals. There have been significant advances particularly in the fields of analgesic treatment and the assessment of pain and distress in animals. The profile of both these subjects was significantly raised in veterinary practice in general after the debate was started in the field of laboratory animal medicine.

The main provisions of the Animals (Scientific Procedures) Act 1986

A significant contributory factor to the introduction of refinement as a principle into scientific procedure establishments was the introduction of A(SP)A and the provisions the Act made requiring establishments carrying out such work to employ named individuals responsible for the day to day health and welfare of the animals housed.

A(SP)A controls the use of 'any experimental or other scientific procedure applied to a protected animal which may have the effect of causing that animal pain, suffering, distress or lasting harm'. A protected animal is any non-human, living vertebrate and also, from 1993, *Octopus vulgaris*. The decision to include the octopus as a protected animal was based on scientific opinion as to the degree of sentience of cephalopods, i.e. it was felt that sufficient evidence was available to show that they had the capacity to suffer. However, since November 1997, the British government has placed a *de facto* ban on the use of Great Apes. Although none of these species has been used since A(SP)A was introduced, this was the first explicit restriction from the otherwise permissive, strictly utilitarian basis of the law. The reason for this ban was, the government stated, 'a matter of morality' (Home Office (a), 1997).

The definition of what is and is not a 'regulated procedure' under the A(SP)A is dependent upon the purpose for which the procedure is applied to the animal. A regulated procedure is something done for an experimental or scientific reason which results in the protected animal experiencing pain, suffering, distress or lasting harm. These terms include death, disease, injury, physiological stress, psychological stress, significant discomfort or any disturbance to normal health, whether resulting immediately or in the long term.

At the same time as banning the use of Great Apes, the British government also introduced a *de facto* ban on the use of protected animals for the testing of cosmetic products. Again, this was previously a justifiable use of animals in the context of a utilitarian cost-benefit assessment.

Humane killing

Killing an animal is not a regulated procedure if done for a scientific purpose in a designated establishment using a method listed in Schedule 1 of A(SP)A (Home Office (b), 1997). It therefore does not require authorization by a project or personal licence (see below). However, 'such killing must be performed by a competent person'. If the method used to kill the animal is not listed in Schedule 1 it must be performed by a personal licence holder and be specified in the project licence.

The licensing system under the Animals (Scientific Procedures) Act 1986

The process of control of animal studies under A(SP)A relies on a system of licences, all of which must be in place before an animal may be used in a procedure. Without all of these planks being in place, no procedure performed for a scientific purpose, however innocuous this might be in terms of the potential suffering caused to an animal, may be undertaken. Failure to obtain the relevant permissions from the Home Office, the government department responsible for the legislation, can result in a custodial sentence, a fine and subsequent failure to obtain authority to carry out scientific procedures using animals at a future date.

The licences concerned are:

1. *Certificate of Designation.* This authorizes the performance of scientific procedures at an establishment which has demonstrated that it has the

required infrastructure to adequately support such work. A Certificate of Designation is also required by an establishment which wishes to act as a breeding or supplying establishment for certain species of animals for use in scientific procedures. The Certificate of Designation consists of the licence or Certificate and a schedule which lists all of the areas of the establishment in which work may be carried out and also what type of work, on which species of animal, may be performed in each of the named areas.

2. *Project Licence.* The Project Licence is the document which authorizes a particular programme of work employing regulated procedures on protected animals. A separate Project Licence document is required for each discrete programme of work at an establishment. A Project Licence is issued to an individual who is responsible for the scientific direction of the work and, once granted, the programme of work may not be varied from what is set out in the project licence except with the consent of the Home Office. Project Licences vary in scope from small, specific programmes to allow a single person to carry out one procedure on limited number of animals (for example, as part of postgraduate degree studies), to a licence containing many protocols, involving a wide range of species and several tens of personnel, for example, an anti-cancer drug discovery programme at a pharmaceutical company.

3. *Personal Licence.* This gives authority to a named individual to perform specific regulated procedures at particular designated establishments, on particular species, with or without the use of anaesthesia. Alone, it does not confer sufficient authority for the holder to carry out animal studies.

Designation of scientific procedure establishments

A Certificate of Designation is issued to an individual at an establishment; that individual is ultimately responsible to the Home Office. Usually this is someone in a position of seniority and who has a significant role in the allocation of budgets with respect to both pay budgets and capital works. This ensures a direct link between the certificate holders' responsibilities in the field of provision of staff and suitable facilities, and their powers to affect these areas. The final decision as to whether or not an establishment is granted a Certificate of Designation lies with the Secretary of State for the Home Office who relies upon the advice of Inspectors. Inspectors are either veterinary or medically qualified and their role under the Act is to advise the Secretary of State on such matters, including the granting of Project and Personal Licences (see below).

All places where scientific procedures are performed must be designated, under the Act. All such establishments must have:

- one or more people responsible for the day to day care of the animals (the Named Animal Care and Welfare Officers – NACWO);
- one or more named veterinary surgeons (NVS) to provide advice on animal health and welfare.

The certificate holder is responsible for ensuring, amongst other things, that:

1. the NACWO and NVS discharge their duties effectively;
2. the fabric of the establishment is maintained in accordance with the *Code of Practice*;
3. all procedures are authorized by personal and project licences and that no unauthorized procedures take place;
4. a protected animal is issued only to a suitably authorized person;
5. records are maintained of the source use and final disposal of all animals protected by the Act in the establishment;
6. all mice, rats, guinea pigs, hamsters, gerbils, ferrets (plus primates, cats, dogs and genetically modified sheep and pigs) are obtained only from a designated breeder and/or supplier (as required under Schedule 2 of A(SP)A).

Responsibilities of the Named Veterinary Surgeon

The primary role of the NVS is to provide for the health and welfare of the animals housed at the establishment. In order to effectively discharge this role the NVS's duties include:

1. making regular visits to all parts of the establishment designated under the Act, at a frequency which will allow the effective monitoring of the health status of the animals;
2. having regular contact with the NACWO(s) and the certificate holder;
3. having a thorough knowledge of the prevention, diagnosis and treatment of disease which may affect the species kept, and of their husbandry and welfare requirements;
4. providing a 365-days-a-year service;
5. supervising the maintenance of health records relating to all protected animals;
6. being familiar with the project licences in use and especially the degree of suffering allowed under each; the expected signs that might

be exhibited by animals undergoing procedures and the steps to be taken to relieve suffering;

7. giving advice to personnel working under the A(SP)A especially with respect to anaesthesia, analgesia, euthanasia, surgical technique, choice of species and the recognition of pain, suffering and distress in these animals;

8. being familiar with all methods of killing listed in Schedule 1 to the Act.

Responsibilities of the Named Animal Care and Welfare Officer

The NACWO has responsibility for the day to day care of the animals. There may be several people each taking responsibility for a discrete part of the establishment. The NACWO has to notify the personal licensee, or make arrangements for the care or destruction of the animal, if the health or welfare of any protected animal gives rise to concern. Additional responsibilities include:

1. being aware of the standards of husbandry set out in the *Code of Practice* and taking steps to ensure these are met;
2. ensuring suitable health records are maintained;
3. ensuring that suitable records are maintained of the environmental conditions of the rooms in which animals are held, and of all the animals bought, bred, supplied, issued used, killed or otherwise disposed of;
4. knowing which areas of the establishment are listed in the Certificate of Designation and the purpose for which they are designated;
5. ensuring that every protected animal in all designated areas is seen and checked at least once daily by a competent person;
6. being familiar with the project licences in use, including severity limits and conditions, adverse effects and humane endpoints.

Project licences

The project licence is the means by which authority is given for a programme of work involving regulated procedures on protected animals to be carried out. It is the primary vehicle through which the Three Rs of Russell and Burch are addressed in A(SP)A. A project licence is granted to individual scientists who must show that they are sufficiently well-qualified in the field of science covered by the project, and also has the experience and project management skills to manage other individuals who will actually carry out the work involving the animals, namely, the Personal Licence holders. The Project Licence sets out:

1. the purpose and scientific justification for the work;
2. the work which may be performed, including the species and number of animals and a full description of the procedures involved, including an assessment of potential severity.

For a Project Licence to be granted there must be a likely benefit from doing the work which will outweigh the cost imposed on the animals (i.e. the adverse effects – pain, suffering, distress or lasting harm). This assessment of cost versus benefit is made by the Home Office Inspector.

Before applying for a Project Licence all applicants must undergo an accredited training course on the role and responsibilities of the Project Licence holder. All Project Licence applicants are required to give a significant amount of detail about themselves and their co-workers, in order to help establish that the work proposed be carried out by personnel who have the required skills and infrastructure available to them to make it a success. The applicant also must show awareness of the need to replace animal use where possible by the use of non-living models, by explaining where such alternatives are used in the work programme and by documenting the literature searches which have been performed to investigate these alternatives.

There are specific areas of work which require the application to be reviewed by persons other than the Home Office Inspector. These are:

1. tobacco or tobacco products;
2. the specific training of practising surgeons in microsurgery;
3. work of substantial severity on non-human primates or work requiring the use of wild-caught primates;
4. applications involving cosmetics.

There is also in place an Animal Procedures Committee (APC) which as well as offering advice to the Secretary of State on matters associated with scientific procedures on animals also reviews licence applications in these four areas. The committee is made up of a mixture of scientists (medical, veterinary and biological) and animal welfarists, as well as at least one member with a legal background.

The reason for APC review of these specific areas of work is the public concern surrounding the use of animals in these areas. For example, research into the smoking of tobacco in the 1970s, has remained in the public consciousness in the form of 'smoking beagles' and this concern has affected all the research in this field. Category 2 (see p. 197), is included because acquisition of manual skills is broadly not deemed to be an acceptable use of animals in Britain. There has never been a tradition in British veterinary schools of using animals in so-called 'wet labs' to teach students the basics of surgery. In many other parts of the world this form of 'practice' is felt to be an essential part of the training requirement of the undergraduate. Indeed, a survey of British professors of veterinary surgery in the 1990s by David Morton, Professor of Biomedical Ethics at the University of Birmingham, found that only one professor was of the opinion that this type of training would add something to the training of veterinary students.

Proposals for work using non-human primates require extra justification because some species, essentially Old World primates, are thought to have a greater capacity for suffering than other non-human animal species. In fact the use of Old World primates requires special justification over and above that required for New World primates. Only captive-bred primates should normally be used. Exceptional justification is required for the use of non-human primates taken from the wild. Any use of wild-caught animals must be made explicit and fully justified in the licence application, that is to say, the use of wild-caught sources must be relevant to the scientific proposal. The use of cats, dogs and equidae also requires extra justification, though not reference to the APC. The main reason for this lies in the political sensitivities associated with the use of these species and their generally closer relationship with humans in terms of their domesticity. There seems to be no scientific argument for saying that a dog requires greater consideration than, for example, a pig, nor indeed a rat for that matter.

In order to enable the reviewer of a Project Licence application to build up a picture of the potential benefits which might be derived from the proposed work, the applicant must provide a detailed scientific background to the project, explaining the hypotheses to be investigated and their derivation. Explanation of how the hypotheses are to be tested and evidence of a complete and up to date literature search must also be given. In addition, the applicant must give concise, specific objectives to be achieved as a result of the programme of work described in the licence, as well as the potential benefits of achieving these.

To further establish the benefits of the work, the applicant must describe the plan of work which will be followed in achieving the objectives. This is done by describing the programme of work and explaining how it will be managed. At this stage the applicant is required to put the need for animal studies into the context of non-animal work, i.e. the use of *in vitro* alternatives as a stage in the process of moving towards the animal model. The applicant must establish that the programme of work is scientifically well designed and is likely to meet the objectives previously identified. In addition, the statistical tests to be applied to the data must be explained in order that an assessment may be made of the attempt made by the applicant to reduce the number of animals used.

With reference to the animal welfare considerations of the work, the applicant must explain how these have been addressed. An example of this might be the use of analgesic regimes or the adoption of humane end-points, and that in addressing these issues the advice of the Named Animal Care and Welfare Officer and the Named Veterinary Surgeon has been sought and taken. Some types of procedures are regarded as particularly sensitive and require careful justification. These are essentially those involving substantial pain, suffering or distress, for example, procedures where death is an end-point or painful disease models such as arthritis. The applicant must clearly explain why such substantial severity is a necessary part of the procedure and why it cannot be replaced by a less harmful procedure.

Assessment of harms

In order to make a more detailed assessment of the potential harms to the animals involved, an index of the separate procedures involving animals and detailed procedural protocols must be provided for the animal work proposed in the programme. The index must set out the severity of the procedures and the animals to be used. The severity limit for each procedure is an estimate of the amount of harm done to an animal undergoing a specific procedure. Only one severity limit applies to each procedure and is classed as either mild, moderate or substantial. However, in the case of procedures carried out on decerebrate animals or animals wholly under anaesthesia from which they are not allowed to recover the limit is unclassified.

The severity limit of any procedure takes into account the techniques applied to the animal during the procedure, the possible adverse effects that the animal might suffer as a result of the procedure and actions taken to avoid, minimize or alleviate these adverse effects. It is an area in which both Named Persons can play an important role in terms of giving advice on the severity and, more importantly, the alleviation or avoidance of pain, suffering and distress. Once decided and set, the severity limit of each procedure must be adhered to. In cases where animals exceed a severity limit, steps must be taken by the licence holder either to terminate the work or apply for a temporary authorization of a higher severity limit if this is felt to be justified. The assessment of the overall severity of a project, which may consist of more than one procedural protocol, each having a different severity limit, reflects the cumulative effect of each procedure; the number of animals used in each procedure; the frequency of use of each procedure; the proportion of animals that are expected to be exposed to the upper limits of severity in each procedure and the length of time that the animals might be exposed to the upper limits of severity.

Overall severity-benefit assessment

An assessment of overall severity is used to weigh the likely adverse effects on all the animals used against the benefits likely to be obtained by performing the programme of work. This is the practical implementation of the utilitarian equation of cost-benefit analysis as applied to the use of animals in science. This process has been further elaborated by the then Chief Inspector of the Animals (Scientific Procedures) Inspectorate in the report of the Animals Procedures Committee for 1993 (Home Office, 1994). Another attempt to produce a similar balance sheet of harm versus benefit was produced by the Institute of Medical Ethics' Working Party on the use of animals in biomedical research in 1991 (eds Smith and Boyd, 1991). Both are valuable insights into how this difficult question can be handled in the circumstances of everyday application.

Ethical review process

The everyday application of some method of ethical analysis of scientific work utilizing animals has become even more important in Britain since April 1999 when the government introduced the requirement that all designated establishments were to put in place their own internal Ethical Review Process (ERP) to cover work under A(SP)A (Home Office, 1998). The remit given to establishments was to establish a process which would:

1. provide independent ethical advice to the certificate holder, particularly with respect to Project Licence applications and standard of animal care and welfare;
2. provide support to Named Persons and advice to licensees regarding animal welfare and ethical issues arising from their work;
3. promote the use of ethical analysis to increase awareness of animal welfare issues and develop initiatives leading to the widest possible application of the three Rs.

The process should involve the Named Veterinary Surgeon(s) and the Named Animal Care and Welfare Officer(s). In scientific procedure establishments both Project and Personal Licence holders should be involved. The guidance also requests that the views of people at the institution not having responsibilities under A(SP)A should be taken into account, as well as giving consideration to the involvement of lay persons from outside the establishment.

As may be seen from the three aims listed above, the remit of the ERP, whilst including the review of research proposals with reference to the likely costs to the animals, the expected benefits of the work and how these conditions balance, is also much wider than just this. It also takes into account promotion of the three Rs, provides a discussion forum for maintaining awareness of ethical issues, retrospectively reviews projects through their lifetime, reviews the accommodation and care given to animals at the establishment in its broadest sense and includes training of staff and monitoring of competence. In terms of the review of licence applications the ERP does not replace the Home Office as final arbiter as to whether or not a research proposal may go ahead. However, the ERP must have approved all applications before they are submitted to the Home Office, therefore it is highly unlikely that an application will be approved by the Home Office but not by an institution, although the opposite may well occur.

Personal Licence

The final licence required under the A(SP)A is the Personal Licence, which acts as a certificate of competence. It is given to individuals and authorizes them to perform techniques on animals as part of a programme of research covered by a Project Licence. Formal education in the use of animals in research is required before a person can apply for a licence and supervision, given during on-the-job training, is the responsibility of a named supervisor. It is of course impossible for an individual to train in a technique using live animals, prior to obtaining a licence, as both the use of animals to obtain manual skills and the performance of techniques on protected animals without a licence are illegal.

Conclusion

This chapter has detailed how significant changes to the ethical review of scientific studies involving animals were introduced as a result of the Animals (Scientific Procedures) Act of 1986. The performance of a 'Utilitarian' harm-benefit analysis on each research proposal, together with the close involvement of veterinary surgeons and other animal care professionals in the application for permission and the Ethical Review Process, have resulted in the use of animals in science becoming arguably the most highly regulated of the specific areas of animal use in Britain. This has had undoubted benefits in terms of improving both the quality of the science and the health and welfare of all animals used.

References

Home Office (1994) *Report of the Animal Procedures Committee for 1993.* London: HMSO.

Home Office (a) (1997) *Supplementary Note to the Home Secretary's Response to the Animal Procedures Committee: Interim Report on the Review of the Operation of the Animals (Scientific Procedures) Act, 1986.* London: Stationery Office.

Home Office (b) (1997) *The Humane Killing of Animals Under Schedule 1 to the Animals (Scientific Procedures) Act, 1986, Code of Practice.* London: Stationery Office.

Home Office, *Circular to Certificate of Designation Holders, Reference 3-4.98.*

Regan, T. (1983) *The Case for Animal Rights.* London: Routledge & Kegan Paul.

Russell, W.M.S., and Burch, R.L. (1959) *The Principles of Humane Experimental Technique.* London: Methuen.

Singer, P. (1983) *Animal Liberation.* Wellingborough: Thorsons.

Smith, J.A., and Boyd, K.M. (eds) (1991) *Lives in the Balance: The Ethics of Using Animals in Biomedical Research.* Oxford: Oxford University Press.

Index